TOOLS

THEODORE GRAY

Bestselling author of *The Elements*
Photographs by Nick Mann

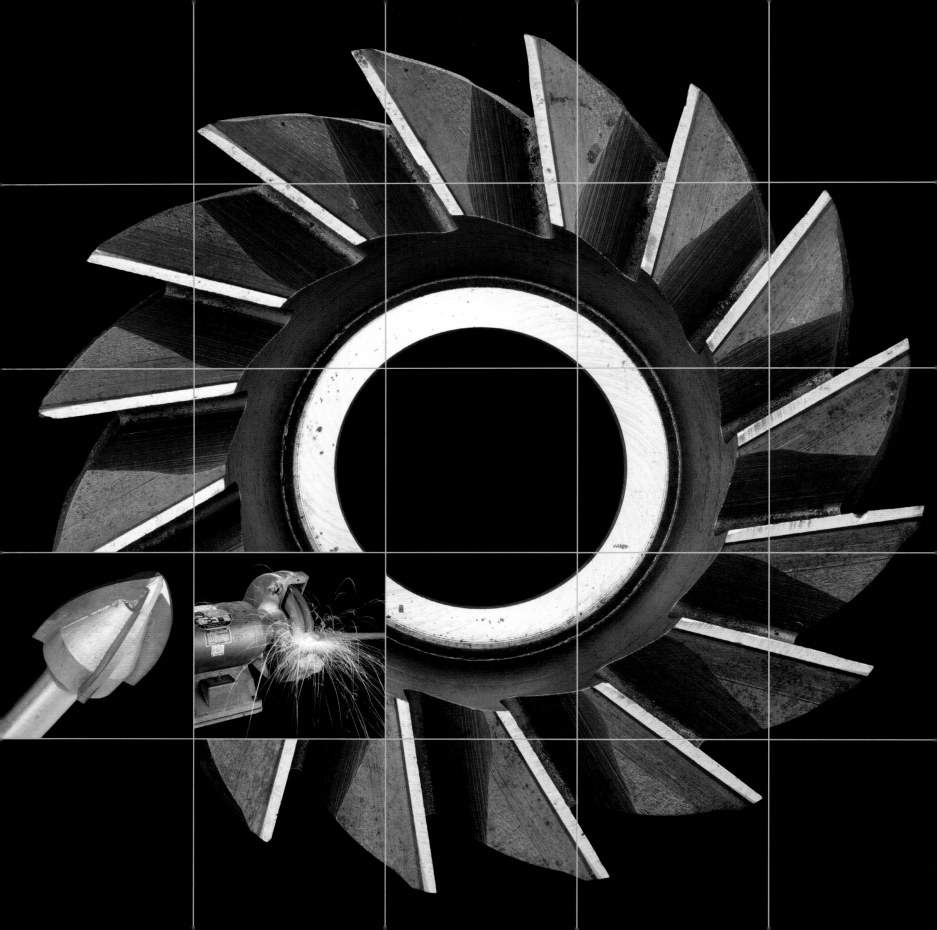

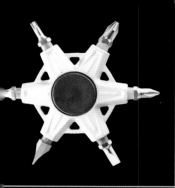

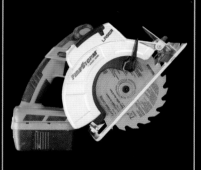

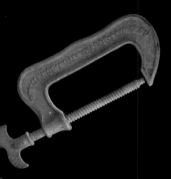

TOOLS

A **Visual Exploration of Implements and Devices** in the Workshop

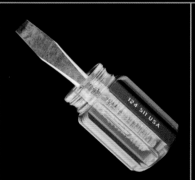
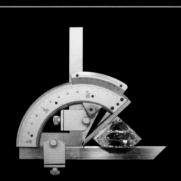

THEODORE GRAY

Bestselling author of *The Elements*
Photographs by Nick Mann

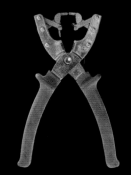

BLACK DOG
& LEVENTHAL
PUBLISHERS
NEW YORK

Black Dog & Leventhal Publishers
Hachette Book Group
1290 Avenue of the Americas
New York, NY 10104

www.hachettebookgroup.com
www.blackdogandleventhal.com

First Edition: October 2023

Black Dog & Leventhal Publishers is an imprint of Perseus Books, LLC, a subsidiary of Hachette Book Group, Inc. The Black Dog & Leventhal Publishers name and logo are trademarks of Hachette Book Group, Inc.

The publisher is not responsible for websites (or their content) that are not owned by the publisher.

The Hachette Speakers Bureau provides a wide range of authors for speaking events. To find out more, go to www.HachetteSpeakersBureau.com or email HachetteSpeakers@hbgusa.com.

Black Dog & Leventhal books may be purchased in bulk for business, educational, or promotional use. For more information, please contact your local bookseller or the Hachette Book Group Special Markets Department at Special.Markets@hbgusa.com.

Print book interior design by Matthew R. Cokeley

Library of Congress Cataloging-in-Publication Data

Names: Gray, Theodore W., author. | Mann, Nick, other.
Title: Tools : a visual exploration of every essential implement and device in the workshop / Theodore Gray; photographs by Nick Mann.
Description: First edition. | New York, NY : Black Dog & Leventhal Publishers, [2023] | Includes index.
Identifiers: LCCN 2022043485 (print) | LCCN 2022043486 (ebook) | ISBN 9780762498307 (hardcover) | ISBN 9780762498291 (ebook)
Subjects: LCSH: Tools. | Workshops—Equipment and supplies.
Classification: LCC TJ1195 .G68 2023 (print) | LCC TJ1195 (ebook) | DDC 621.9—dc23/eng/20221012
LC record available at https://lccn.loc.gov/2022043485
LC ebook record available at https://lccn.loc.gov/2022043486

ISBNs: 978-0-7624-9830-7 (hardcover); 978-0-7624-9829-1 (ebook)

Printed in China

1010

10 9 8 7 6 5 4 3 2 1

INTRODUCTION

ALL MY BOOKS GROW from something I care a lot about. My books about chemistry come from an early desire to play with things that burn enthusiastically (and an actual college degree). My lifelong interest in how things work is the result of me being more comfortable with mechanical things than with people. This book is the most personal of all.

Tools have been a central part of my life for as long as I can remember—literally my earliest memories are of tools. One sticks out in particular: at an age when I could barely see over of the edge of the table, I wanted to drill a hole through a nail.

I had an idea to make an automatic rubber band gun, but my design required drilling a hole crosswise through a nail so it could pivot around that point. Based on my experience at that age with handheld drills, this was plainly impossible. There was no way anyone could hold the drill point steady on the curved surface of the nail, and besides, I couldn't imagine how there could be a drill in the world that small.

We were living in my grandfather's house in Switzerland at the time, so I brought the idea to my uncle to see if he could help me. He took me down to the machine shop in the lower levels of the house and proceeded to blow my little mind with a machine the size of a refrigerator, yet so nimble and precise it was able to put a tiny hole perfectly through the center of the nail.

My memory is not clear enough to say if that giant machine was a large drill press, a small vertical milling machine, or perhaps a jig boring machine. Regardless, it was no doubt the finest available Swiss or German precision tool. Putting a 1 mm hole through the middle of a 3 mm nail was child's play for this machine. (Literally, what with me being a child and all.)

I have never forgotten the power of that tool. It is one of many that have woven themselves into who I am today. This book is the story of those tools, but also many new tools I have discovered, some even while writing this book. When you go down the rabbit hole of looking for variations on a theme, you encounter a delightful, surprising, and never-ending parade of clever options.

It's an expensive rabbit hole, and with my tool addiction, writing a book about tools is possibly the worst thing that's ever happened to me. So . . . uh . . . enjoy the book!

THE DEWALT PEOPLES

TOOLS ARE NOT just incidental to life. Civilizations are defined by the tools they used. "Stone Age," "Bronze Age," and "Iron Age" all refer to the materials used to make tools during those times. It gets much more specific. For example, the "Clovis Peoples" were residents of the Americas in ancient times. We don't know what they called themselves, but we have named them for their characteristic style of stone arrowheads, known as Clovis points. This regional flavor to tools has persisted up until very recent times. Well into the last century workshops in Switzerland would be filled with tools made in Switzerland or Germany. Garages in America would be filled with "Made in America" tools by Craftsman, Stanley, or Milwaukee.

This tribalism persists even to the present day, but in a less geographically focused way. I, for example, was long a member of the "DeWalt Peoples." An archaeological dig in my shop would find an inordinate number of DeWalt brand tools, linked by a trail of very expensive yellow batteries. (The batteries often cost more than the tools, so you want to keep adding tools from the same brand to share batteries.) The DeWalt Peoples hated the Milwaukee Peoples, pitied the RYOBI crowd, and entirely failed to notice the Black+Decker camp.

In recent years, as has happened with so many other products, the world of tool diversity has become a lot smaller. Walk into any establishment selling tools anywhere in the world and you'll find pretty much the same array of screwdrivers, hammers, pliers, drills, and so on. There will be a larger or smaller variety depending on the size of the store, and occasionally you'll find a delightful local specialty, but by and large it's the same old same old.

In large part this is due to the dominance of China as the source of nearly all commonly used tools (and quite a few of the less common ones as well). Milwaukee Tool, for example, is now owned by a company based in Hong Kong. Is this a bad thing? Not really. Though as a DeWalt partisan it pains me to say it, Milwaukee is today perhaps the single most respected brand for professional-grade contractor's power tools. They make more kinds of tools than you can imagine, and sell them at serious prices to serious people who use them hard all day every day.

Good tools have always been expensive, and in the past they were often your only choice. Today you can still get expensive, high-quality tools, but you also have the option of getting what are often perfectly good tools for very little money. For a young tradesman starting out, or an older one starting over, this can be a life-changing fact.

In this book I show equal love to all tools, cheap and expensive, old and new, plain and fancy. I feature both pristine tools fresh out of the box and those worn down by use or disuse. The new ones are beautiful, like airbrushed models in a cordless nailer commercial. But it's the rougher ones that show a deeper beauty, their patina reminding us of the lined faces of the old.

You find them in estate auctions and antiques stores, often rusted from that sad time in a tool's life after their owner becomes too weak to care for them, and before they find their way to a new life. Sometimes the seller has awkwardly spiffed them up, like a scruffy date cleaned up for dinner with the parents. Other times they are in ragged bags, moldy and badly in need of a shower. Either way these are tools that have been loved, that have built a life for someone, and lived that life with them. I hope that in this book Nick Mann and I can show you their beauty inside and out.

WHAT IS A TOOL?

———

THE CONCEPT OF a "tool" is one of the oldest, most universal, and most foundational of all ideas. It's right up there with "language" and "chartered accountancy" in defining who we are as a species.

Depending on how broadly you define the term, we use tools to do nearly everything in our lives, from getting out of the tool we use to sleep better at night (a bed), to using a small pressure washer on our teeth at night (a water flosser). I like this definition to separate tools in the broadest possible sense from things that are not tools:

A tool is a *catalyst*.

In chemistry a catalyst is a substance that makes a chemical reaction happen faster than it otherwise would, *while itself remaining unchanged*. Because it is not consumed by the reaction, a catalyst can keep working as long as you keep feeding in more reactants. Similarly, a tool can keep working as long as you keep giving it material to work on. Wood is a reactant, and the chisel is a catalyst that makes the carving go faster than if you used your teeth.

Unfortunately this definition is far too broad to base a book on. Even if you stick to a much narrower meaning, there are a *lot* of tools. So I'm going to restrict myself to covering things that most people would call a tool, typically an implement or device that you'd expect to find in a home shop—plus some interesting variations to show how the same ideas manifest unexpectedly.

To create this book I started with all my own tools: the ones I grew up with, built my house and farm with, and use today. To those I added many more I found at auctions, estate sales, antiques stores, hardware stores, and building centers, as well as on Reddit, eBay, AliExpress, at markets in Shenzhen (by virtual tour due to Covid) and in person at markets in Bangalore, from friends and relatives, and in a few junk heaps. I took a snapshot of each one with a ruler for scale, gave it a catalog number, and recorded where it was, either at home, at my farm, or, in most cases, in a numbered crate stacked on shelves in my studio. In all I enumerated about twenty-five hundred tools, of which only about a quarter fit on the pages of this book.

While I show some exotic, highly specialized tools, by and large the tools here are ones used by me or people very much like me. This isn't to say that any one person *needs* that many different tools: it's more that, for any given category of tool, there are endless delightful variations, any one of which will do the job but each of which has unique advantages and disadvantages.

Which is right for you? Much as with wands, the tool chooses the user. It lurks on a store shelf waiting for just the right person to walk by, then it leaps out, showing off its style and utility by its smooth curves and thick, satisfying handle. You'll know when the right one has found you. Over the years a lot of tools have assaulted me with the need to buy them.

HOW THIS BOOK IS ORGANIZED

YOU MIGHT NOTICE that the table of contents of this book looks just like a periodic table. This may seem like a silly conceit—and maybe it was when I first started toying with the idea of how to arrange the tools in this book. My publisher and I discussed numerous ways to sort the tools into categories. I wanted to highlight one type of tool on each two-page spread, and cover around a hundred types of tools, which coincidentally is about as many elements as there are (118). As I started exploring the idea of a "Periodic Table of Tools," I worried that 118 would be way more types of tools than I could name, but in fact, no, it's about as many as I came up with in trying to break down my collection into sensible divisions.

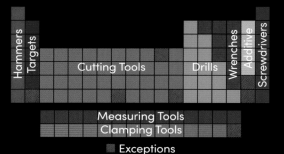

Of course these hundred-or-so types of tools can be grouped into larger categories. For example, hitting tools is a group composed of hammers, mallets, sledges, picks, axes, power hammers, and just to complete the thought, nail pullers to undo what the hammers have done.

So what's a place you find about a hundred individual types of things arranged into about a dozen larger groupings? If your most successful book is about the periodic table of the elements, well, the answer is obvious. And as a final clincher the URL periodictableoftools.com was available, and now I own it and have put a greatly expanded list of tools there for you to explore.

In arranging this book, I have followed the basic properties of the table of elements. Within each column of the periodic table the elements share similar properties, and they get heavier the farther down you go. So, in my periodic table of tools, each column contains related tools, which get bigger, stronger, and heavier as you go down the column. (The exception to this rule is the diagonal line that separates metals from nonmetals in columns 13–16, which in tool world translates into a diagonal line separating drills from wrenches.)

Just for fun I tried to make a few analogies between tool and element properties. For example, column 17 of the periodic table is the halogens, fiery dangerous elements that burn anything they touch. So column 17 of the table of tools contains those that use heat: welders, soldering irons, casting furnaces, and laser cutters. Element 29 is copper, so in that spot I have put non-sparking tools made of brass and bronze, which are alloys primarily of copper. (But don't read too much into every placement: tool-element analogies only go so far.)

I hope you have as much fun romping through this periodic table as I did organizing it and populating each of the 118 squares.

A NOTE
ON SAFETY

WHEN I WAS SMALL, I once asked my dad: What is the best way to cut yourself? After some discussion, we figured out that I meant to ask: What activity is most likely to result in your accidentally cutting yourself? His answer was using your thumb held against a saw blade to guide the start of a cut in a piece of wood (which is, of course, how it's done).

Tools are *dangerous*. Almost any tool can hurt you: personally I've hurt myself with a lot of the tools in this book at one time or another. But I've only ever hurt myself with tools that seem relatively innocuous. I've stabbed myself with a screwdriver countless times. Scraped off some skin with a wood rasp. Hit my thumb with a hammer and splashed molten lead on myself.

I have never been hurt by a table saw, miter saw, welding torch (okay, I've dropped a couple of balls of hot steel on my bare feet), chain saw, milling machine, or any of the other seriously life-threatening tools I've used. I'm willing to bleed a little in the interest of getting the job done, but will not knowingly risk permanent injury. Blindness is *right out*. So I evaluate each situation in terms of a worst-case scenario, and take precautions accordingly.

I encourage you, before using any tool, to make your own decisions about what risks you are or are not willing to take. Almost all the tools in this book can hurt you, and they will if you don't have a clear understanding of how they operate or you are careless with them. Having said that, I am not going to give you any further safety warnings about any of the tools I talk about. If I did, this whole thing would be nothing but lawyer-like warnings about how you're going to cut your head off with a micrometer.

Be careful, be safe, be sensible, and if you hurt yourself with a tool, recognize that only you could have prevented that injury, not me, not this book, and not the two-page safety warning the tool came with, which you didn't read. The only thing that might help is my dad telling you how to cut yourself with it: guiding a saw blade is one of the few ways I have never cut myself with a hand tool.

CONTENTS

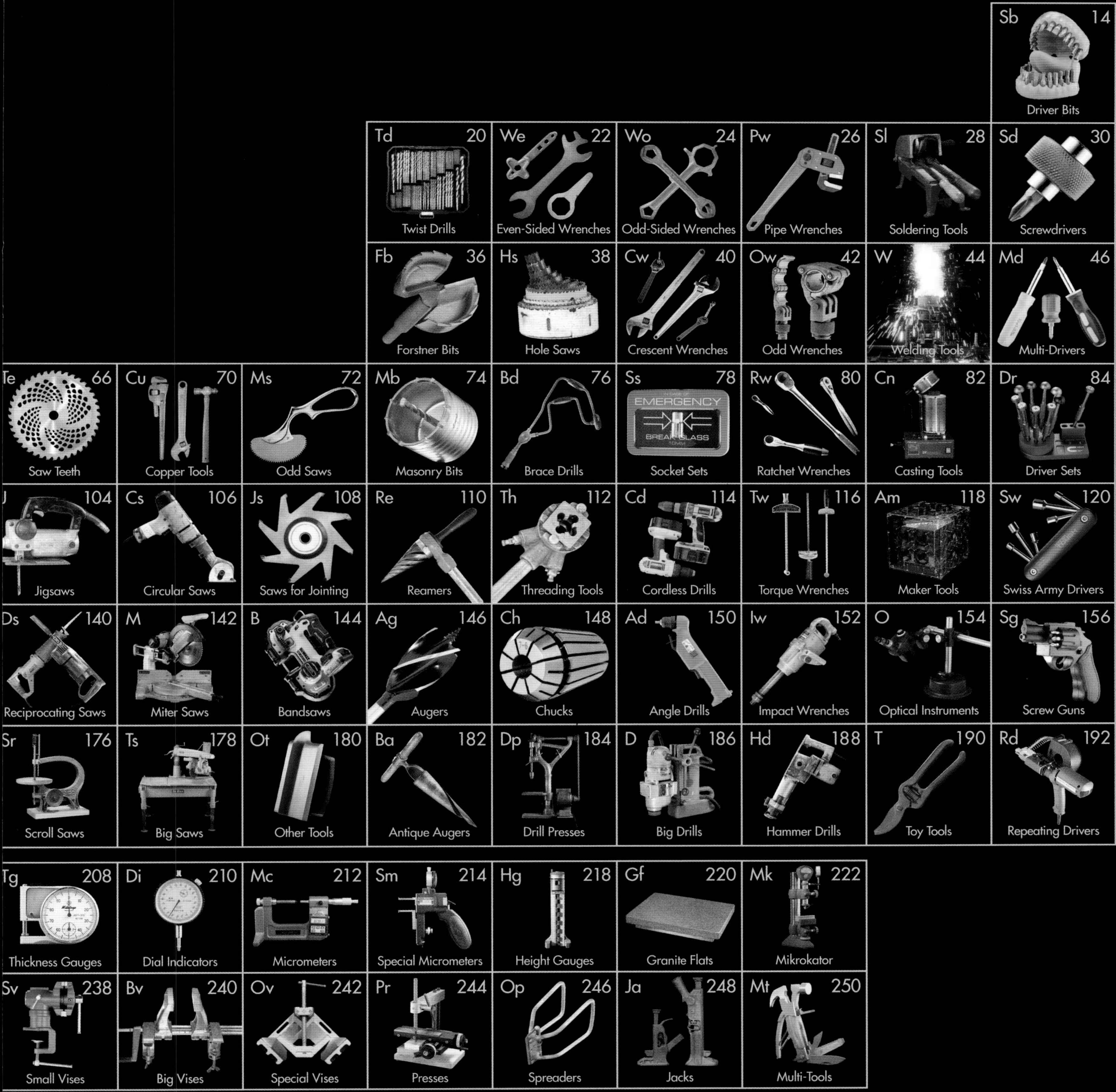

																Sb 14 Driver Bits

This is a periodic-table-style layout of tools. Each cell contains an element symbol, a number, an image, and a caption:

Sb	14	Driver Bits
Td	20	Twist Drills
We	22	Even-Sided Wrenches
Wo	24	Odd-Sided Wrenches
Pw	26	Pipe Wrenches
Sl	28	Soldering Tools
Sd	30	Screwdrivers
Fb	36	Forstner Bits
Hs	38	Hole Saws
Cw	40	Crescent Wrenches
Ow	42	Odd Wrenches
W	44	Welding Tools
Md	46	Multi-Drivers
Te	66	Saw Teeth
Cu	70	Copper Tools
Ms	72	Odd Saws
Mb	74	Masonry Bits
Bd	76	Brace Drills
Ss	78	Socket Sets
Rw	80	Ratchet Wrenches
Cn	82	Casting Tools
Dr	84	Driver Sets
J	104	Jigsaws
Cs	106	Circular Saws
Js	108	Saws for Jointing
Re	110	Reamers
Th	112	Threading Tools
Cd	114	Cordless Drills
Tw	116	Torque Wrenches
Am	118	Maker Tools
Sw	120	Swiss Army Drivers
Ds	140	Reciprocating Saws
M	142	Miter Saws
B	144	Bandsaws
Ag	146	Augers
Ch	148	Chucks
Ad	150	Angle Drills
Iw	152	Impact Wrenches
O	154	Optical Instruments
Sg	156	Screw Guns
Sr	176	Scroll Saws
Ts	178	Big Saws
Ot	180	Other Tools
Ba	182	Antique Augers
Dp	184	Drill Presses
D	186	Big Drills
Hd	188	Hammer Drills
T	190	Toy Tools
Rd	192	Repeating Drivers
Tg	208	Thickness Gauges
Di	210	Dial Indicators
Mc	212	Micrometers
Sm	214	Special Micrometers
Hg	218	Height Gauges
Gf	220	Granite Flats
Mk	222	Mikrokator
Sv	238	Small Vises
Bv	240	Big Vises
Ov	242	Special Vises
Pr	244	Presses
Op	246	Spreaders
Ja	248	Jacks
Mt	250	Multi-Tools

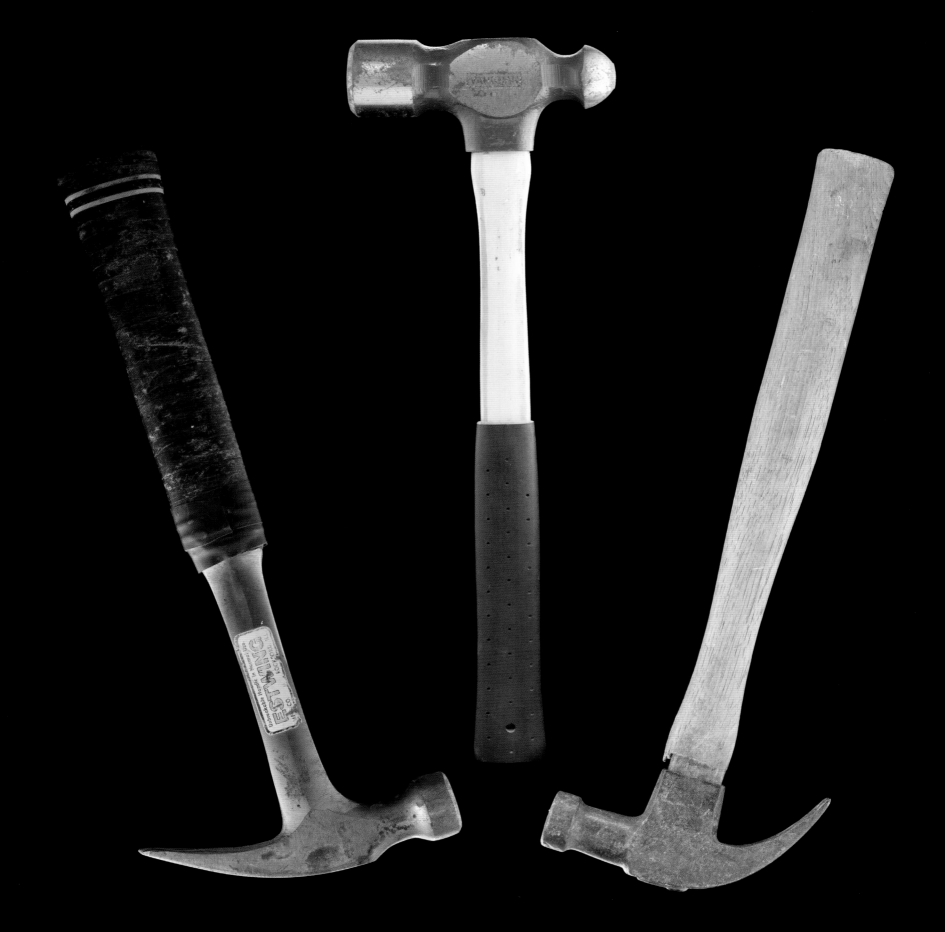

HAMMERS

HAMMERS WERE THE first tools: they are where tools began. Ever since our ancient ancestors first tied their favorite bashing rock to the end of a stick, we have been improving the original design. Something hard and heavy at the end of something long and thin is the basic physics of every hammer.

As the hammer evolved, the hard, heavy thing went from brittle rock to tough but softer bronze, and finally to the forged and hardened steel of a modern framing hammer. For the long, thin handle, many today still prefer the wood of our ancestors, but new options include fiberglass, steel, and exotic titanium. There are advantages and disadvantages to each. Wood rots and steel rusts, which gives a certain advantage

to fiberglass. Titanium is light and strong, but very expensive. In any case, there's no way to know which material you'll prefer without using each for a few days of heavy hammering.

The claw at the back end of most of today's hammer heads is used to pull out nails. It might look like a modern innovation, but the first combination hammer and nail puller dates back to Roman times, and came not long after the first forged iron nails. Only in the last sixty years—the blink of an eye in the history of the hammer—has the first serious competition arrived to challenge this ancestor of all tools, in the form of power nailers and powered versions of the tools (see the next page).

◀ This is a chipping hammer, but one that's well on its way to becoming an adze.

◀ The three hammers you are most likely to encounter are a straight-back rip hammer for large nails, a curved-back claw hammer for smaller nails, and a ball-peen hammer for general hitting.
Left to right:
Claw Hammer
Ball-Peen Hammer
Rip Hammer

▶ Peening hammers come in many shapes and sizes, from the large ball-peen on the left, to this tiny jeweler's hammer. They are used for shaping and hardening metal by repeated and precise pounding.

◀ Duplex nails have a second head which keeps the first one elevated for easy pulling. They are handy for temporary construction, when the nail and the thing it's securing are not meant to stay in place forever.

▲ You can't get much swing going with this stubby thing, but it's handy for hammering a nail in a tight spot, or if you can't find your real hammer.

▼ There's a continuum from blunt hammer heads meant for nails to those that are closer to an axe or adze, used to chip away at something. This chipping hammer is the first stage in that transformation.

▲ I built a fence around my whole yard using this as a hammer to knock each board into place. Because it was there, and my hammer wasn't. (The boards were screwed together so I wasn't using it on nails.)

GRIPNAIL

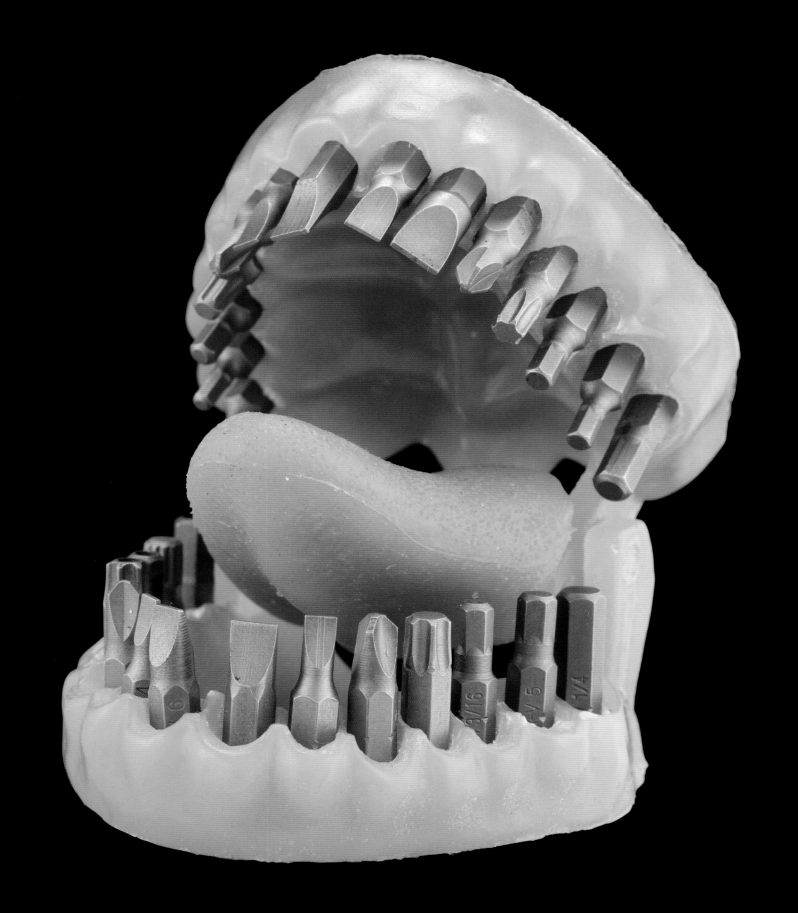

DRIVER BITS

THE DESIGN OF the basic slotted or flat blade screwdriver is about five hundred years old. It has persisted over the centuries mainly because the easiest way to make a screw is with a flat head that has a slit down the middle of it. And for all those centuries people have been struggling to keep the flat blade from slipping out and jamming into the work surface or a finger (whichever it meets first).

In the last century Phillips screws with a plus-shaped indentation and Robertson screws with a square indentation have become popular, largely because they are self-centering. They work great, but are just the tip of the iceberg—er, screwdriver—when it comes to screw head improvement. Over the years dozens of different styles have been invented,

and some have become popular in particular industries.

The tip of a screwdriver needs to be at the end of some kind of handle or power tool to make it useful, but the great diversity of tip styles means that you generally need to have a lot more bits, each with a different tip, than handles. This explains the popularity of driver sets that include one handle and dozens of interchangeable bits. On this page we're looking at the tips in their purest form, in driver sets meant to be used with one of the many handles you are assumed to already have.

If you're too impatient to twist a screw all the way in, you can always go back to the older technology of hitting nails on the head, but do it in style using one of the fancy hammers on the next page.

▲ This clever adapter holds a screwdriver bit and goes on the end of an electric drill. It automatically stops when the screw is a precise depth below the surface.

▼ A dial on the back lets you adjust the depth at which it will stop.

◄ If ever there was a reason for 3D printers to exist, this artisanal screwdriver-tip holder is it! The squishy rubber tongue is amazing. The fact that it makes you think about which types of screwdriver tips are most like incisors, canines, and molars is a pure delight.

▼ This colorful bit set covers what was for several decades the trifecta of driver tips: square drivers for construction, Phillips bits for drywall and manufactured goods, and slotted drivers for antique things that need fixing.

▼ Recently the Torx style has become popular for decking and framing (large construction screws). They also come in colorful sets.

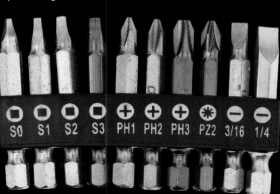

S0	S1	S2	S3	PH1	PH2	PH3	PZ2	3/16	1/4

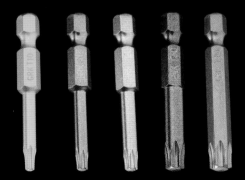

◄ Phillips bits used on drywall screws tend to wear out because they are used with depth stops that allow them to "cam out" and spin when the screw is seated. So you can buy them literally by the bucketful.

▲ To keep people from pulling their products apart, some manufacturers use exotic screws that require a screwdriver you don't have. A comprehensive security bit set represents a world of frustration for these manufacturers.

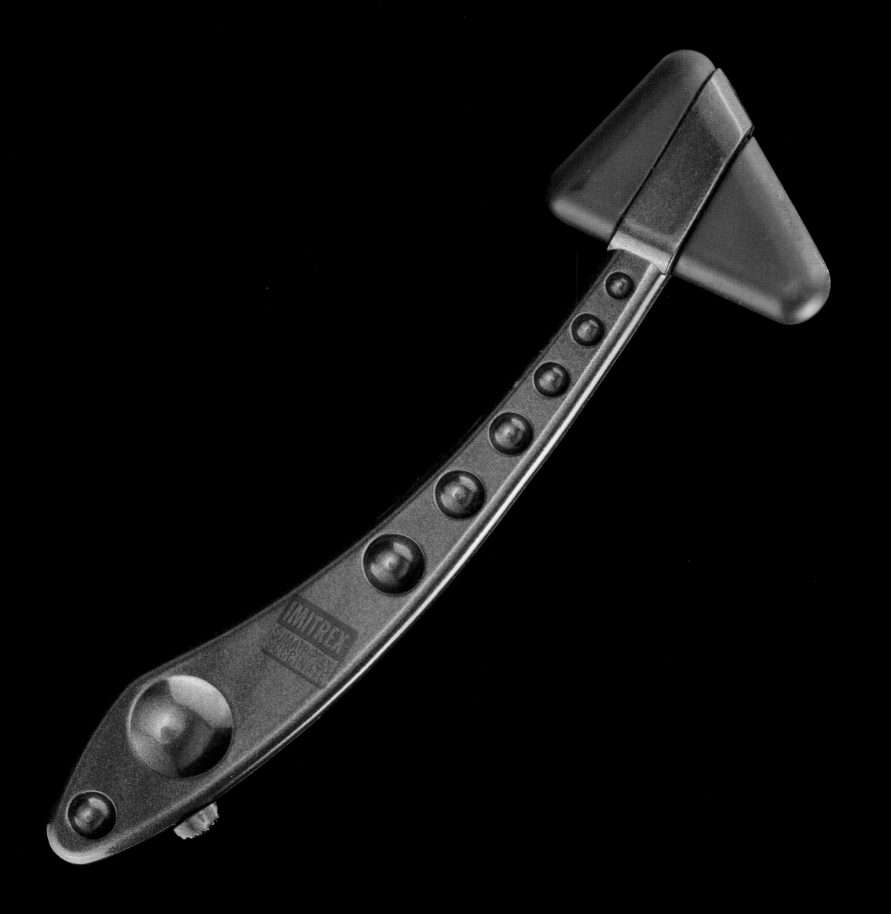

FANCY HAMMERS

MODERN HAMMERS are sold by weight. Heavy ones are used for big nails, lighter ones for small nails. Steel is the ideal material for a hammer because it's hard and dense. Yet there are some *very* expensive hammers with heads made of titanium, which is quite possibly the worst idea in the history of hammers.

Titanium is about half the density of steel, so a titanium hammer head of the same weight needs to be almost twice as big as a steel one. Instead, titanium hammers are often made lighter, and promoted with the claim that they are more efficient because their lighter weight means you can swing them faster, and thus impart more energy per swing.

Even if this were true, which it isn't, the whole argument is ludicrously irrelevant: if a lighter head were better and more efficient, why not just make *steel hammers with lighter heads*? The answer is they do, but people use the heavier ones because they work better for larger nails.

Presented with this devastating rebuttal, titanium-headed marketing people will sometimes resort to mumbling about the modulus of elasticity of titanium. This is also irrelevant because titanium, while strong for its weight, is much softer than steel, meaning that most titanium hammers have steel striking faces on them. Even if the modulus of elasticity made a difference (which it doesn't), the steel face would negate this effect.

All that said, I have no complaint about hammers with titanium *handles,* and am prepared to believe that they are superior. Perhaps they absorb vibration better or allow more of the total weight to be concentrated in the head, where it belongs. But the laws of physics prevent a wooden-, fiberglass-, or steel-handled hammer with a titanium head from making any sense at all, and that is a hill I will die on.

In any case, once you've picked a hammer, and learned to ignore your friends who say you picked the wrong one, you may want some of the accessories on the next page, all designed specifically to be hit with a hammer.

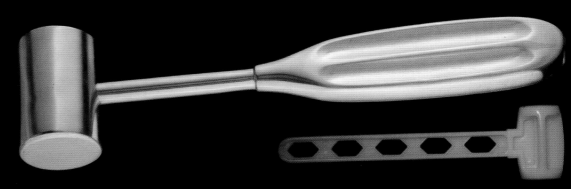

▶ Aluminum seemingly makes zero sense as a material for a hammer: it's lighter and softer even than titanium. But it finds its place in this meat tenderizer, whose head needs to be large, rustproof, cheap, and not too heavy.

◀ Usually when you hit yourself with a hammer, that's a bad thing. But when a doctor hits you with this rubber reflex hammer, you're meant to get a kick out of it.

◀ I only bought this titanium hammer as a sample of the element titanium in my element collection. As a hammer, it's nothing to me.

STILETTO
TITANIUM
14

▲ This hammer is made of a fancy metal—stainless steel. It's a dental hammer meant for hammering chisels, gouges, or whatever other ghastly things dentists hammer into your teeth. The stainless steel allows it to be sterilized in an autoclave.

▲ This hammer really is trying to have it both ways. It's meant for hammering down tent stakes while camping. So which is it supposed to be: heavy for hammering or light for camping? They decided to go with glow-in-the-dark so you can find it at night.

Standard
Bench Made
Dies SIZE 1/4

STAMPS

THERE'S A SAYING, "If all you have is a hammer, every problem looks like a nail." The converse is also true: if your problem is a nail, every tool looks like a hammer. Punches and stamps are not nails, but they are designed specifically to be hit with a hammer, to transmit, concentrate, and shape the force of the hammer blow and deliver it in a precisely targeted way.

Number and letter stamps are used to mark leather, soft metal, or even mild steel. Nail sets countersink nails (driving them slightly below the surface, so the hole can be filled and painted over, making the nail invisible).

Center punches are used for making a small indentation in the precise location where you want to start drilling a hole. Often the most accurate way to locate the center punch before whacking it is to use an awl or scribe to scratch two intersecting lines that cross exactly at the point you want the hole. You can then gently feel with the tip of the center punch until you find the spot where the intersecting scratches trap the tip. This is more accurate, more reliable, and faster than trying to do it visually.

Why would you want to make an indentation where you want to drill a hole? Because it keeps the drill bit from wandering, allowing you to, with practice, start a hole very precisely even with a hand-held drill.

▲ Letter stamps can be hammered or pressed. This hydraulic press uses fairly large letter stamps designed specifically for marking leather belts.

◀ Hardened steel number stamps can be used on any material up to and including mild steel. This set is not missing a stamp: you use the same stamp for 6 and 9.

▶ Nail sets have slightly cupped ends designed to not slip off the head of a nail as it's sunk into the material.

▶ This gorgeous dapping set caught my eye at a jewelry makers' trade show. I didn't need it, but that's beside the point when it comes to a tool set of this magnificence. The ball-end punches are used together with the dimpled block to form metal sheets or bars to the desired radius. (There are twenty-four punches and 4 x 6 = 24 matching dimples on the block.)

▼This set is missing one. Actually, it's missing 4.

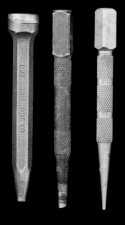

◀ This optical center punch has a clear magnifying lens with crosshairs to sight the exact location where you want the hole. Once the location is set, you can remove the lens while holding the barrel and insert the pointed center punch.

◀ Hole punch kits come with many sizes of punch and one handle, which you hit really hard with a hammer to make a clean hole in a piece of leather, cloth, rubber, or similarly soft material.

▲ This razor-sharp punch would dull instantly if used on wood, but that's OK because it's meant for punching skin, for example to remove a mole or add a large hole to your ear.

▲ These spring-loaded center punches don't need a hammer. You push down hard on the handle to build up pressure in a spring, which eventually snaps and kicks the point into the material.

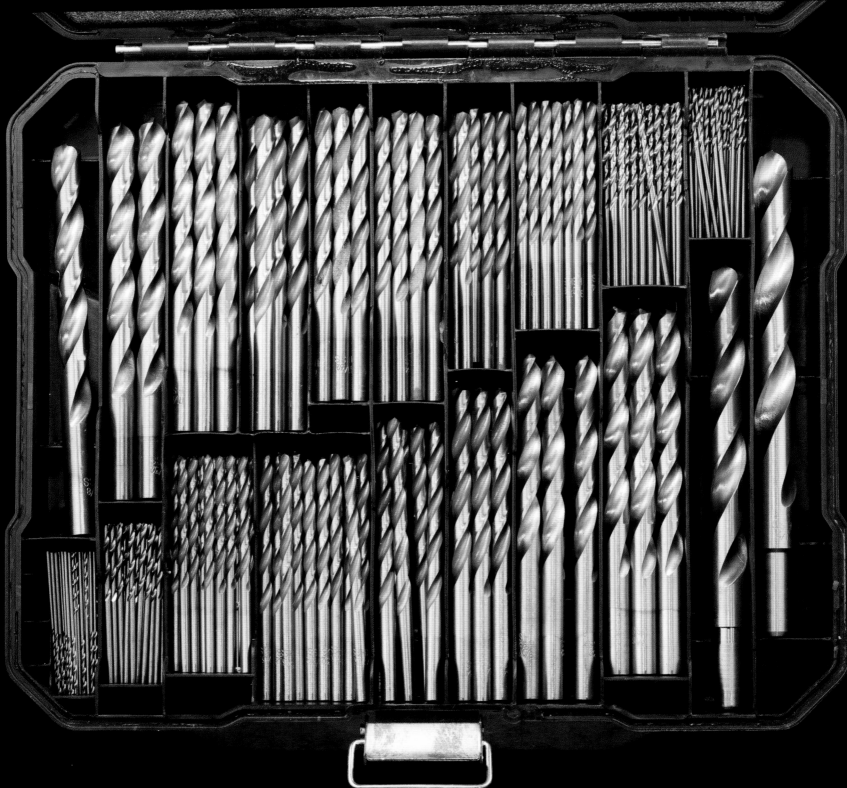

TWIST DRILLS

TWIST DRILL BITS are designed with spiral "flutes" that act like a grain auger to carry the chips from the material you're drilling up and out of the hole. The shape, pitch, and number of flutes you use—and the shape and sharpness of the tip—depend on what you're drilling. We'll meet quite a range of them in the coming pages.

Because you need a different drill for every diameter of hole, drills are almost always found in sets of between a dozen and 115 (a number specific to Imperial sets). There is something very satisfying about a complete set of bits, but owning one is to live on the edge of danger. There is a lingering anxiety that's impossible to shake. Sooner or later, one of those bits is going to get lost or broken.

You promise yourself that you're going to put away each one as soon as you're done using it. It's going to be OK this time! But it never is. And once you reach a certain age, you know it. You know that your set's youthful shine and perfection, like your own, is doomed. Nothing will ever match the pure and fleeting joy of your first full set of bits.

So enjoy your youth while you have it. Run while you are strong, love while you can love without fear. Don't listen to me, buy that expensive brand-name 115-piece drill bit set and believe in your heart that it will always be there for you, every bit, even the smallest. There is plenty of time to be old and cynical later. At least you'll always have your memories.

The tools on the next pages won't fill the hole in your heart, but they can help fill the holes you drill with all these bits.

◀ When I saw this set of twist drill bits, I just about fainted with joy. It's like a taste of immortality. Instead of having one bit of every size, it has several of only the most common sizes. You can use a 1/8-inch bit, lose it, and still have a complete set. This is a collection of drill bits you can trust and settle in with for a long time.

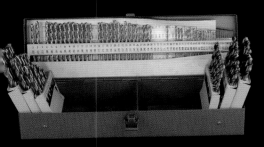

▲ The number 115 in a standard complete set comes from 29 fractional sizes from ¹⁄₁₆ inch to ½ inch in steps of ¹⁄₆₄ inch, plus 26 letter sizes from A to Z, plus wire gauge sizes from 1 to 60. The vast majority of these bits will never be used. As you can see from the missing bits, I've had this set for a while.

▲ Brad point drills work only in wood. Their sharp points and knife edges would instantly fold over if used on metal.

▼ Long bits are used to drill holes where it's hard to reach, like inside a wall. Rarely would you use one to drill a hole anywhere near as deep as the bit is long.

▼ The most common length of bit is called jobber length (different for every diameter, but standardized as a set). That's what you find in the ordinary sets shown on this page. These screw machine bits are shorter than jobber bits, which makes them stiffer and less likely to go off center. (The name, like "jobber," is historical: these bits have nothing to do with screws, they are just shorter.)

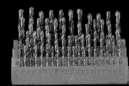

▲ The very shortest bits are called spotting bits. Their job is to make a pilot hole in exactly the place you want to start a bigger hole: being so short makes them very stiff and unlikely to wander off center.

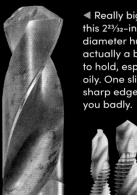

◀ These very short bits with built-in countersinks are called center drills, because their main use is making a hole for a lathe center. They can also be used as spotting bits.

◀ Really big drills, like this 2²³⁄₃₂-inch (69 mm) diameter hunk, are actually a bit dangerous to hold, especially when oily. One slip and the sharp edge can cut you badly.

▲ These clever bits combine a drill with a tap, letting you make a tapped (threaded) hole in one pass.

▲ This drill is for bone. It's so long that you could, for example, drill all the way down the middle of a leg bone to install a titanium stabilizing rod. A reader once sent me pictures of exactly this being done to their leg and I'm going to spare you the sight.

EVEN-SIDED WRENCHES

THERE AREN'T NEARLY as many wrench shapes as there are screwdriver tips. Most of them are regular polygons, varying only by how many sides they have: one, two, three, four, five, six, seven, or eight. On this page we'll look at those with an even number of sides, then move on to odd-sided wrenches on the next page.

Square nuts were popular in the past because they are easier to make, and many plumbing fittings have nuts or rings with eight sides because the more sides you have, the less material is wasted between a circular center and the outer, flat sides.

But six-sided wrenches are by far the most common and make up probably 99.9 percent of all wrenches.

Adjustable wrenches are versatile, but single-piece-of-metal, six-sided hex wrenches are still fundamental, and every toolbox should have at least one set. Unlike adjustable wrenches, fixed hex wrenches can fit in the tightest spaces. They are stronger because there is no joint to flex or loosen. And they are much faster to use precisely because they aren't adjustable: once you have the right size in hand, you can slap it on and off with no fumbling around.

◀ Box-end wrenches can have very thin sides, as you can see in this extreme example of a six-sided wrench.

▼ Open-ended wrenches need proportionally thicker sides. This multi-wrench for hex nuts calls itself "tactical," and I have absolutely no idea what that's supposed to mean.

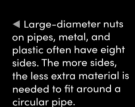

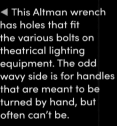

◀ This Altman wrench has holes that fit the various bolts on theatrical lighting equipment. The odd wavy side is for handles that are meant to be turned by hand, but often can't be.

◀ Rather large, rather odd wrench.

◀ This octagonal wrench is designed for the wire wheels on an MGB Midget Triumph.

▶ This emergency gas shutoff wrench could be described as a two-sided wrench: it engages the flat tab on a gas valve.

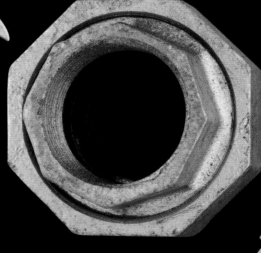

◀ Large-diameter nuts on pipes, metal, and plastic often have eight sides. The more sides, the less extra material is needed to fit around a circular pipe.

▲ Some exotic cars use large octagonal nuts instead of separate lug nuts to hold the wheels in place. The 250 to 300 foot-pounds of torque listed on this nut is a *lot* of torque.

▼ Square-headed nuts and valve heads were once common. They can be turned easily with a standard open-ended or crescent wrench, but a dedicated square wrench will give you more torque.

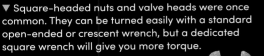

▲ Water pipe plugs often have square heads.

▲ Drain plugs, on the other hand, often have square holes, because they are meant to lie flush with the floor.

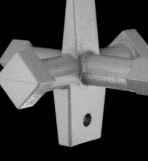

▲ Strictly speaking, this square drain plug wrench belongs with the screwdrivers, because it drives from the inside, not the outside. But it's so big I'm going to classify it as an honorary wrench.

▲ This eight-sided valve head is designed for the most versatile wrench of all: your hand.

ODD-SIDED WRENCHES

AS A GENERAL RULE, if a bolt head has an odd number of sides, it's meant to be hard to turn without a special tool. Fire hydrants are a good example: five-sided heads are the most common, with three and seven being a bit harder to find. This results in all sorts of fun nonstandard fire hydrant wrenches, as well as odd-sided wrenches needed to open smaller water faucets in public locations. Odd numbers of sides can also be found on things meant to be hard to steal: anti-theft lug nuts, for example.

What's beyond the ones we've seen so far? Although there are nine-sided and twelve-sided spline drive heads, these are more like gears, not nuts with flat sides: I'm not aware of any flat-sided wrenches with more than eight sides. However, if you go all the way up to an infinite number of sides, forming a smooth circle, there are wrenches for that, coming up next.

◀ There are said to be seven-sided fire hydrant wrenches, but so far I have only been able to find three and five. The eight-sided opening is for generic fittings, and the peg holes are for hose rings.

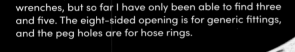

▲ A wrench with one side might seem logically impossible, but there are some tools that you could describe that way, including this one, which catches on the grooves of certain kinds of slip nuts and vise screws.

▼ This thing is called a chain whip. No, it's not what you think, it's a one-sided wrench that works by catching on the teeth of a bicycle gear.

▶ *This chain whip is exactly what you think it is.*

▲ As with three-sided bolts, five-sided bolts are used for security purposes, because they require an uncommon wrench to loosen them.

▲ Three- and four-sided heads are found on some water faucets in public places, for example on the wall outside my old studio. Which is why I have this wrench.

▼ This cabinet lock can be opened with a triangle wrench. It's less secure than a key, but more secure than a square or hexagonal head. The recess makes vise-grip pliers useless.

▶ Fire hydrant heads are common in many cities, and here's a wrench to open them.

▼ For some godforsaken reason, Toyota decided it was necessary in some of their cars to use a five-sided bolt head on the mechanism that lowers the spare tire. I found this out the hard way, stranded with a flat tire and no five-sided wrench.

▲ These are heptagon (seven-sided) lug nuts for car wheels, the idea being that the average car wheel thief doesn't have a wrench that will fit them. Neither does the average tire shop, so be sure to keep the adapter they came with.

PIPE WRENCHES

PIPE WRENCHES are nasty brutes. They intentionally damage anything they're used on. That's because on a round pipe there are no flats or splines for a wrench to grip, so you have to make your own. Used with any force, a pipe wrench will leave score marks where its teeth bit down into the metal.

The key to a pipe wrench is the adjustable jaw, which is designed to tilt back and forth. When it tilts away from the handle, the opening becomes slightly larger. When it tilts toward the handle, the opening gets smaller. To use the wrench, you tighten the jaws down on the pipe while the movable jaw is tilted away from the handle. When you start turning the handle, the jaw is pulled closer, and thus becomes tighter. The harder you turn, the harder the jaw grips.

If you turn the wrench in the other direction, the jaw is instead pushed away from the handle, and becomes looser. That means pipe wrenches have an automatic ratchet-like behavior: they can be moved back and forth, advancing the pipe a bit more each time, without you having to adjust the jaws. If you want to turn the pipe in the other direction, you have to flip the wrench over and put it on the other side of the pipe.

If you want to avoid marking up the pipe, or the pipe is delicate and thin-walled, there are other choices. Strap, chain, and collet wrenches grip smoothly all the way around, but can't turn as hard without slipping. If you want to avoid pipe wrenches entirely in your plumbing endeavors, there is another way: soldering.

▲ Chain wrenches, including this odd one from India, can be used on large-diameter iron or plastic pipe. They automatically self-tighten just like a normal pipe wrench.

▼ Oil filter wrenches create a small amount of friction all the way around.

◀ This bendy-handled pipe wrench is hilarious, like some kind of cartoon character. I can't quite put my finger on which one. Maybe something from a Tim Burton movie?

▲ 6-inch (150 mm)

▲ 8-inch (200 mm)

▲ 10-inch (250 mm)

▲ 12-inch (300 mm)

▲ 18-inch (450 mm)

▼ 24-inch (600 mm)

▼ 36-inch (900 mm)

▼ This lightweight aluminum-handled wrench gripped a pipe so tightly that the handle bent before the jaws slipped. No human could have done this bare-handed. Someone used a "helper" pipe slipped over the end of the handle to create extra leverage.

▶ Old pipe wrenches are among the most common finds in antiques store tool sections. They are just too lovely for anyone to throw away, and they never break.

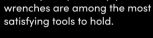

▲ Oddly-shaped old pipe wrenches are among the most satisfying tools to hold.

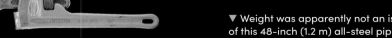
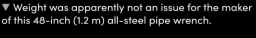

▼ Weight was apparently not an issue for the maker of this 48-inch (1.2 m) all-steel pipe wrench.

SOLDERING TOOLS

SOLDERING AND BRAZING are techniques that use one type of metal as a sort of glue to hold together pieces of another type of metal that has a higher melting point. The most common example is using tin-lead solder to hold together copper wires. A soldering iron with a hot tip is touched to the wires until they are hot enough to melt the solder when it's added to the joint. Copper melts at a much higher temperature than solder, but when liquid solder comes in contact with a clean copper surface, it "wets" the surface, and on cooling sticks to it to form a strong mechanical and electrical connection.

Soldering is also commonly used to join copper water pipes. Since the use of lead for this purpose is banned in many countries, solder made with some mixture of tin, silver, bismuth, copper, and antimony is

used instead. Soldering pipes is high stakes: if you don't clean the pipe and fittings properly, you'll get a dirty joint that leaks water, and you'll have to take the whole thing apart, dry everything, and start over. Done right it's tremendously satisfying to watch the solder instantly flow into the joint and bleed out on all sides.

Brazing is the same as soldering, but at a higher temperature range. You might, for example, braze together steel parts using bronze (a mixture of copper and tin). The brazing material has a much higher melting point than tin-lead solder, but still much lower than steel's melting point.

Beyond brazing comes welding, which uses temperatures hot enough to melt the metals you are joining. Or you can dispense entirely with heat and just use screws to join your metals instead.

▶ Even the most humble plumbing torch, which this is not, delivers far more heat than a soldering iron, because the flame plays directly on the pipes.

◀ Before the introduction of propane torches in the 1950s, torches for plumbing ran on liquid fuel. The tip needed to be preheated by burning some fuel in a little tray under the tip. This is why, even though I have several of these, I've never dared light one.

◀ Representing the least convenient form of cordless soldering, these "sad iron" antiques have to be heated in a furnace, then used to do a bit a soldering before being returned to the fire.

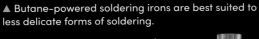

◀ When I was a kid I soldered together *so many things*. But I'm not *that* old: this antique soldering iron probably predates me by a couple decades.

▼ My current "rework" soldering station includes both a soldering iron and a mini heat gun that blows a thin stream of air hot enough to melt solder (which is useful for surface-mount chips).

▲ Butane-powered soldering irons are best suited to less delicate forms of soldering.

▼ Adding pure oxygen, even a tiny bit as in this mini torch, makes the flame *much* hotter.

▶ For really extreme cordless soldering, you used to be able to get thermite-powered soldering irons. The cartridges contain a mixture of iron oxide (rust), aluminum powder, and moderators that, when ignited, burns *very* hot.

▲ This hot-melt glue gun is like a soldering iron for wood or cardboard. Or you could say that solder is like hot-melt glue for metal.

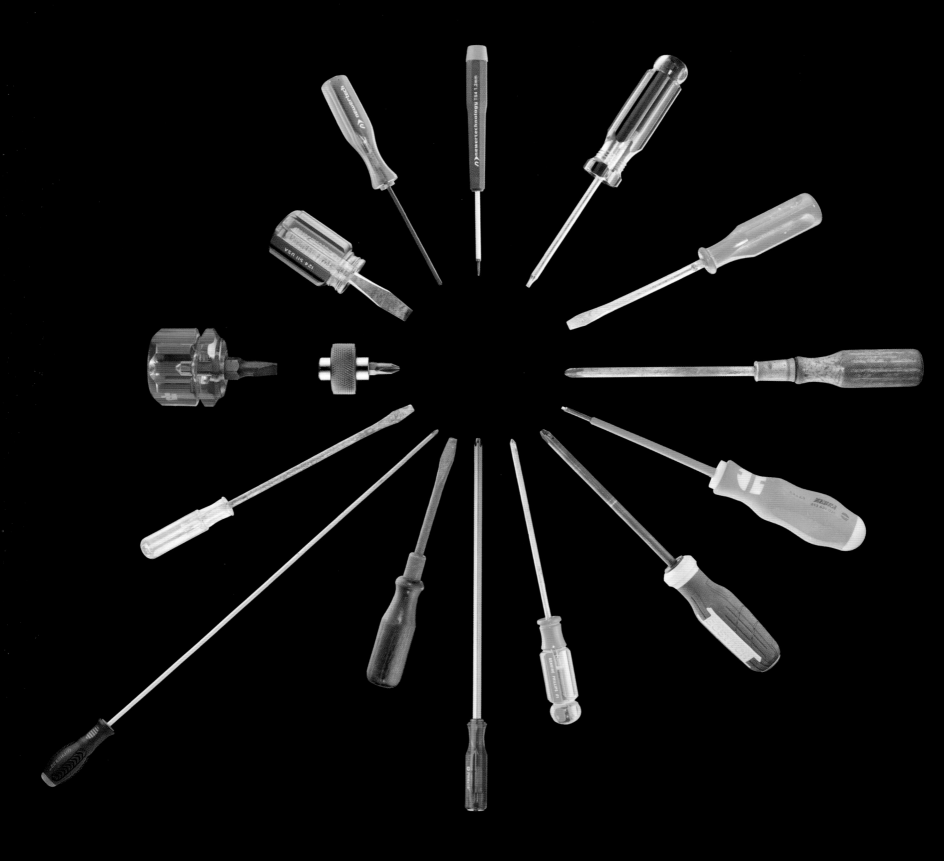

SCREWDRIVERS

FOR GENERATIONS—centuries in fact—screwdrivers were simply a piece of metal with a flat blade and wooden handle. Today we have an endless variety of multi-headed screwdrivers, power screwdrivers, cordless electric pencil screwdrivers, and so on. But nothing has yet replaced the basic, single-function, manual screwdriver.

One reason for this is that nothing beats your basic short manual screwdriver for reaching a screw at the bottom of a deep, narrow hole—something you find very commonly embedded in the plastic cases of appliances and toys that tend to break a lot and need taking apart.

Like the simple hand chisels they resemble, simple screwdrivers can be beautifully made and satisfying to hold in the hand. Or not. Either way they are among the most useful of all tools.

◀ I have screwdrivers ranging in length from under an inch (25 mm) to over two feet (670 mm) long. The really short ones also have to be relatively wide so there is enough handle to grab, and some of the really long ones are perhaps as much prybar as they are screwdriver.

◀▶ Wood is an attractive material for screwdriver handles. Attractive, but not very practical. It's not as strong as plastic, and doesn't last unless it's taken care of like fine furniture.

◀ The steel shank of this Irwin screwdriver continues on through the whole handle and makes for an exceptionally strong screwdriver.

▶ This is the flattest right-angle screwdriver I know of.

▼ This specialized driver fits over and turns screw-in hanging hooks (such as you might hang plants or sausages from).

◀ Cellulose acetate, a type of plastic that is often yellow for some reason, is a great material for screwdriver handles. It's even used for chisel handles because it can survive decades of hammering.

▼ Screw pliers? These are sold for one purpose: adjusting the screw that holds together the blades of a pair of scissors. They let you press the screwdriver bit into the screw very hard without the danger of it slipping or camming out.

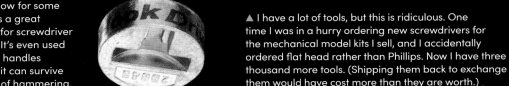

▲ I have a lot of tools, but this is ridiculous. One time I was in a hurry ordering new screwdrivers for the mechanical model kits I sell, and I accidentally ordered flat head rather than Phillips. Now I have three thousand more tools. (Shipping them back to exchange them would have cost more than they are worth.)

MALLETS

THERE'S NO PRECISE definition that distinguishes a mallet from other categories of hammer. It's mostly a question of size, shape, and who you're talking to whether you call it a hammer, a mallet, a sledge, or a maul.

Mallets tend to have wide, flat striking surfaces, because they are meant to deliver their force "gently" over a wider area, rather than in the sharply concentrated form delivered by a hardened steel hammer. Many mallets are made to be softer than the thing they are hitting, so you find a wide range of materials, with brass, plastic, rubber, and wood being the most common.

Aside from the hardness of the head, there is also the question of how fast the head comes to rest when it lands. Mallets with solid heads, no matter what they're made of, necessarily come to rest quickly upon impact. If you want to deliver energy more slowly, over the course of maybe a tenth of a second instead of a thousandth of a second, you can use a dead blow mallet, which has a hollow head loosely filled with steel or lead shot (pellets) that spread out while you are swinging the mallet. When the head reaches its target, the pellets crash into the face from the inside, but not all at once. You get a dull thud and no bounce, which is good for knocking parts into place—after which you might want to use one of the tools on the next page to hold them there.

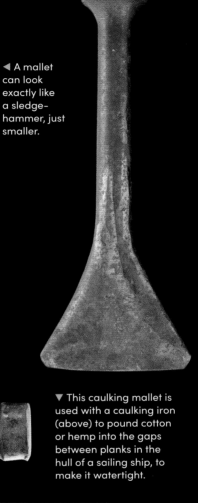

◀ A mallet can look exactly like a sledge-hammer, just smaller.

◀ Arranged in order of decreasing hardness, these mallets are used instead of traditional steel-head hammers to avoid leaving marks on progressively softer materials. A soft iron mallet is used on hardened steel, brass on iron, lead on brass, and leather on leather.

▼ This caulking mallet is used with a caulking iron (above) to pound cotton or hemp into the gaps between planks in the hull of a sailing ship, to make it watertight.

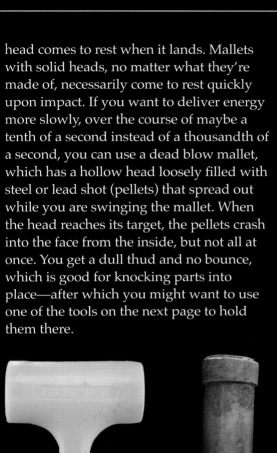

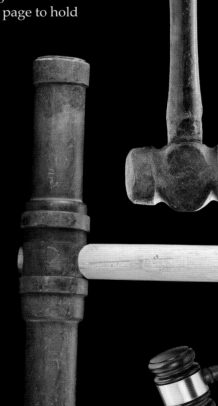

◀▶ If you want to seriously bonk someone, these wooden mashers may be a good choice.

▶ A plastic dead blow mallet (often called a dead blow hammer) will gently knock wood or metal parts into place. Don't use it on anything pointed, like a nail, or the head could split open on impact.

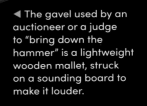

◀ The gavel used by an auctioneer or a judge to "bring down the hammer" is a lightweight wooden mallet, struck on a sounding board to make it louder.

RIVETS

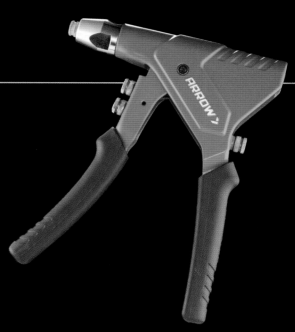

THE POP RIVET seems to have fallen out of favor in recent decades. You can still buy them, but I get the feeling that the pendulum has swung in favor of sheet metal screws for most applications where you might have once used a pop rivet. My guess is that it's the advent of cheap, powerful cordless electric drill/drivers and the invention of self-drilling, self-tapping screws that spelled the end of the age of pop rivets.

Pop rivets are not like the hot rivets you see being hammered into place in old movies (more on those later). They are applied cold with a tool that pulls rather than hammers. Referring to the stages of pop rivet application shown on this page, you can see that a stem, most of which gets thrown away, is pulled into a grommet-like part, deforming it so it ends up clamping the materials together. An advantage over nuts and bolts is that you only need access to one side of the material to apply them, but that's true of screws as well.

The accordion rivet tool on the left is one of my very favorite tools because of how clever and elegant it is. And that's despite the fact that I've never used it, in stark contrast to the tools on the next page.

▲ Most people never get to experience the joy of an accordion-style pop rivet tool. The common ones are squeeze-driven.

◄ This magnificent rebel, a "Lazy Tong" pop rivet tool, uses an accordion to cleverly translate about 2 feet (600 mm) of hand movement into less than an inch (2 cm) of rivet stem movement, magnifying the force of your hand by about 30–1 (even more near the end of the stroke). Notice how the bars get thicker the closer you are to the business end. The whole accordion works together to create the overall leverage ratio, but the force accumulates on the end that is resisting movement.

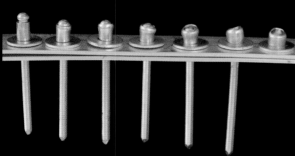

▲ The stages of pop rivet applications, from left to right. A rivet is inserted from the bottom, and a washer (optional) is placed on the top side. The pop rivet tool pulls the rod (which is a bit like a nail with a rounded head) downward, spreading out the grommet. When the head is fully seated, the rod breaks off, leaving the rivet in place.

▶ If you can get to both sides of the material, rivets can be applied with a press like this, which squeezes a rivet or grommet flat while spreading it out.

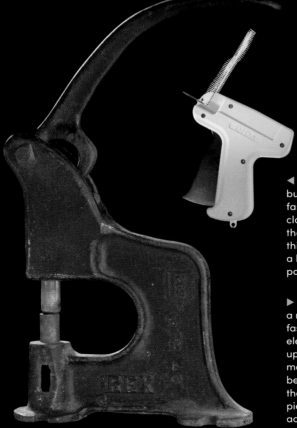

◄ Not exactly a rivet, but this tagging gun fastens price tags to clothes for sale, using those annoying plastic things that are, sort of, a bit like rivets holding paper to cloth.

▲ Again not exactly a rivet, but this is a clever gun used to apply, tighten, and trim off zip ties.

▶ Yet again, not exactly a rivet. This exotic plastic fastening tool uses an electric current to heat up a zigzag piece of metal, which can then be melted down into the surface of a cracked piece of plastic, joining it across the gap.

FORSTNER BITS

THERE ARE TWO THINGS that make drilling wood fundamentally different than drilling metal. First, wood is *much* softer than metal. Even the very hardest hardwood is nowhere near the hardness of lead, aluminum, or copper, the softest common metals. So you can drill much bigger holes in wood than you can in metal, with much less effort.

Second, wood has grain, which you can imagine as thousands of strong threads all lined up and held together with relatively weak glue. This creates problems unique to wood. For example, if you try to cut across the grain, individual threads will get pulled out and make the edge of the cut rough, or even ruin the surface around the hole. That's called tearing, and it happens if you use dull tools or tools not suitable for wood cutting.

The solution is to cut the grain with a sharp blade, like a knife edge, before removing wood from one side of the cut. That's why the main feature of most wood cutting bits is that they have knife edges around the outside of the bit, which reach the wood before the raking blades that remove material from inside the hole. The purest example of this idea is called a Forstner bit, a tool I have spent a lot of time using.

Forstner bits are known for being able to drill at any angle through the grain, and even into the end grain. This is extraordinarily tough to do because it requires cutting many more threads with every pass of the cutting edge. These bits can even make difficult holes that enter a board at a slant, but only if they are held firmly in a drill press.

On the next page we'll meet some other ways of dealing with grain, but Forstner bits are so wonderful they deserve their own page.

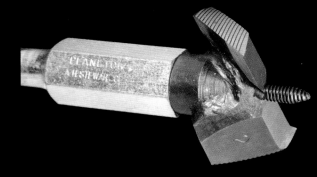

▶ This variation on a Forstner bit adds a tapered screw tip, which allows the bit to pull itself into the wood. This sometimes lets you use the bit as a hand-held tool, as long as you and/ or your power drill are strong enough to keep the bit going at the rate dictated by the screw thread.

◀ I love my Forstner bit set so much. It was pretty expensive. This is the bit from the set that I used to drill all the holes in the blocks of walnut that make up my wooden periodic table table.

▲ Here are 150 drilled and routed walnut blocks ready to be assembled into a periodic-table table.

◀ When you drill with a Forstner bit, all the wood inside the hole gets turned into nice big curled shavings. This can really add up.

▼ Under each of these removable engraved tiles is a hole drilled with my largest Forstner bit.

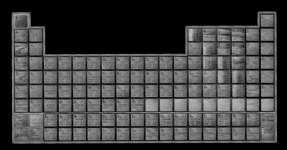

▲ This set of interchangeable Forstner bits includes three shanks, and a bunch of different interchangeable bit heads that screw into the shanks. Seems like a lot of trouble and expense to avoid having a fixed shank on every head.

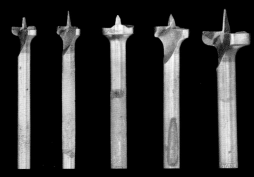

▲ These Forstner bits look like you could use them in a hand-held drill, and you sort of can, but watch out! They tend to jump out and run all over the place as soon as the outer edge touches the wood. A drill press is best.

HOLE SAWS

AN INTERESTING CLASS of drill bit–like tools makes holes by cutting only a ring of material, rather than chopping up everything inside the hole. This includes hole saws, plug cutters, and tenon cutters. A hole saw is just what it sounds like: a saw wrapped into a circle to saw out a hole. They are great for cutting very large diameter holes with much less effort than if you tried to carve out the center.

With plug cutters and tenon cutters the goal isn't to make a hole: that's just a byproduct. It's what gets pulled out of the hole that we're interested in. Plug cutters extract round plugs, like wooden corks, that can be used to fill in other holes or cover up screws. Tenon cutters leave a rounded peg on the end of a square piece of wood, which can then be glued into a hole called a mortise. Mortise-and-tenon construction is common in quality furniture and barn construction, as is the use of fasteners that require the tools on the next page.

◀ Hole saws for wood and drywall come in sets that store compactly one inside another. A small number of arbors and pilot drills work with the whole set.

▼ Plug cutters work to make a smooth inner cylinder, which you remove and use elsewhere, leaving a hole you don't care about (usually in a leftover piece of wood). The bit on the left makes straight-sided plugs, while the bit on the right makes tapered plugs that can be hammered in for a tight fit.

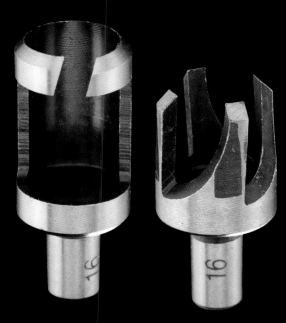

▶ This is a plug cutter for bones, used to make plugs for transplants.

斯钉取出器 10.0mm KD2020no (1)

▲ This is a plug cutter for pineapples.

▲ Plugs made of contrasting wood can make attractive inlay patterns.

▶ This tenon cutter, a type of hollow drill, makes a smooth cylinder, like a plug cutter, and also cuts a smooth, flat bottom around it. The result is a square wooden bar with a round rod sticking out of it, ready to be glued into a round hole.

▶ Drilling a square hole in wood is easier than it might seem. You just put a hollow square chisel around a normal drill bit and attach the whole thing to a machine able to push the chisel down really hard.

CRESCENT WRENCHES

CRESCENT IS THE NAME of the company that invented crescent wrenches, but the name long ago became generic for this style of adjustable wrench. Despite their limitations, if there were a list of tools essential to the maintenance of civilization, the crescent wrench would be right up there with hammers, vise-grip pliers, and can openers.

The main problem with crescent wrenches is that they tend to loosen themselves as you use them. Each time you remove and reapply the jaws to a bolt, the adjusting screw wiggles just a bit looser, until the jaws slip off the bolt and you bang your knuckles into the conveniently placed sharp corner. I usually retighten on every turn. This slows things down, but I like my knuckles with the skin on them.

Given the obvious convenience of one tool for every size bolt, and the obvious problem of loosening, there have, of course, been many attempts to make a better version of the crescent wrench, some more successful than others.

The most common "improvement" is the introduction of some form of ratcheting action, where, much like a pipe wrench, the jaws automatically open enough to let the wrench slip around to the next set of flats when the wrench is turned backward. None of these "improved" crescent wrenches work very well. Another attempted upgrade is an adjusting screw that releases so you can rapidly adjust the jaws. These wrenches aren't worth the extra cost and size in the head, but at least they work reasonably well, unlike some of the wrenches on the next page.

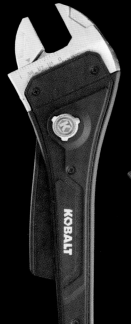

▶ This variety isn't usually called a crescent wrench, though the design is basically the same. It's weak in terms of force, but that's okay because it's designed to turn large slip nuts on plumbing fixtures, which don't require much torque.

◀ The standard crescent wrench has changed very little over many decades, and versions from different manufacturers look nearly identical. The Crescent company itself no longer makes crescent wrenches in the US: they now sell Chinese-made wrenches under their brand name.

▶ The jaws on this one get a bit tighter each time you squeeze the handle, and lock at that separation until you press the release button. The whole thing is too big to fit many places.

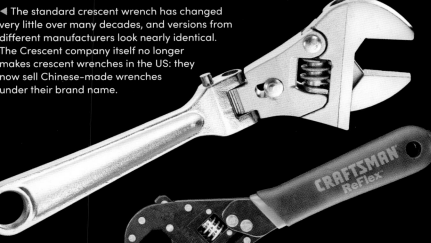

▲ This articulated crescent wrench also optionally ratchets. It isn't a completely silly design, but you lose a lot of leverage if you bend the handle.

▲ In this design, the whole adjusting screw slides out when the wrench is turned backward, providing an automatic ratchet action, but only as long as the bolt is already fairly tight (otherwise the bolt just turns backward with the wrench).

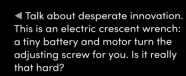

◀ Talk about desperate innovation. This is an electric crescent wrench: a tiny battery and motor turn the adjusting screw for you. Is it really that hard?

▶ This "miner's wrench" adds a hammer face, acknowledging the fact that people are going to use wrenches as hammers. For added convenience, there's also a ratchet drive on the other end.

ODD WRENCHES

THERE ARE A NUMBER of peculiar members of the wrench family. As is usually the case in life, the rare ones are not precious, they are just bad. If they were useful, people would make more of them and they would not be rare.

To be fair, there are also wrenches that are odd and rare because they are specialized for uncommon applications, or because they have advantages in rare circumstances, or because of the rare history that led to their existence.

And there are probably also wrenches that are really amazing but just haven't had their day in the sun. Maybe the company was lousy at marketing, or some evil corporation stamped them out to eliminate competition for their inferior wrenches. In any case, here are some of my favorite oddball wrenches.

◀ This superb Parmelee wrench is smooth and grips like a collet. It leaves no mark even on soft copper but can only be used on a single diameter of pipe.

▲ A wrench with a twist! Which is purely decorative and means the movable jaw can't be removed, as it can on normal monkey wrenches.

▲ This venerable rarity was made during WWII in the J.A. Henckels factory in Solingen, Germany, which was, and is to this day, known for its high-quality knives.

▲ This is probably the rarest form of crescent wrench because it's the least useful. Yes, the two sides are different sizes, but does that really make this wrench more useful than putting something else entirely on the other end? Or having a more comfortable handle?

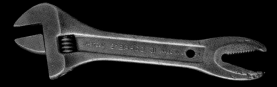

▲ In theory the adjustable end of this wrench works on nuts and bolts in good condition, while the alligator end is for rounded-over fasteners that can't be gripped well with flat jaws. In practice vise-grip pliers work better.

▼ This style is called a dog bone wrench and comes in standard and fancy designs. The oversize heads and weak construction limit their usefulness.

▲ If there's a dog bone wrench, why not a cat face wrench? Cute, but useful only when the nut or bolt is completely out in the open with no obstructions around it.

▶ "Spuds" are plumbing fixtures that connect a pipe to a porcelain toilet. Spuds have large-diameter nuts that lock them in place. A thin-jawed wrench like this might be fine for applying a new spud, but good luck loosening an old corroded one!

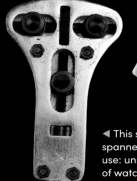

◀ This surprised-looking spanner wrench has a specific use: unscrewing the backs of watches and the retaining rings on optical devices.

WELDING TOOLS

WELDING IS LIKE soldering without the solder. Instead of solder you melt the actual metal being joined (and optionally add some more of the same kind of metal) to turn two pieces into one without anything coming between them. Welding is significantly more difficult than soldering because it requires much higher temperatures and because you are actually melting the edges of the pieces being welded together. If you mess up soldering, you can just remelt the joint, take it apart, and try again. If you mess up welding, you may well have destroyed the pieces you were working on.

There are two common ways to weld. You can either point a torch burning a mixture of oxygen and acetylene at the parts to be welded, or you can run an electric current through an electrode touching the metal, creating a very hot electric arc at the point of contact. Arc welding is easier and somewhat safer because there is no explosive gas to deal with, just a superhot spark. I quickly learned to use a wire-feed arc welder to connect angle iron. In fact, the very first thing I ever welded, after a few minutes' practice, was a bracket that is still holding up a section of my house. (If those welds fail, the roof could collapse, but I'm not worried. The welds are good. I think.)

Other forms of welding are *much* harder (and I can't do any of them). Aluminum is notoriously difficult to weld because it conducts heat so well that there is a very fine line between melting just the edge of a piece and melting the whole thing. As you are working, heat is spreading rapidly throughout the piece, and you can't tell when it's all about to fall away in a puddle: unlike steel, aluminum melts before it starts to glow.

▲ A spot welder joins two thin pieces of metal in one . . . spot. It's simply a transformer that delivers a jolt of very high current through its two thick copper jaws, melting a bit of the two sheets where they touch.

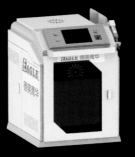

◄ Laser welding is not yet common due to the high cost of the machines, but it can do amazing things with very thin, difficult-to-weld materials. I have never wanted a machine as much as I want this one: I just don't have any reason to have it.

◄ Welding is not just for metal. This tightly focused heat gun along with plastic welding rods (just like the metal ones) can join certain plastics just as an arc welder joins metal.

◄ Thermite welding is easily the most exciting way to join two pieces of steel. In this example about ten pounds of iron oxide and aluminum powder react to form white-hot liquid iron, which drops down into a mold, joining two sections of train track into one.

▶ A "stick welder" is just a big transformer. It converts relatively high voltage from the wall socket into the low voltage and high current needed for welding. The current is fed into the joint through a welding rod (the "stick"), which is consumed and becomes the material of the weld. This venerable beast from the 1960s has a crank that lets you move the secondary coil away from the primary to reduce the welding current, or closer to increase it.

▶ Acetylene welding and cutting torches are beautiful and powerful tools, but not to be used lightly. Explosively flammable compressed gases demand respect.

▶ A wire-feed welder delivers its electric current through the end of a continuous spool of welding wire fed at a constant rate out the end of a gun. The wire becomes the weld. This is by far the easiest type of welding for beginners.

◄ Plasma cutters are the perfect companion to wire-feed and stick welders. They use electricity and air to cut steel like butter, letting you make pieces to be welded into pretty much anything you like. Even the cheapest plasma cutters will effortlessly cut ¼-inch (6 mm) thick steel.

▲ Named after the Roman god of fire, a vulcanizer heats liquid rubber in the presence of sulfur, causing cross-linkages to form that effectively weld new tread onto a tire.

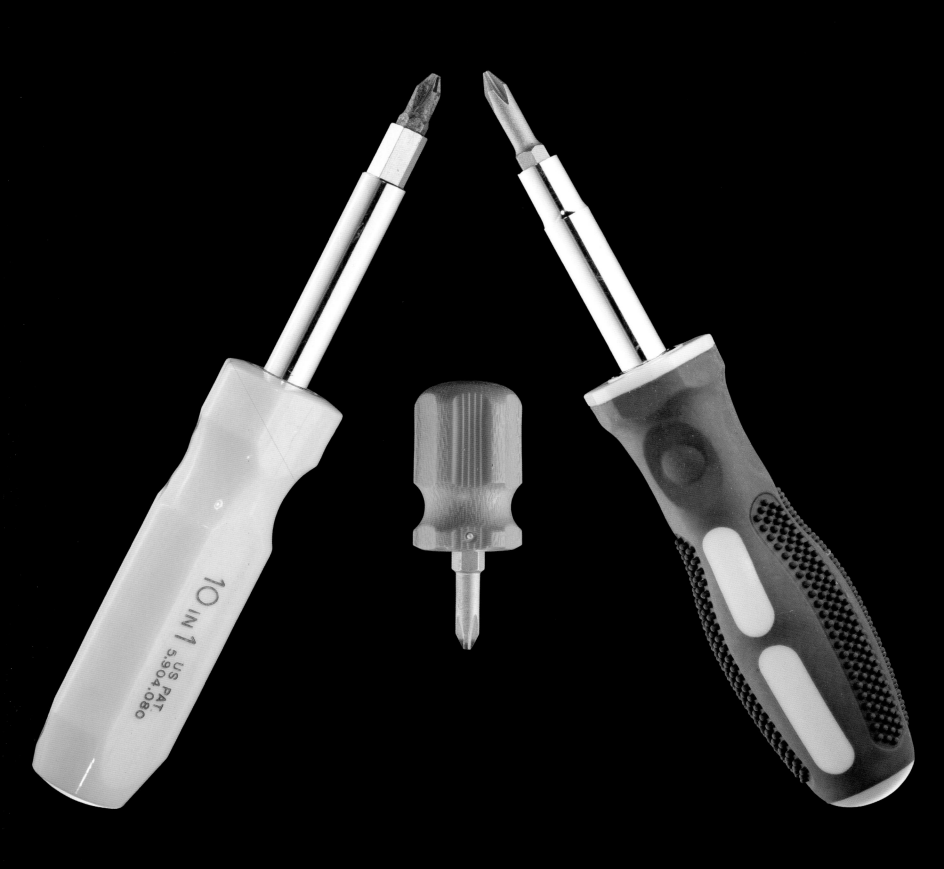

MULTI-DRIVERS

THERE ARE TWO popular kinds of multi-headed screwdrivers: incredibly useful and annoying. The sensible kind have a reversible main shaft and a reversible bit on each end, giving a total of four screwdriver tips, any of which can be accessed with at most two flips. As a bonus, the ends of the main shaft work as nut drivers when the double bit on the end is removed.

The annoying kind have a fixed handle with a hex socket on the end, usually with a magnet at the bottom. And they have about half a dozen individual bits mixed up in a compartment in the handle. It takes longer to switch bits, and they are more likely to get lost. I really don't like this type. On the other hand, for specialized applications you can use any of dozens of different types of bits, not just the standard slotted and Phillips you can get with the flip-type screwdriver.

In between these two options is a version that stores the bits in an accessible place, neatly organized. Not as robust and fast as the flip type, but a lot better than a jumble of bits in the handle.

◄ The basic six-function flippable screwdriver has two slotted and two Phillips bits, and two sizes of nut driver. Fancy models have an extra level of flip-ability at each end, giving you eight screwdrivers and six nut drivers! Stubby ones have just one flip level.

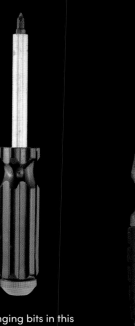

▲ Changing bits in this annoying screwdriver requires dumping all of them out of the handle to search for the one you want. Not recommended.

▲ This type of screwdriver is not bad, if you need a variety of exotic tips.

▲ This flip driver might be a great idea if it were made better: you can choose any two screwdriver bits, or one screwdriver and one drill, and flip between them rapidly.

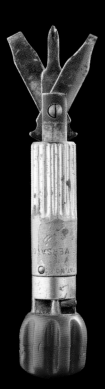

▲ This type of multi-headed screwdriver died out some decades ago and is quite difficult to find, probably because it's cheaply made and likely to break.

▲ Snowflakes! So fun but work only in a few situations.

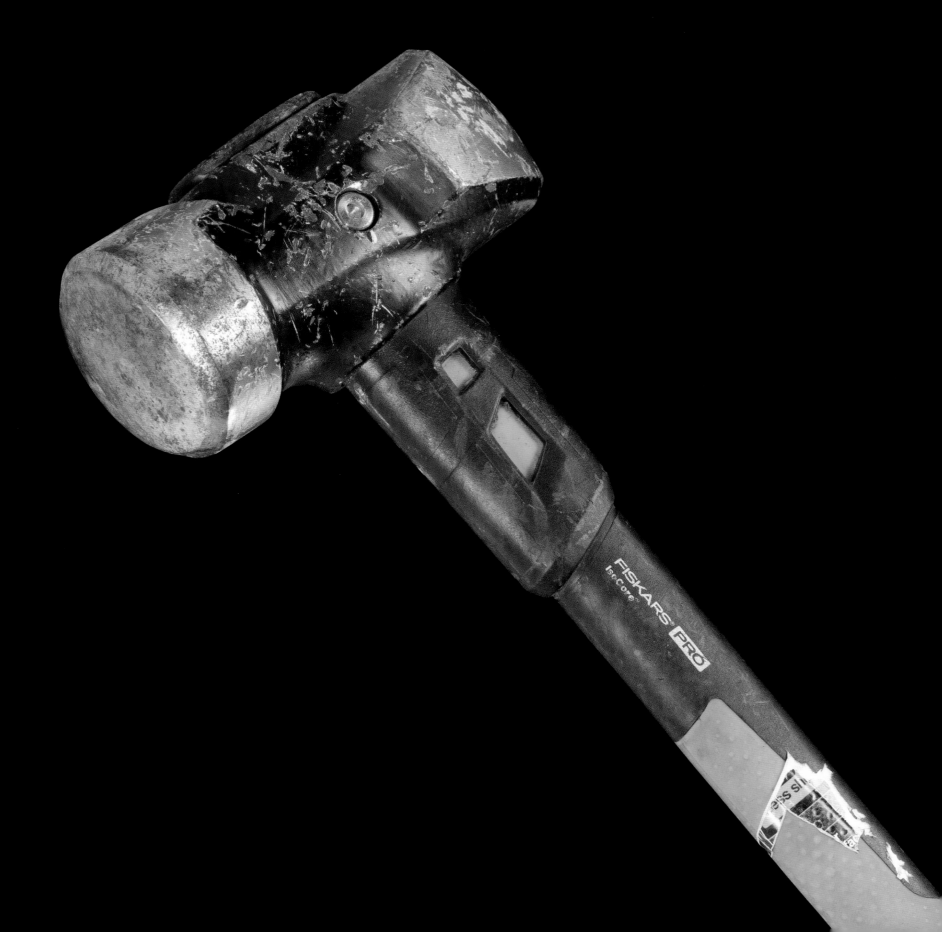

SLEDGES & AXES

THE ONE THING you can say definitively about a sledgehammer is that it's big and heavy—up to 20 pounds (10 kg) or more. Sledgehammers are used to break up concrete, pound in metal stakes, or knock down statues of people no longer in favor. The classic sledge has two flat heads. If one side is wedge-shaped, the tool is known as a splitting maul. If one or both sides are shaped into a blade or a point, then it's an axe, adze, hatchet, or pick.

There's an old philosophical puzzle about an axe that goes: "This is my grandfather's axe. My mother replaced the handle and I replaced the head. It is my grandfather's axe." Or is it . . . ? If you think the answer is no because no part of the original axe remains, consider that the same is true of you. By the time you turn sixteen, no atom in your body remains from when you were born. Every part

of the original you has been replaced, and yet you still have to show your birth certificate to get a driver's license, as if that is somehow relevant.

Anyway, if you want the full story on the philosophy axe parts, google "Ship of Theseus," but for now back to practical axes. The classic wood-chopping axe has a blade that is parallel to the handle. A small axe is called a hatchet, and it does pretty much the same thing as an axe, but with less intensity. If the blade is turned 90 degrees to be crosswise to the handle, the axe becomes an adze, which is used for more delicate shaping of wood. Traditional log cabins, for example, are made from logs that have been felled with an axe, then straightened and flattened with an adze.

Sledgehammers are usually associated with destruction, but they can sometimes be used for construction as well.

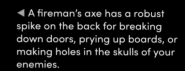

◄ A fireman's axe has a robust spike on the back for breaking down doors, prying up boards, or making holes in the skulls of your enemies.

◄ A slash hook or bill hook is used to quickly cut down brush, branches, small trees, and victims in horror movies.

► This beautiful curved-blade carving adze was hand-forged in Indiana.

◄ This sledgehammer was brand new two months before the picture was taken. These things take, as well as give, a beating.

▼ Long sledge, maximum whack.

◄ Post mauls are very heavy and have wide faces that spread the impact over the whole end of a wooden post, to avoid splitting it.

▼ Two-sided axes have one thick, sturdy edge for heavy chopping and another finer, sharper edge for delicate shaping and trimming.

► Splitting mauls work on logs and zombies. The handle is not supposed to be bent.

▲ The stereotypical "peace pipe" of old Westerns was a pipe for smoking tobacco, but shaped like a type of hatchet called a tomahawk. It is the proverbial hatchet of the phrase "bury the hatchet," or I guess if things didn't go well during the negotiations, you could bury the hatchet more literally, in your newfound enemy.

▲ Short sledge, still hurts.

MANUAL NAILERS

IF YOU'RE GOING to be driving a lot of nails, what you want is not a hammer, but rather a nail gun or a stapler that automatically drives its fasteners down in one whack.

The key difference between a nail and a staple is that if the material being held is thin and flexible, it can potentially slip around a nail head and come loose. A staple, on the other hand, will trap some of the material between its two prongs, so no matter how flexible the material, it can't get loose without either tearing or pulling out the staple. Nailing woven fabric, for example, is pointless, but stapling it is an effective way of holding it down.

Because of this difference, manual nailers are rare: most nails are meant for thick, stiff materials and are too big to be

comfortably driven by hand in one blow. Later we will meet a variety of power-assisted nailers that can drive even the largest construction nails effortlessly.

Manual staplers, on the other hand, are very common. While there are large staples and power staplers to drive them, small, easily driven staples are the norm, starting with the common office stapler for fastening papers together. Similar but thicker staples can be driven with squeeze-handle staplers, which gather up energy from the long travel of their handle and release it suddenly when the handle is fully squeezed. The same staples can be driven much faster with a hammer stapler, a clever tool that works like a hammer that automatically feeds a new staple every time you hit something with it.

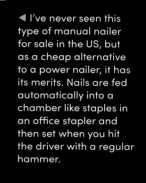

◄ I've never seen this type of manual nailer for sale in the US, but as a cheap alternative to a power nailer, it has its merits. Nails are fed automatically into a chamber like staples in an office stapler and then set when you hit the driver with a regular hammer.

◄ This floor nailer drives specially shaped nails diagonally into the joints of tongue-and-groove flooring. When you hit the round rubber knob with a small sledgehammer, the nailer not only sets the nail but also simultaneously drives the floorboard tight up against the one next to it. I redid the floor in my house without one of these nailers because they are expensive. Decades later I bought one cheap at an auction. A case where "better late than never" is just not true.

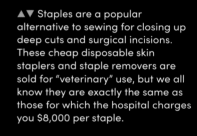

▲▼ Staples are a popular alternative to sewing for closing up deep cuts and surgical incisions. These cheap disposable skin staplers and staple removers are sold for "veterinary" use, but we all know they are exactly the same as those for which the hospital charges you $8,000 per staple.

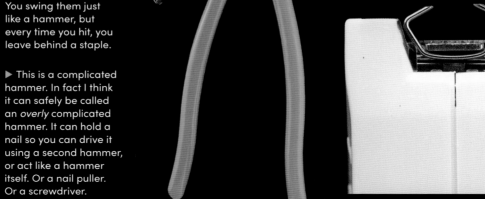

▲ Hammer staplers are a lot of fun to use. You swing them just like a hammer, but every time you hit, you leave behind a staple.

► This is a complicated hammer. In fact I think it can safely be called an *overly* complicated hammer. It can hold a nail so you can drive it using a second hammer, or act like a hammer itself. Or a nail puller. Or a screwdriver.

▲ The classic hardware store manual stapler is barely able to get a staple all the way into soft wood, but that's fine for temporary work.

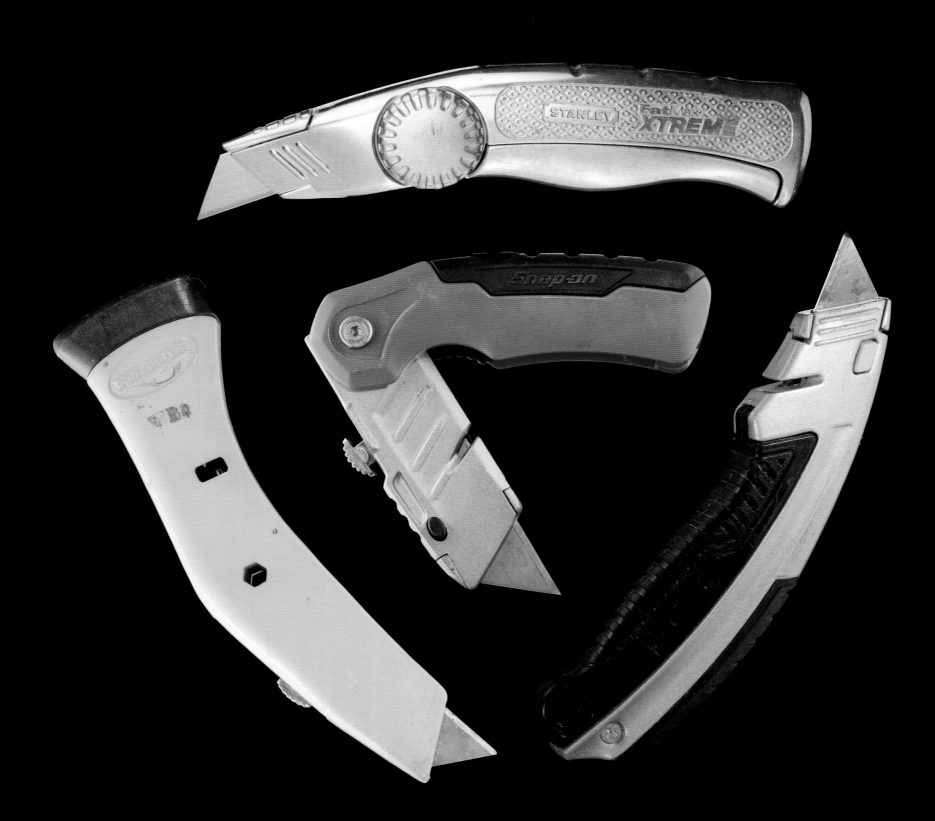

KNIVES

KITCHEN AND POCKET KNIVES are beyond the scope of this book, but there are a lot of knives that are very much shop tools. The obvious example is the common utility knife. These come in a dizzying array of styles, and finding a clever new design of utility knife is a highlight of any trip to the hardware store.

The replaceable nature of utility knife blades is the key to their usefulness. There is always a tradeoff between sharpness and durability. A very sharp blade must have a steep V angle between its two edges, making the edge weak and easy to bend over, nick, or chip.

You have to be careful not to damage the permanent and very sharp blade of a pocket knife, but with utility knives you just throw the old blade away and slide in a new one. If you're cutting rough material, or cutting against something abrasive like concrete, you may be replacing the blade literally every few minutes. And that's just fine, because blades are cheap, come in packages of a hundred, and are designed to be abused in the most egregious ways.

The material of the blade can make all the difference, and everything from stone (literally in the Stone Age) to metal has been used. Even today, the sharpest knives—though not always the most practical—are made of materials closer to stone than metal.

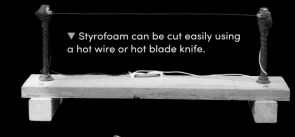

◀ The sharpest steel blades are surgical scalpels. This flexible one is meant to be squeezed between two fingers to form a curved knife to cut out moles and other skin growths. (I got a pack of them, intending to deal with a mole myself, before coming to my senses.)

▼ Styrofoam can be cut easily using a hot wire or hot blade knife.

◀ Never leave a hardware store without a new and better utility knife. Otherwise, how will you end up with way too many?

◀ Fractured glass—like in this volcanic obsidian spear point—is second only to diamond in sharpness. Even today, obsidian scalpels are sometimes used by surgeons because they are sharper than steel (though more delicate).

▲ Ancient peoples who didn't have access to obsidian used widely available and relatively hard silica rocks instead, agate in this reproduction example.

▶ This keychain knife is just so cute. And dangerous! Who thought razor-sharp keychain knives were a good idea?

▶ Ground and polished ruby crystal knives are extremely sharp and stay that way for a long time, if treated carefully. This "swivel knife" is used for cutting patterns in leather.

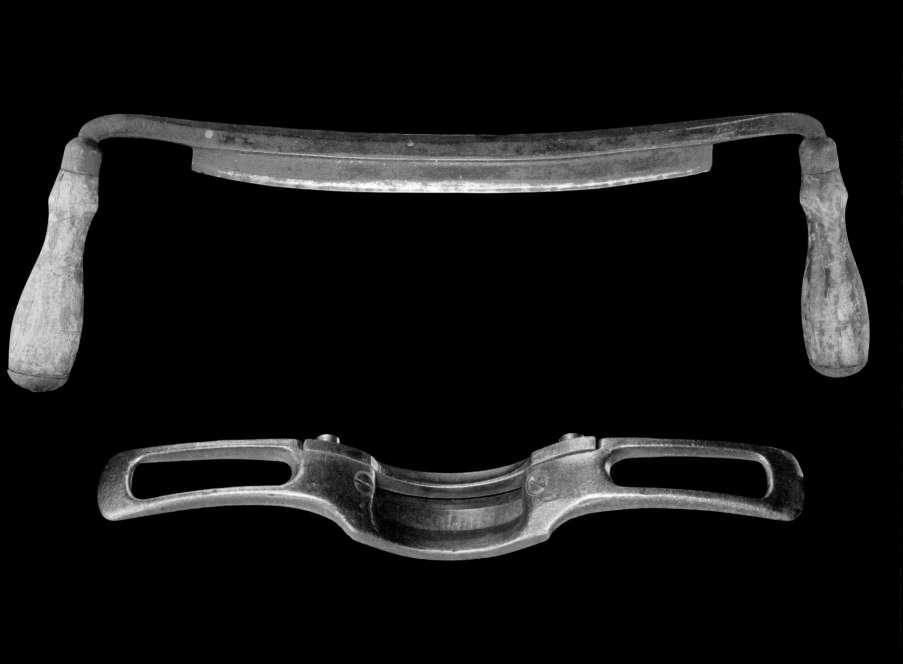

SCRAPERS

THERE ARE TWO KINDS of scrapers: those you push and those you pull. Push-type scrapers are almost like chisels and are typically used to remove relatively soft material from a smooth and harder surface. For example, paint from metal, or burned-on food from a glass stovetop. If you use a push scraper on a soft surface like wood, it just digs in, which is rarely what you want, and if it is, you should probably be using a chisel.

Pull-type scrapers are used to smooth, shape, or fine-tune softer surfaces. The classic drawknife is used to cut away large amounts of wood or bark each time you pull it toward you. A spokeshave is similar, but more refined because of its depth stop.

Surprisingly, scrapers are also used to shave down metal surfaces, including steel. It might seem like you can't possibly cut away much steel just scraping it by hand, and that's true, you can't. But with careful and repeated checking against a granite flat, you can hand-scrape a milled or ground surface to be flatter than by any other method except lapping.

Scrapers have a single blade, but what if that's not enough? What if the job calls for *a hundred* scraping blades all in a row? Read on.

► This is a scraping tool for smoothing and refining the insides of holes and other hard-to-reach areas in machined metal parts.

◄ Both drawknives and spokeshaves are pulled toward you. The difference is that the former have only a blade, while the latter have a sole plate that limits the depth of cut, sort of like a block plane.

◄ A nice old cast-iron wood scraper I got from the shop room of an abandoned high school.

► This looks like an awl, but it's actually a scraper for clay or wax. It's an artist's carving tool. (Or at least that's what I've used it for—it may have some other official purpose I'm unaware of.)

ALEXEN.MODELS
PJ0081

ANGEL SCRAPER FOR GUNDAM
N MILITARY MODEL KITS

2.0mm 1.7mm 1.5mm 1.2mm 2.5mm 2.7mm 3mm 3.5mm 0.2mm 0.5mm 0.7mm 1mm

▲ Sometimes the job requires an intentionally soft scraper. This nylon version avoids scratching delicate surfaces.

Film Peeling Tool

▲ This delicate finger-worn scraper is used by model makers to round over the edges of tiny parts.

▲ A tungsten carbide blade makes this scraper last nearly forever without needing to be sharpened.

▲ Every one of the Mechanical GIFs model kits I sell comes with one of these plastic scrapers. It's used to remove the protective film from acrylic parts without scratching the surface.

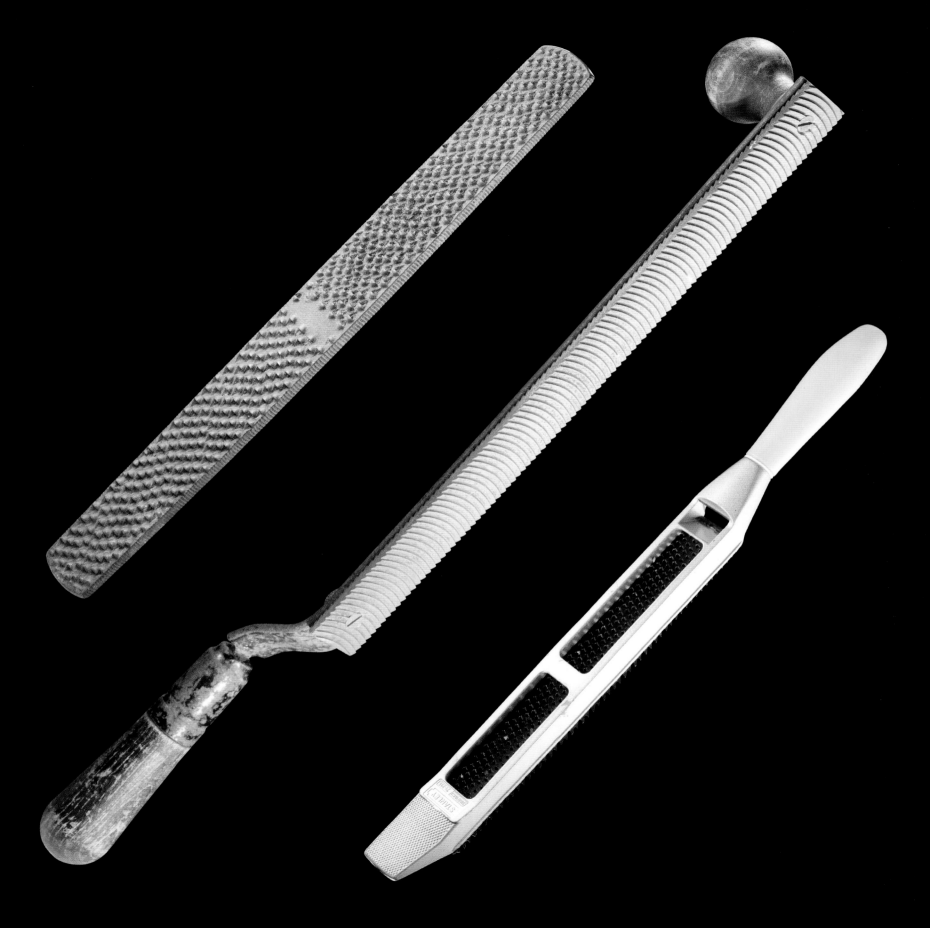

THE COARSEST FILES are called rasps and are used for the free-form shaping of wood. They have large, sharp, triangular teeth and leave a rough surface that must then be filed and sanded smooth. Files with smaller, more closely spaced teeth can be used on both wood and metal. Those with teeth cut in two or three directions cut faster but leave a rougher surface than those with a single straight row of teeth.

Files are made by using a hardened steel chisel-like tool to cut or raise the teeth while the metal of the file itself is in an annealed (soft) state. The file is then hardened by heating it red-hot, then quenching (cooling) it rapidly to a lower temperature. (The details of exactly how hot to make it and how quickly to cool it are rich with history and differ depending on the alloy used to make the file.)

Hardened steel files are among the hardest common tools. They can cut almost any other tool in the shop, including those made of lesser hardened steels. This of course means that they are brittle: a chisel made as hard as a file would soon have a ragged, chipped edge. Files can be so hard because they have a *lot* of sturdy thick teeth. Over time, if used on hard materials, some of the teeth will break off, but the file will keep working just fine with a fair number of broken teeth.

◀ Wood rasps have big, widely spaced, aggressive teeth to rapidly shape wood.

◀ A "float" is a type of file that can be used almost like a plane to smooth surfaces, round edges, or aggressively remove material.

◀ These rasps are made a lot like cheese graters—and the same company sells those too.

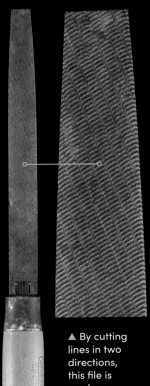

◀ You could use this rasp on wood or cheese, but it's designed for feet.

▲ By cutting lines in two directions, this file is made more aggressive for either wood or metal filing.

▼ Files come in a lot of different shapes and sizes. Flat and curved files are for filing outside edges, while round, square, and triangular files are for inside curves and holes.

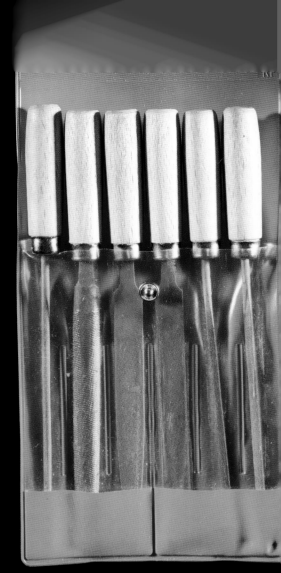

▲ Mini file sets are nice for detail work.

▲ If you have a lot of filing to do on metal parts, a pneumatic power filer can save your arm.

▲ Some files are a bit like permanent, reusable sandpaper, with a fine random pattern rather than defined teeth. This nail file, for example. (Human nails, not steel ones.)

SNIPS

SNIPS ARE SCISSORS: tools with blades that pass by each other, creating a shearing action. But they're designed to take on more workshop-oriented tasks. Some of these tools are really just overgrown scissors, while others work in novel ways.

For example, tin snips are like extra-thick scissors with long handles that provide lots of leverage for cutting thin sheet metal. They can weigh several pounds and often require two hands to operate. By the way, "tin" in the name *tin snips* does not refer to the metallic element tin nor does it describe the material from which the snips are made. It's used generically to refer to the material the snips will cut: any kind of thin sheet metal, usually steel, aluminum, or copper, almost never actual tin.

A major annoyance when using tin snips is that sheet metal, unlike paper or fabric, does not just flop or bend away from the scissors when you make a long cut. Instead, it has to be forcibly angled down on one side and up on the other, taking care not to crease it. Cutting curves can be quite difficult, but specially made left-cutting and right-cutting tin snips are available, depending on which direction of curve you're making.

Nibblers get around this problem by removing a narrow strip of material, like two scissors very close to each other, leaving room for the blade in between and allowing the tool to make sharp curves.

Where shearing tends to fail is on material that is either brittle, which tends to just crumble, or very stretchy, which deflects the blades and squeezes between them. For those sorts of material you may be better off using two blades that meet, like those on the next page.

▲ These power cutters for carpet and cardboard have a squarish rotating blade that spins continually. The square shape means that a gap is always opening and closing, just like with scissors, but without the jerky motion.

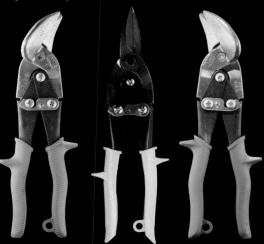

◀ This pair of tin snips is one of the first tools I bought for myself, and I've always enjoyed the feel of it. The blades are made of hardened steel, but aluminum handles lighten the tool quite a lot, while providing strength and stiffness.

▼ Tin snips for making left-curving, straight, and right-curving cuts.

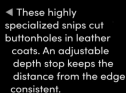

◀ These highly specialized snips cut buttonholes in leather coats. An adjustable depth stop keeps the distance from the edge consistent.

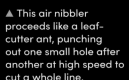

▲ This air nibbler proceeds like a leaf-cutter ant, punching out one small hole after another at high speed to cut a whole line.

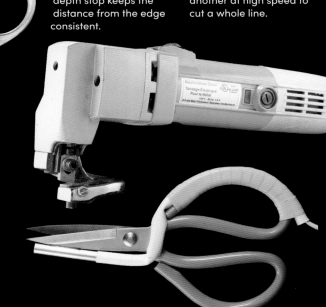

◀ Sheet metal shears work just like electric scissors with really thick blades.

◀ These would be ordinary scissors if not for the heating element fastened to one blade, which turns them into tools for cutting synthetic fabrics, which melt at low temperatures.

NIPPERS

NIPPERS HAVE BLADES that meet each other head-on, creating a pinching action instead of a shearing action, which is sometimes a more effective way of cutting hard and ductile things like wire. ("Ductile" means the material is able to stretch and deform without breaking. Wire, for example, is very ductile, but paper is not.)

If you try using shearing blades on steel wire or nails, the two blades may separate and bend, rather than cut, the material. But if the blades meet head-on in a pinching action, the twisting force is eliminated, and they can push harder without getting out of alignment.

A subtle issue with wire nippers is that the final "snap" when the cut finishes sends a shock wave down the length of the wire. If you're just cutting a length of wire, that's no problem, but if you're trimming the leads of an electrical component, the shock wave may damage the component internally. In this case it's best to use shearing wire cutters, or at least use the nippers gently to cut without creating a harsh snap.

Shears have two blades that pass each other, nippers have two blades that meet, but what if you had multiple blades that all move together in the same direction? That's the subject of these two pages.

▶ Need more leverage without long handles? Add compound leverage! The handles move a longer distance to deliver more squeeze with less effort.

◀ This nipper doesn't have handles at all: you pull the plug out to separate the blades, then push it down. It's a pill splitter.

◀ I had to ask the internet to find out that these are "sugar nippers," used to chip off little bits of sugar from a sugar cone. Google "sugar cone" today and you'll get nothing but ice cream cones, but if you googled the term in the 1800s, you would have found these solid cone-shaped blocks of sugar.

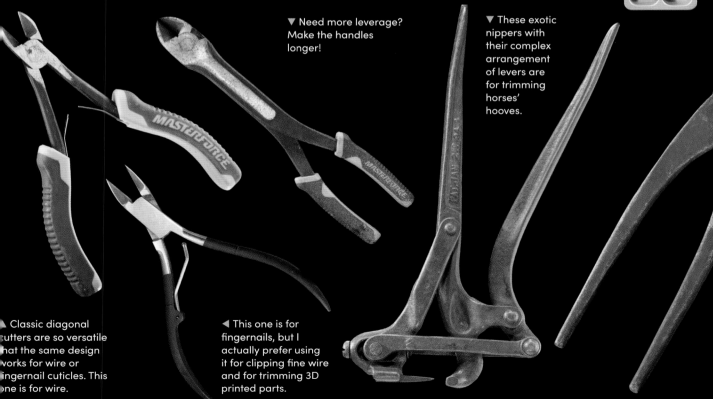

▼ Need more leverage? Make the handles longer!

▼ These exotic nippers with their complex arrangement of levers are for trimming horses' hooves.

◀ Classic diagonal cutters are so versatile that the same design works for wire or fingernail cuticles. This one is for wire.

◀ This one is for fingernails, but I actually prefer using it for clipping fine wire and for trimming 3D printed parts.

◀ These are not actually nippers or cutters, despite their appearance. They are pliers designed to reach into a link in a chain and pry it open.

WOOD SAWS

SAW TEETH COME in three main configurations: a row of small chisels, a row of small knives, or a very thin grinding wheel.

Traditional rip saws for cutting wood along the direction of the grain have teeth like tiny chisels, which scoop out the wood. Crosscut saws, for cutting across the grain, have tiny knife edges that slice the grain on either side of the cut before scooping it out. Without these knife edges, the saw would tear the surface of the wood.

Modern handsaws have a more complicated tooth structure that works well both for ripping and for crosscutting. They are also induction-hardened, a form of heat treatment that allows them to stay sharp for a very long time. The hardening is applied only to a thin layer around the teeth, while the rest of the blade and the core of each tooth remains softer, making them both tough and hard.

Modern hardened saws are unambiguously better than old unhardened ones, but they have one downside: they can't be sharpened without destroying the thin hardened layer. Fortunately, steel is highly recyclable and buying a new blade is cheaper than sharpening an old, unhardened blade. And if you're a casual sawyer, you will probably never have to change or sharpen a blade, because the saw will stay sharp longer than you will. Some people do painstakingly sharpen unhardened saw blades, but this is largely an exercise in meditation and historical reenactment rather than in practical woodworking.

The harder the material you're cutting, the smaller the teeth need to be, making them increasingly tedious to sharpen. By the time you get to saws for cutting steel, the teeth are so small *no one* tries to sharpen them.

◄ This saw is about as long as it can be before needing a handle on the other end, and a second person to operate it.

▼ Backsaws have a stiff rail down the back to keep them perfectly straight. This extra-long one is from a miter box, but they come much smaller, down to tiny dovetail saws.

◄ Bone saws, for surgery and butchering (or both if you're a terrible surgeon), have teeth very similar to saws for wood. This would indicate that bone is similar in hardness to wood, which it is, and leads to the observation that many tools are happy to cut or drill through your bones just about as fast as they go through wood.

▼ Old saws were often decorated with chip carvings in the handle. These, like many old tools, were lifelong possessions.

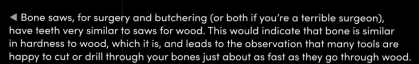

▼ This old crosscut saw has an interesting variation: a set of teeth on the top of the blade for cutting through nails, so you don't ruin the sharp teeth on the bottom.

▼ If you don't have a chain saw, and you don't know anyone who does, and there are no tool rental companies within a hundred miles, then you—and a friend—can use a saw like this to cut through immense logs and tree trunks. It might not even take you a whole hour. Many people choose instead to hang these old saws on the wall in their workshop or den as decoration.

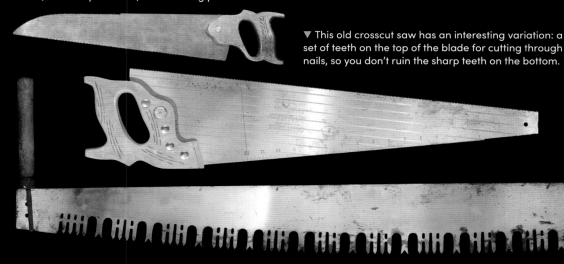

HACKSAWS

HACKSAWS ARE FOR cutting metal. They typically have a lot more teeth than wood saws, and better quality ones are made of high-speed steel, an alloy normally reserved for drill bits and other power cutting tools. The blades need to be hard because hacksaws are meant for cutting steel. (But try to cut a steel file and you will get nowhere: files are *much* harder.)

Hacksaws have replaceable blades because they're impractical to sharpen. There are just too many teeth. The best thing you can do to save money replacing blades is to always push the saw all the way from one end to the other. As my grandfather said, you paid for the whole blade, you should use the whole blade!

High-speed steel blades will last a long time when cutting soft metals or plastic, but when used on steel the blade will dull faster than you think. Switching to a new blade can be an eye-opening experience when you realize just how dull the old one had become. Which is why, like utility knife blades, hacksaw blades are sold in packs of fifty.

As a general rule, the thicker the metal you're cutting, the more widely spaced the teeth of the saw should be. If the teeth are too close, there won't be enough room between them for chips to accumulate before the blade exits the other side of the cut. Or if they are too far apart, thin material can get stuck in gap between them, stopping the saw. Ideally you want a minimum of three teeth in contact at all times. These and other factors go into the shape of all the teeth you'll see on the next pages.

▲ This saw for cutting frozen meat is frankly the best-built hacksaw I own. The stainless steel frame is impressively robust, and the locking handle is strong and convenient.

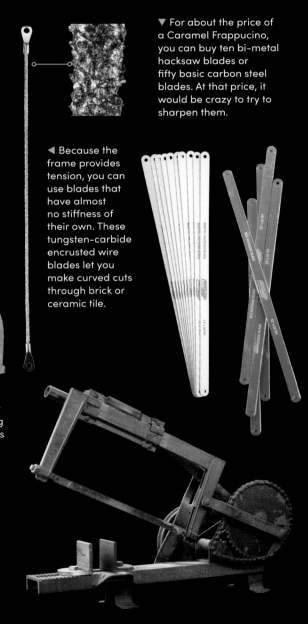

▼ For about the price of a Caramel Frappucino, you can buy ten bi-metal hacksaw blades or fifty basic carbon steel blades. At that price, it would be crazy to try to sharpen them.

◀ Because the frame provides tension, you can use blades that have almost no stiffness of their own. These tungsten-carbide encrusted wire blades let you make curved cuts through brick or ceramic tile.

◀ This double-sided hacksaw can hold two different blades, one coarse and one fine-tooth, at the same time.

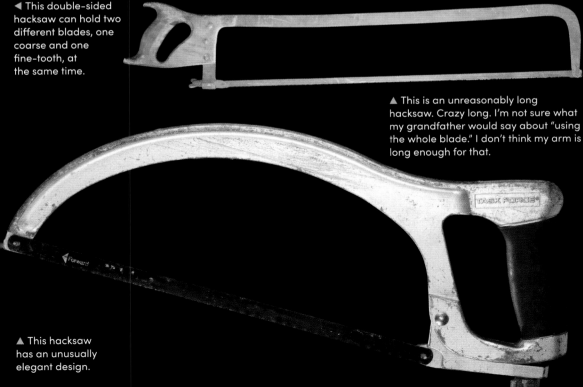

▲ This is an unreasonably long hacksaw. Crazy long. I'm not sure what my grandfather would say about "using the whole blade." I don't think my arm is long enough for that.

▲ This hacksaw has an unusually elegant design.

▲ Antique "Iron Mike" saws are ordinary hacksaws with a belt-driven power mechanism that does the sawing back and forth for you.

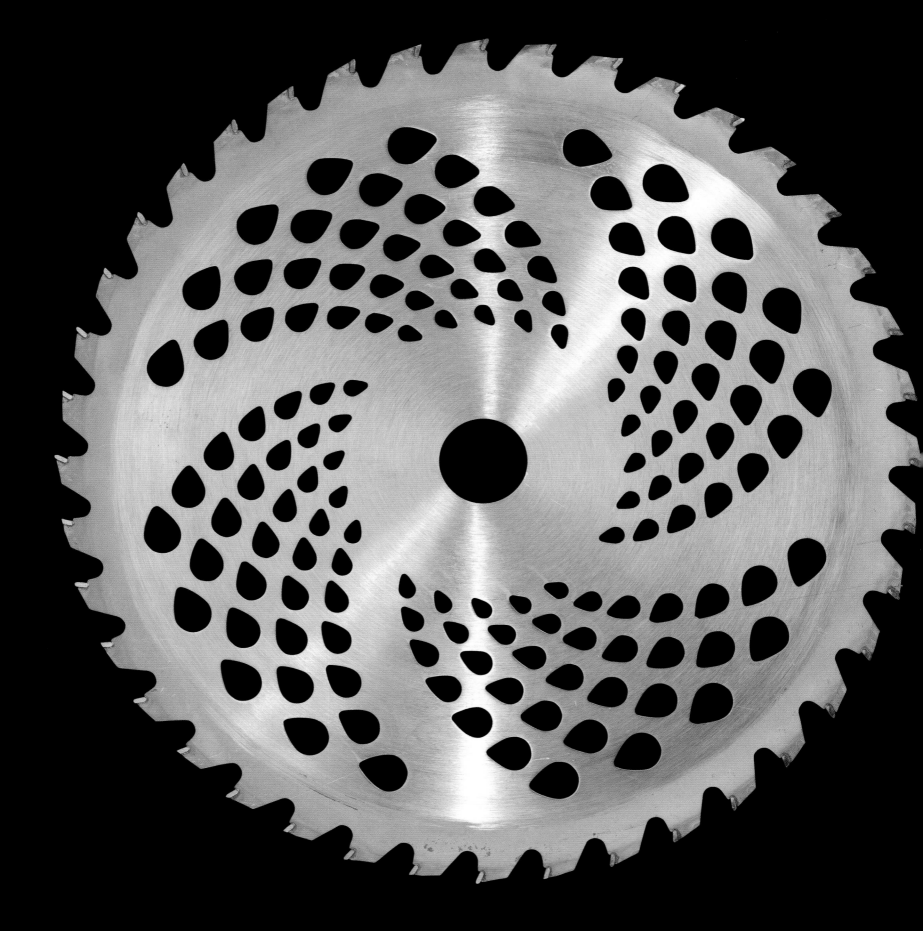

SAW TEETH

SAWS ARE ALL ABOUT the teeth: the rest of the blade is just a carrier to get the teeth into the action. A lot of art and science goes into the shape and positioning of saw teeth.

Teeth on circular saws are characterized by their "hook angle," meaning how far the tooth leans away from perpendicular to the direction of the cut. A positive hook angle, leaning into the cut, makes for an aggressive, grabby saw that pulls itself into the cut. A negative angle, leaning away from the cut, makes the blade push itself back from the cut, increasing safety and giving you more control because it requires that you

push the blade in constantly, or it will just stop cutting.

The amount of space *between* the teeth is also important, because that's where chips accumulate before the tooth comes out the other side of the material. If you're cutting thick, soft material, a log for example, there needs to be plenty of room between the teeth to hold all of the accumulated wood chips. But if you're cutting something thin or something very hard, you don't need much space because not much material will gather on each pass. The very hardest of materials, glass and stone, require teeth so small you can hardly call them teeth at all, as we'll see on the next page.

▲ This hay knife, used to cut bales of hay, looks like a wood saw with comically oversized teeth. This makes sense because a bale of hay is a lot like a piece of wood with comically oversized grain.

◀ This is not actually a circular saw blade. It's meant to be mounted on the end of what is normally a string trimmer (Weedwacker) to make it exponentially more dangerous. The large number of holes make it lighter, reducing the gyroscopic effect.

▼ Saws for wood can have teeth spaced anywhere from less than ⅛ of an inch (3 mm) to over 2 inches (50 mm).

◀ Bone saw

◀ Rip saw

◀ Crosscut saw

◀ Modern Hand saw

◀ Extra-long saw

◀ Two-man saw

◀ Sawmill bandsaw

▼ Hacksaw and jigsaw blades for cutting metal have more teeth for thinner sheets. Blades for wood are bigger and sharper.

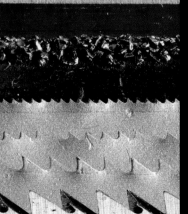

◀ Knife edge

◀ Carbide

◀ Thin metal

◀ Medium metal

◀ Thick metal

◀ Fine wood

◀ Rough wood

▲ One of these is an insulation saw used to cut fiberglass or foam insulation. The other is a bread knife. Can you tell which is which? (Hint: The bread knife is all metal.)

SAW TEETH

▼ Old plain steel circular saw blades don't last very long. Carbide-tipped circular saw blades are much more expensive, but they stay sharp nearly forever with casual use. Blades for metal and plastic cutting have teeth with a negative hook angle: they lean away from the direction the blade is rotating.

◄ Abrasive rebar cutting

◄ Abrasive steel cutting

◄ Diamond concrete cutting

◄ Carbide-tipped fine wood cutting

◄ Fine wood cutting

◄ Rough wood cutting

◄ Carbide-tipped Trex plastic cutting (negative hook angle)

◄ Carbide-tipped rough wood cutting

◄ Carbide-tipped aluminum cutting (negative hook angle)

◄ Carbide-tipped steel cutting

Very hard materials, like concrete, ceramic, porcelain tile, brick, and hardened steel are best cut with abrasive wheels rather than traditional saw blades. The key feature of an abrasive blade is that it doesn't try to have an edge that stays sharp. Instead, it has countless tiny sharp edges that break off and fall away when they get dull, exposing new sharp edges.

Cut-off blades meant for cutting steel rebar have a fiber mesh inside that keeps the grit layer from flying apart when the blades are spinning rapidly. (WEAR SAFETY GLASSES AND A FACE SHIELD BECAUSE THEY DO FLY APART ANYWAY.) They start out typically 14 inches (35 cm) in diameter, but keep working until only half that diameter is left.

Diamond blades for cutting concrete have many tiny diamonds embedded in a steel disk. The edge feels almost smooth to the touch because the diamonds don't stick out very far. (They don't need to because the concrete won't move out of the way even a tiny bit.) Over time these protruding diamonds break off, rendering the surface actually smooth, at which point the blade would stop cutting—except that the steel disk is also slowly wearing away, exposing new diamonds.

Here's the tricky part: if the steel is too tough and wears away too slowly, the blade will go dull and stop cutting well. If it wears away too quickly, the (expensive) blade will not last long, and many unbroken diamonds will be wasted.

How tough should the steel be? Well, that depends on what you're cutting, which in the case of concrete means what type of rocks were added to the mix–the "aggregate" that is combined with cement to form concrete. What type of rocks are used in concrete? Well, that depends on *where you are.*

Concrete is a very local product. It's mixed up with rocks from the nearest quarry, and then delivered by cement truck no more than a few dozen miles from where it was made. This is why companies that sell diamond concrete saws have *detailed maps* that show which model of blade you should buy based on your exact location. Try to imagine the layers of civilization and technology that had to be built up before it was possible to even conceive of such a map, let alone gather the massive volume of detailed information needed to create it.

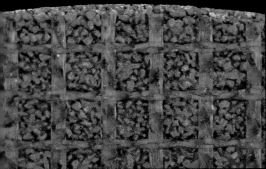

▲ Abrasive disks are used to cut steel. They "grind through" rather than cut.

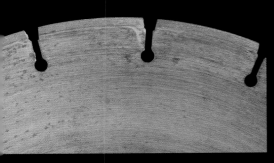

▲ Diamond blades may have a continuous edge but often have gaps that allow cooling water to flow through the cut, and minimize the distortion caused by expansion of the metal as it heats up.

▲ A tile saw is a form of miter saw that uses a water-cooled diamond abrasive blade to cut ceramic tile. I bought this one to make the floor in my round house, which required making two angled cuts on *every single tile* so they would fit into the twenty-eight-sided design of the floor.

■ Soft   Medium Soft   ■ Medium   ■ Medium Hard   Hard

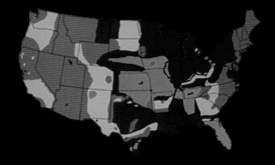

▲ This map shows the hardness of aggregate stone used in concrete in different parts of the United States. This determines which blade will cut best and last the longest.

▶ This measuring tool has a micrometer that allows a rental company to measure the diameter of a diamond blade before and after a customer uses it, to within one ten-thousandth of an inch (0.002 mm). That way they can charge by the amount of blade used.

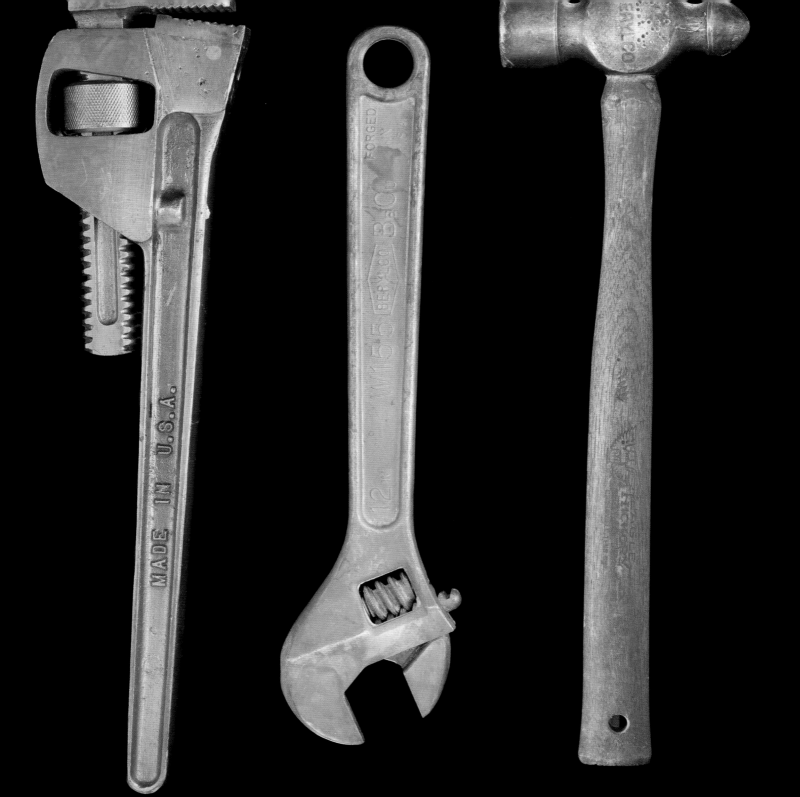

COPPER TOOLS

MOST BRASS AND BRONZE tools exist for one reason: they don't create sparks like steel tools. A spark from a slipped wrench or a falling hammer may be catastrophic if explosive gas is present. The downside is that copper-based alloys are much softer than steel. But who cares when the choice is between needing to replace your tools more often and needing to replace your head because it got blown off?

There are two common alloys used for these types of tools: aluminum bronze (80 percent copper plus aluminum, iron, and nickel) and beryllium copper (98 percent copper plus beryllium, cobalt, and nickel). Beryllium copper tools are stronger, but in exchange they are more expensive and dangerous to modify, because grinding beryllium copper can release toxic beryllium-containing dust. Special procedures and regulations govern its machining or grinding.

A less common reason to use copper tools is that they are non-magnetic, or nearly so (beryllium copper again is superior). If you brought a common steel wrench anywhere near an MRI machine, you would be asked to leave the hospital and never come back. The tremendously powerful magnets in these machines are always on, and they can tear a tool out of your hand from several feet (a meter) away.

Finally, copper alloys are highly corrosion-resistant, so in marine environments or chemical plants where a lot of corrosive chemicals are present, their relative softness may be a small price to pay for them not rusting to dust in just a few months. And yes, again beryllium copper is the better performer.

That concludes this brief intermission in honor of element 29 in the periodic table. We will now return to our regularly scheduled discussion of saws.

◀ The brass and bronze versions of common tools can easily be twenty or more times as expensive as their common steel cousins. From left to right: aluminum bronze pipe wrench, beryllium copper crescent wrench, beryllium copper hammer.

▼ There is little reason to make block planes for wood out of brass, other than that they're so pretty.

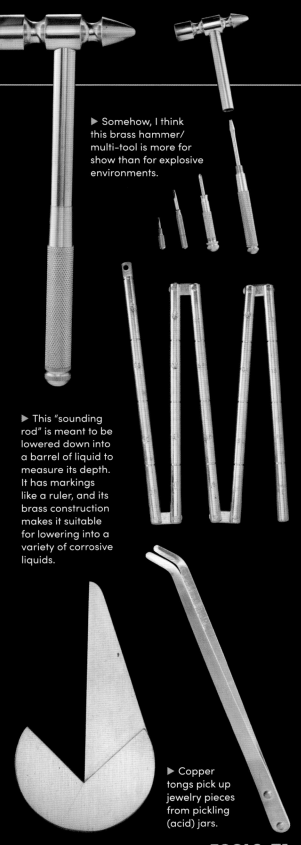

▶ Somehow, I think this brass hammer/multi-tool is more for show than for explosive environments.

▶ This "sounding rod" is meant to be lowered down into a barrel of liquid to measure its depth. It has markings like a ruler, and its brass construction makes it suitable for lowering into a variety of corrosive liquids.

▶ Copper tongs pick up jewelry pieces from pickling (acid) jars.

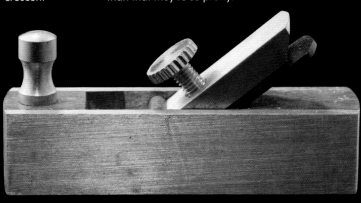

◀ Aluminum bronze tools are less expensive and still just as pretty. Just not as hard as the higher-class beryllium copper versions on the left.

▶ A tool like this center-marking gauge is made of brass only to avoid having it rust.

ODD SAWS

THIS IS THE PAGE for all the *other* saws I couldn't fit elsewhere. There isn't really any common theme to these saws other than that I find each of them either interesting or amusing. And now that I've run out of saws to talk about, it will be back to drills on the next page.

◄ I'm not sure what situations call for this curved bone saw, but isn't it lovely?

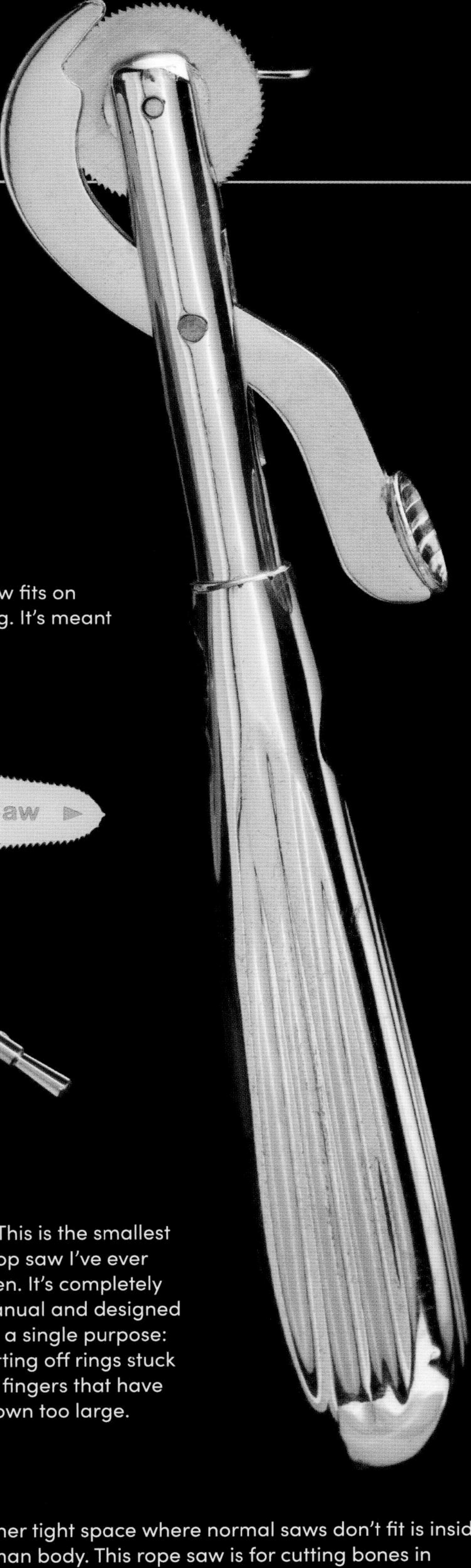

◄ A keyhole saw has a stiff, wedge-shaped blade and is designed for cutting out an opening in the center of a board from a starting hole. I like this one because the handle is where it belongs: right behind the blade for maximum pushing comfort.

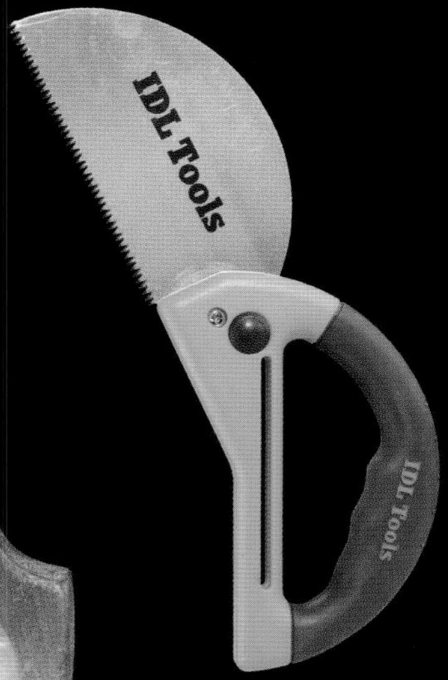

▲ Don't you hate single-function hair clips that just sit there holding your hair without doing anything else? This one is much better because it is also a saw and a hex wrench.

◄ This very fine-toothed pull saw fits on your finger like a dangerous ring. It's meant for delicate model-making.

Designed By Illman

⚠ Beware the Sharp Edge of Saw ▷

IDL Tools

IDL Tools

▲ I don't *think* there's any advantage to the shape of this handsaw, but it is cute the way it armadillos into a ball.

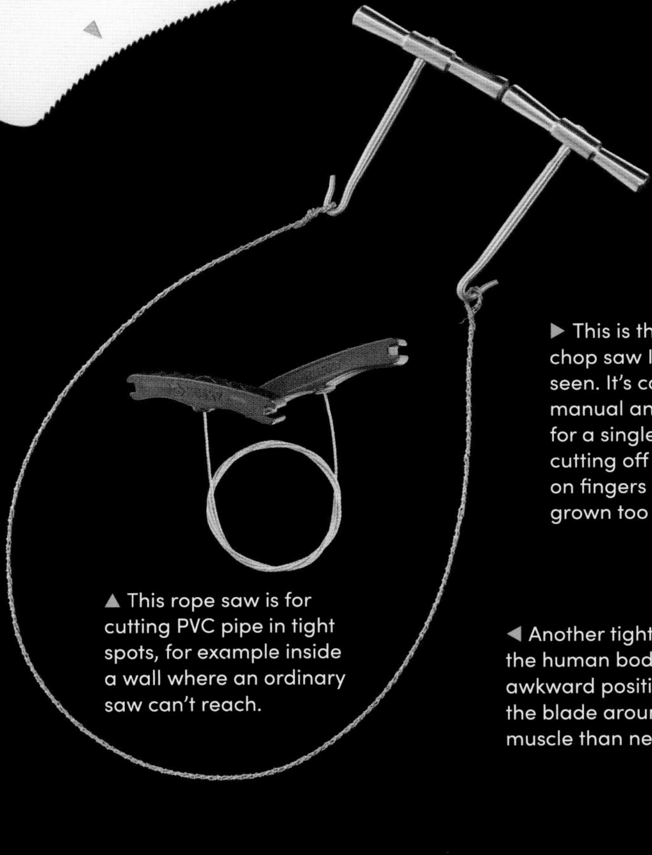

▲ This rope saw is for cutting PVC pipe in tight spots, for example inside a wall where an ordinary saw can't reach.

▶ This is the smallest chop saw I've ever seen. It's completely manual and designed for a single purpose: cutting off rings stuck on fingers that have grown too large.

◄ Another tight space where normal saws don't fit is inside the human body. This rope saw is for cutting bones in awkward positions. The handles detach so you can thread the blade around the bone without cutting away any more muscle than necessary.

MASONRY BITS

STEEL DRILL BITS are sharpened using stone grinding wheels. This works because when steel rubs against stone, the stone wins. But what if you want to drill through stone? You need something harder than steel.

Diamond is the obvious choice, but there are issues. As of now, you can't easily buy solid diamond bits with machined cutting surfaces. Diamonds are also, for the time being, notoriously expensive. Tungsten carbide (usually referred to simply as carbide) is a lot more practical, and it's the most common choice for extra-hard drill bits. It can be formed into solid pieces, and diamond grinding equipment can be used to shape and sharpen it, just as if it were steel. It's more expensive than steel, but not unreasonably so.

In some cases, the entire drill bit is made of one piece of solid carbide. I have a number of these, but they are quite expensive and, in small diameters, actually quite delicate. (Tungsten carbide is very hard, but that very hardness makes it brittle. One wrong move and *snap*, there goes your tiny fancy drill bit.)

More common is to have small chunks of carbide, often simple sharpened rectangular blocks, brazed onto the end of steel shafts. This makes for inexpensive but tough and long-lasting drill bits that can power through concrete, stone, brick, ceramic, or glass. Bits made this way are also useful for cutting metal and even wood: in those cases, tungsten carbide is used not because it's necessary, but because it lasts much longer without needing to be sharpened.

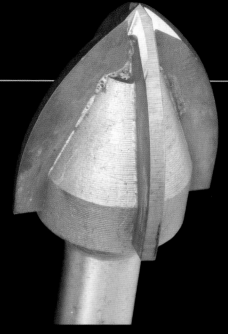

▲▼ Spear-point bits for cutting glass or fine-grained porcelain have a solid wedge of tungsten carbide (or a set of four shaped in a cross) brazed to a steel shank. They cut almost like metal bits, with more of a shaving action than hammering (because otherwise the glass would shatter).

◀ What a magnificent bit! This 4-inch (100 mm) diameter concrete hole saw has massive carbide teeth and a robust centering drill. Though not as expensive as diamond coring bits, a single one of these can cost as much as the hammer drill needed to drive it.

▲ Stone is hard, but brittle, which makes it surprisingly easier to drill through than softer but tougher materials (such as steel). This simple carbide-tipped masonry bit can be driven with a relatively small hand-held hammer drill, which would never work with a similarly large bit going through metal.

▶ This expensive carbide bit is designed to cut through concrete with embedded steel reinforcing bars (rebar). Steel requires a sharp bit, while concrete needs a blunt bit, so this is a tough combination to get through.

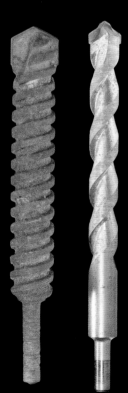

◀ Masonry bits have a surprisingly wide range of flute styles. The super-tightly coiled ones are for drilling extra-hard concrete, where the bit will spin many times without making much progress.

▶ Masonry bits tend to be longer than bits meant for steel, because many common walls are 8-inch-thick (200 mm) concrete, brick, or cinderblock. Very few walls are made of 8-inch-thick steel.

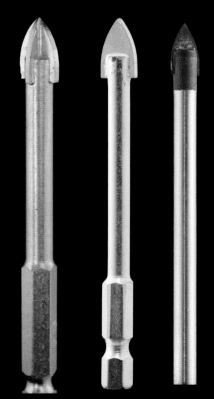

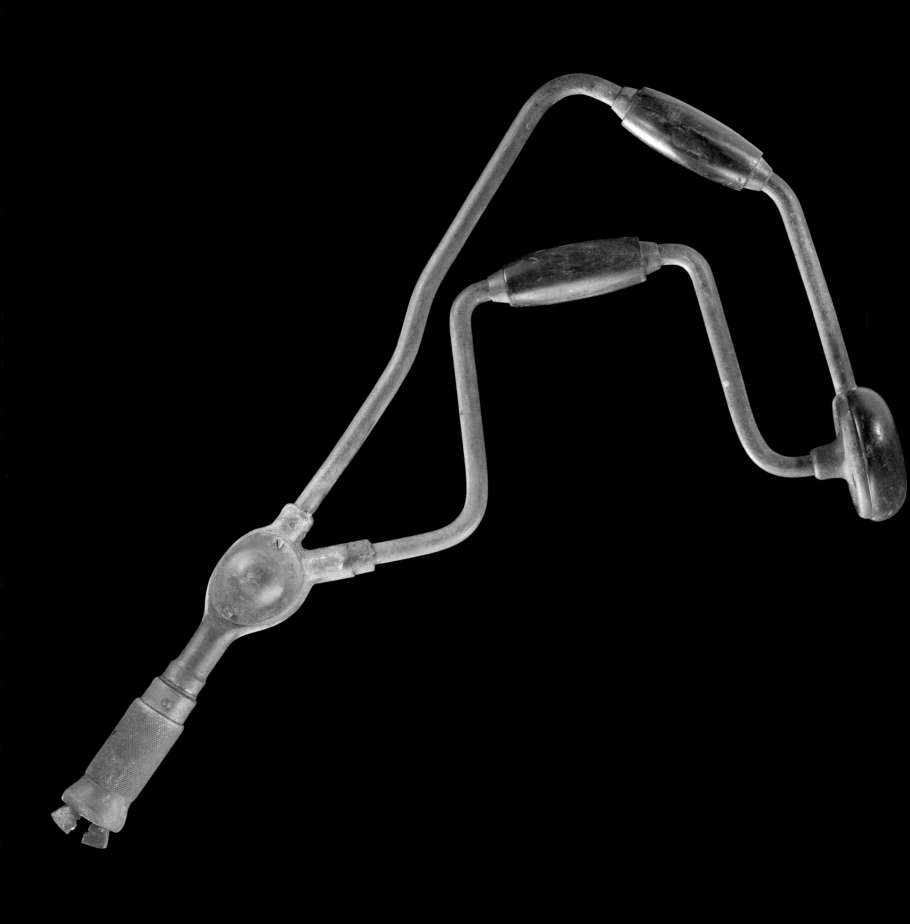

drill small-diameter holes in wood or metal—and even in masonry, with a lot of effort.

To turn a large-diameter bit requires torque more than speed, so the gears in an eggbeater drill are counterproductive. The older brace drill design turns the bit only as fast as you are cranking the offset handle, but it can transmit as much force as you can deliver with your whole arm.

Electric alternatives existed, but a lot of people used these manual styles because the power ones were heavy and difficult to control. Thinking about how young people today will likely never see a tool like this in use is just one of many ways I have of making myself feel old. Of course, I never use them either, because modern cordless drill/drivers are just so very much better at the job.

◀ This exotic variation on a bit brace lets you drill holes up against a wall or in a corner.

▶ All these drills will go through bone at about the same rate, but only the stainless steel ones are designed for that purpose. The red-handled one was my drill when I was a kid, and fortunately never went through even a single one of my bones.

you engage either the inner or the outer ring on the large gear, changing the rotational speed. The flat plate on top is for leaning into the job for more pressure.

▶ The oldest brace drills were not much more than a crank with a bit holder. The design was first used in the 1400s, but this one can't be anywhere near that old.

▶ Spiral drills are another ancient design. The simplest have a slider that makes the bit spin when it's moved up and down. Newer designs, in common use late into the last century, have an enclosed spiral, and they spin when you push the handle down, much like a "Yankee" screwdriver.

SOCKET SETS

OWNING A COMPLETE SET of socket wrenches and ratchet drive handles is a sign of a serious tool user. Socket sets can be very expensive, but they're worth it if you find yourself with a lot of nuts and bolts to drive. Because nuts and bolts come in a variety of sizes, many of which are commonly used, the sets are necessarily large.

To use a socket you need a ratcheting handle with a square peg that fits in the square hole on the back of the socket. There are a small number of standard sizes of this square peg, with ¼-inch, ⅜-inch, ½-inch, ¾-inch, and 1-inch covering all but the very largest sockets. (Interestingly, there is no metric standard for these pegs: the imperial sizes are used all over the world.) Each size peg covers many different sizes of socket, so the three smallest sizes, as found in a typical home socket set, cover dozens of socket sizes.

Read on to see the beautiful variety of ratchet handles you can get to go with your sockets.

◀ The most oft-missing socket in any automotive shop is the 10 mm, because that is the most common size of bolt head used in cars, both foreign and domestic. This survival kit ensures that a 10 mm socket is always on hand. Break glass in case of emergency!

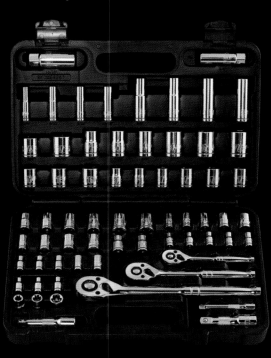

▲ I'm not even going to try to compete with the huge socket sets that serious mechanics keep. This is my little set; there are many like it, but this one is mine. And I've got several more like it in different locations. And drawers full of random other sockets.

▲ Sadly the closest I have to a proper socket set is this darling 9-inch (230 mm) tall salesman sample of an exotically expensive Snap-On tool chest.

▶ A nut threaded far down on a long bolt requires a deep socket. *Very* long bolts require a pass-through socket, which needs a special pass-through handle, which will not work with other sockets. You're seeing all the way through the socket to the black on the other side.

▶ These gadgets are meant to drive bolts at odd angles, but you lose a lot of torque in the process. They are to be avoided if possible.

▲ A lug wrench, used for changing the tire on your car by the side of the road, typically has a different size of socket on each end.

▶ This hundred-year-old socket set looks almost handmade. At the time it was made, square nuts were common, so the set includes both square and hex sockets.

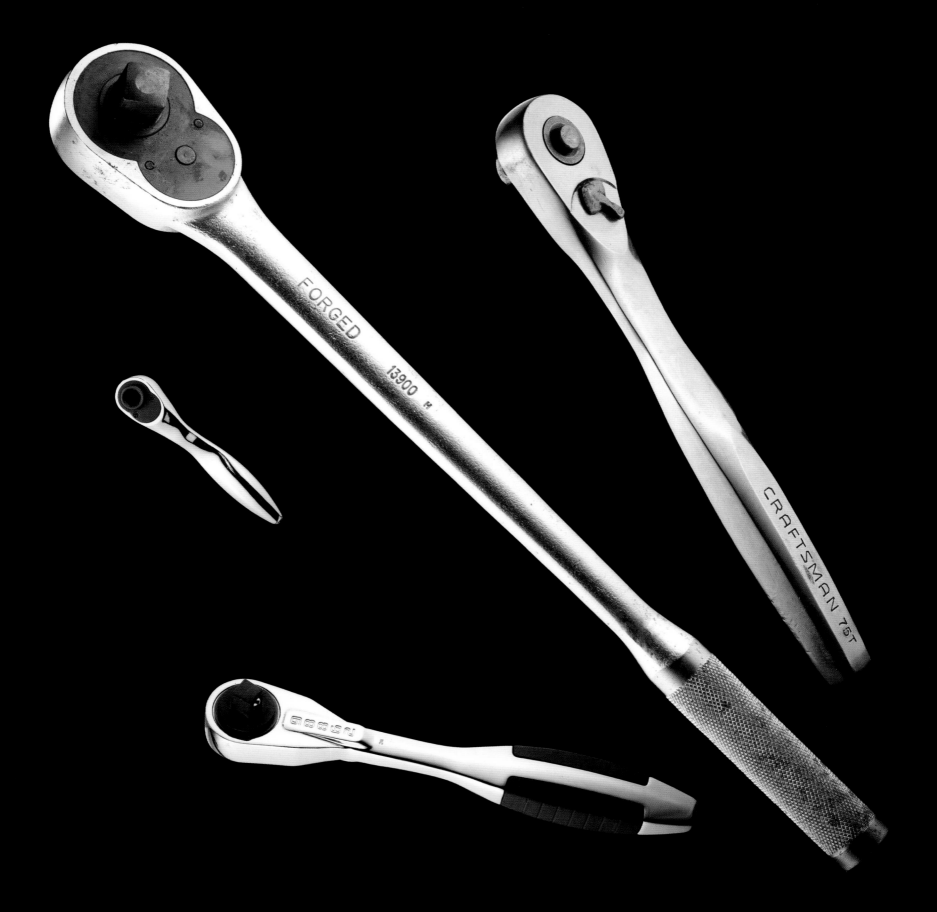

RATCHET WRENCHES

TO USE THE SOCKETS on the previous page you need a ratchet handle. Together this combination is one of the most useful tools in any shop. It is the tool of choice for most mechanical assembly and disassembly where the fasteners are larger than normal screws. The ratchet mechanism allows you to move the handle back and forth while the socket keeps going in the same direction. The best of these wrenches are both strong enough to stand up to every ounce of strength you have, and fine-toothed, so moving the handle back by only a small amount clicks to the next stop, allowing you to use the wrench in tight spaces. It can be very frustrating if you only get one or two clicks, wasting most of the available range of motion, or no clicks at all, making the wrench useless.

The most primitive ratchets have just a few large teeth and a single "pawl" that jams into one tooth at a time. A wrench like that may have to turn as much as 30 degrees (if it has twelve teeth) per click. Smaller teeth reduce the distance needed to turn the handle, but you can't just make the teeth smaller: the pawl would not be strong enough.

The solution is a multi-tooth pawl that engages with many teeth on the ratchet wheel at the same time. The wedging action of the mechanism means that the harder you turn, the harder the teeth are jammed together, and the combined surface area in contact is as large or larger than it would be for a single large tooth. I have not tested this myself, but in all the tests I've seen of ultra-fine-tooth ratchets, the square drive peg always shears off before the ratchet mechanism fails.

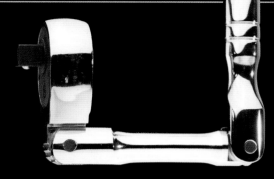

▲ The handle of this articulated ratchet bends in two places! You can turn it into a crank shape, which is actually quite useful for quickly spinning a loose nut. Or you can do this with it.

◀ Ratchet handles can get pretty short, but this is ridiculous. Actually, it's useful for small-diameter fasteners in tight spots: I use one with our sewing machines.

◀ Ratchet wrenches are among the most satisfying tools to hold in your hand, whether they are cute and dainty or suitable for use as a murder weapon. The feel is solid, and the good ones are nearly indestructible, accurately machined, and carefully finished.

▼ The mechanism inside the highest–tooth–count wrench available has a remarkable 160 teeth, giving it a click every 2.25 degrees of rotation. Two pawls, one on each side, engage 12 teeth each with the outer ring.

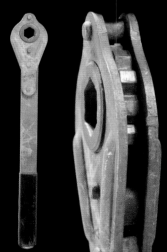

▲ This old ratchet handle has only twelve teeth.

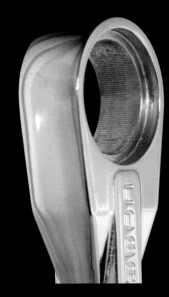

▶ This ratchet has no teeth at all, and thus makes no clicking sound: perfect for library work! You still need to turn it about one degree before the internal mechanism engages and locks the rotation.

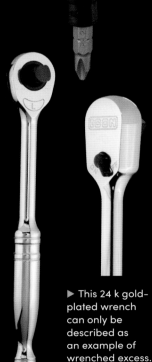

▶ This 24 k gold–plated wrench can only be described as an example of wrenched excess.

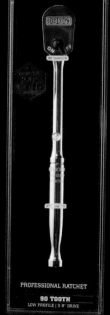

PROFESSIONAL RATCHET
90 TOOTH
LOW PROFILE | 3/8" DRIVE

KerrLab _____ _____ Auto Electro Melt™

℃ EUROTHERM   2116

OP1
OP2
MAN

OPERATION
▼ ▲ Press to view or adjust chamber set point
temperature 1120° C/2050° F max.
See owners manual for complete instructions

CASTING TOOLS

I'VE DONE A fair bit of metal casting. When I was in high school, I would get scraps of zinc roof flashing from a local junkyard and melt them down either with a propane plumbing torch or a stove burner (or both at the same time, which annoyed my mom). Then I would cast the zinc in plaster molds made by the ancient lost-wax technique: I carved a wax original, poured plaster around it, and then melted the wax out in the oven (again annoying my mom).

Later, when I had some money, I got a couple of dedicated precious-metals melting cups. These lovely electrically heated furnaces melt a pound or three of copper, silver, or gold in a graphite crucible. The liquid metal can be poured right out of the cup like a morning coffee.

Molds can be made of plaster or machined out of graphite, both of which I've done many times. But the most common method for making molds, especially for casting iron, is to use casting sand pounded in around a wooden form in the shape of the piece you want to make. It always surprises me that this works at all. The secret is in the sand, which has small amounts of clay and/or organic binders mixed in to make it hold its shape.

Many tools are made by casting: if it says it's made of "cast iron," that is literally true. Casting produces rough shapes, perfect for a pipe wrench handle, for example. Smaller tools that need a precise shape, like those on the next page, are generally forged and then machined.

◀ Melting cups like this have sophisticated proportional-integral-differential (PID) controllers that automatically measure the thermal characteristics of the material being melted, then bring the temperature *just* up to the melting point without overshooting. This protects both the metal and the heating elements.

▼ This is the most complicated machined mold I've made. It's used to cast chain links around each other, forming a complete chain where every link is solid, no joints.

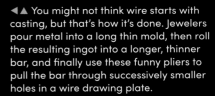

◀▲ You might not think wire starts with casting, but that's how it's done. Jewelers pour metal into a long thin mold, then roll the resulting ingot into a longer, thinner bar, and finally use these funny pliers to pull the bar through successively smaller holes in a wire drawing plate.

▲ This was one of the first things I made from scrap zinc roof flashing. I carved the original from wax, poured plaster around it, baked out the wax, and then poured metal into the mold. Nothing remains of the mold: the wax was recycled and the plaster smashed up.

▶ Injection molding is a form of casting where the liquid (often plastic) is forced into the mold under pressure. I just have this little guy: usually injection molding machines are closer in size to a bus.

DRIVER SETS

I ADMIT TO A CERTAIN unnatural fondness for small precision screwdriver sets (even beyond my unnatural fondness for tools in general). Every time I think I've found the perfect set, better than any I've seen before, I always find another, even better one, a few months or years later. A comfortable mini-screwdriver with a ball-bearing spinner on the end (which rests against your palm as you push it against the screw) is a thing of joy.

Although the vast majority of all the screws in the world are either slotted or Phillips drive, there are many other drive styles, and there are many sizes of slotted and Phillips bits. This leads to many different screwdriver sets that offer one or another subset of possibilities.

Some of these sets excel by having *many* different bits. In the arms race between manufacturers forever trying to frustrate you by using a driver shape you don't have, and screwdriver manufacturers trying to liberate you from that brand of evil, it is never more than a few months before new bits are available. Worst case you can always make your own. I once had to file my own tiny "pentalobe" screwdriver to get into my MacBook for an emergency repair, just after arriving in a small town in Germany where Macs were considered unserious.

If you just can't get the bit you need, you can always resort to the tools on the next page instead.

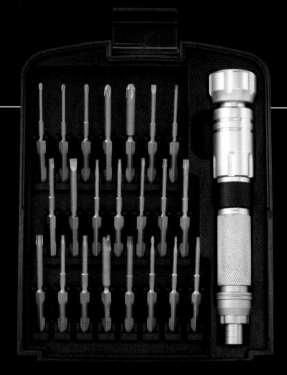

▲ This is my current favorite set. The handle is amazing, the bits are great, and it has everything you need for both MacBooks and iPhones. The set on the left page is more beautiful, but this one is more useful.

▶ Who can resist a cute little mini ratchet set? Not me: I want every one I see.

◀ Words cannot describe the deeply satisfying nature of this cell phone repair screwdriver set. The holder spins like the wheels of an Italian sports car (if it had ball bearings made in Germany). The individual spinner caps are so perfectly made that they spin seemingly forever, like a built-in fidget spinner on each screwdriver.

▼ Once upon a time, my favorite precision screwdrivers were ones like these that came in a set from RadioShack. I now realize that they were terrible, but I didn't know that at the time. Dozens like these have infiltrated my shop, home, and office, creeping in at night or hiding in auction lots.

▲ For quite a few years this was my favorite screwdriver set. I got several to keep in different places. But the handle was never quite right.

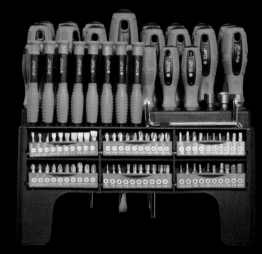

▲ Individual screwdrivers are very cheap to make: even full-sized ones can be made for a few cents each, which allows large sets like this to cost under $20.

PICKS & PRY BARS

SOME TOOLS ARE for building things. Picks and prybars are mainly for destroying things, or at least taking them down or apart.

I have a lot of snarky things to say about titanium hammer heads, but I change my tune when it comes to crowbars. These tools don't need to be heavy or particularly hard to do the job of prying. They just need to be strong, which is something titanium excels at. Weight for weight, titanium is significantly stronger than steel, measured by its resistance to bending or breaking (which is different from its resistance to denting from impact, which is lower than that of steel).

I'm told that titanium crowbars have an unusual fan base: undersea construction workers. This makes sense because not only does titanium resist corrosion, it's also closer in density to water than are steel tools. If you drop a heavy steel tool while floating 100 feet (30 m) underwater, the sudden loss of ballast could send you shooting up to the surface. The loss of the titanium equivalent causes less of an imbalance.

Crowbars and similar prying tools are sometimes also used for hammering— the titanium Halligan bar on the left even has a specific hammering surface. But if a swinging blow is needed to plant a tool before using it to pry, a pickaxe is a better choice, and it should be made of steel because hardness and sufficient weight are key. See previous rant on titanium hammers.

◄ The classic miner's pick can be used to break rocks or dig and pry them loose from the earth.

▼ Brick hammers are used to shape bricks by chipping off pieces of material.

◄ The Halligan bar, named after the New York City firefighter who designed it, is used for breaking down any sort of door, window, or wall that needs breaking down to get to a fire. Halligan bars are normally made of steel, but this military version is made of solid forged titanium, which makes it light, strong, and expensive. It includes a prybar for opening doors, a blunt adze for chopping and splitting wood, a hammer for general pounding, and a brain spike for finishing off zombies.

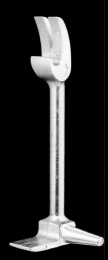

▼ Titanium crowbars are normally too expensive for casual use, but occasionally some geopolitical event will cause a dip in the price. I got this titanium crowbar and nail puller for very reasonable prices during a glorious period when Russia was dumping titanium onto the world market.

▶ Prybars don't have to be strong to be useful: these plastic tire levers work fine because rubber bicycle tires are even softer and the plastic won't damage the metal rim of the wheel.

▶ But sometimes you do need a prybar to be very strong. This forged steel mini-prybar is used to pry apart sheet metal and body panels in aircraft and cars.

▲ This Halligan bar is only 6 inches (150 mm) long, because it's actually a bottle opener.

RE fundamental to
f wood. Large framing
the structure, finish
d roofing nailers
es. Battery-powered
tting better, and
rs are nifty, but the
neumatic nailers
sed air). If you've ever
nstruction noise and it
chances are it was a

ailer is a very simple
ases compressed air
e-diameter cylinder,
own onto the nail.
eeping to supply
r and direct the nail
o go, instead of firing
-oom. (It is a basic

feature of nail guns that they won't fire
unless their nose is being pushed down
onto a surface. The 2022 film *Kimi* provides
a rare semi-realistic nail gun self-defense
scene in which the heroine uses duct tape
to hold the nose back.)

Power staplers are similar in construction
to nailers and are used to fasten fairly
thin material together. They're used a
lot by furniture manufacturers to fasten
upholstery fabric to the wood frames of
sofas and chairs. Electric staplers work fine
for fastening fabric, paper, or house wrap to
walls, but the ones sold in hardware stores
are not strong enough for anything more
than that. Pneumatic staplers are quite a bit
more powerful: larger ones can be as strong
as a small pneumatic nailer, which makes
sense since a stapler needs to drive in two
spikes instead of just one.

m nailer (for small nails)
ompress air in a cylinder
y to drive a nail. In other
ler with the compressor
ss, and hoseless, but heavy.

▲ I've used this pneumatic stapler to fasten together
wood garden lattice panels. Nails would not be strong
enough, and screws would take too long. Staples are
best for both home- and factory-made lattice.

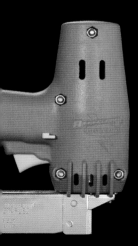

overgrown office staplers,
k just like o e staples

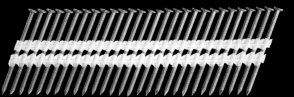

◄ Large framing nails usual
they can fit tightly next to e
head nails like these are als
to put in a new strip more f

Schnitze mit Schnitermeissel
➤➤➤➤ Marke Pfeil ◄◄◄◄
Die Marke der höchster Leistung

Schw ✠ Fab

CHISELS

THE TWO TOOLS that woodworking snobs get most worked up about are chisels and block planes. Perhaps it's a character flaw of mine, but I really don't have much use for either, so I've chosen to focus less on common wood chisels and more on the variations that I find fascinating.

The difference between a knife and a chisel is that a knife edge is typically beveled on both sides, but most chisels are beveled on one side only. The other side is perfectly flat right up to the very edge. This is important because it allows the chisel to lie flat against a wood surface and cut off anything that sticks out, even the tiniest bit,

above the surface. It also allows the chisel to cut vertically down into a block of wood, leaving perfectly straight, flat sides in the hole (typically called a mortise).

There is a crude end to the chisel spectrum. Cold chisels are for cutting or breaking iron that has not been heated (in contrast to tools used to forge hot iron). Brick chisels are for scoring bricks, and masonry chisels do the same for harder rock and concrete. These chisels have an edge, but it's very dull. They are impact tools more than cutting tools.

When the edge of a chisel is made so narrow that it becomes just a point, you've arrived at the tool on the next page.

◀ These chisels are a legacy of my mother's upbringing in the Steiner School philosophy. Along with a considerable volume of nonsense, this philosophy emphasizes equality and the dignity of handcrafts (which explains why she learned to carve and I learned to knit).

▶ Steiner School graduates have a distinctive carving style that I associate with my childhood in Switzerland. I think my mom made this box, but if not, she easily could have.

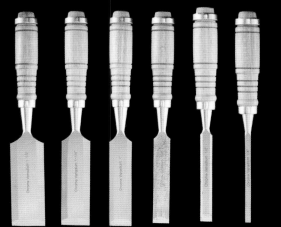

◀ As with saws and drills, chisels made for bone look alarmingly like those used for wood, except made of stainless steel, without any gaps or joints where bacteria could hide.

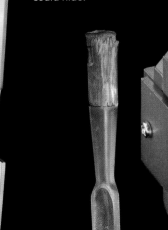

◀ Chisels for wood need to be very sharp, and even the best quality ones need to be sharpened frequently to keep the edge keen enough for comfortable use. This cheap set even more so.

◀▲ If you use a router to carve out a pocket for a hinge or door strike, you're always left with rounded corners. A corner chisel (one old and one new) makes them square in one whack.

◀ Cold chisels are blunt and brutal.

▲ If it looks like a very wide cold chisel, it's actually for splitting bricks.

▲ Chisels for dirt are called shovels: you dig a hole just the same way you carve a mortise. I love the look of history and thrift in how this one has been cobbled and mended.

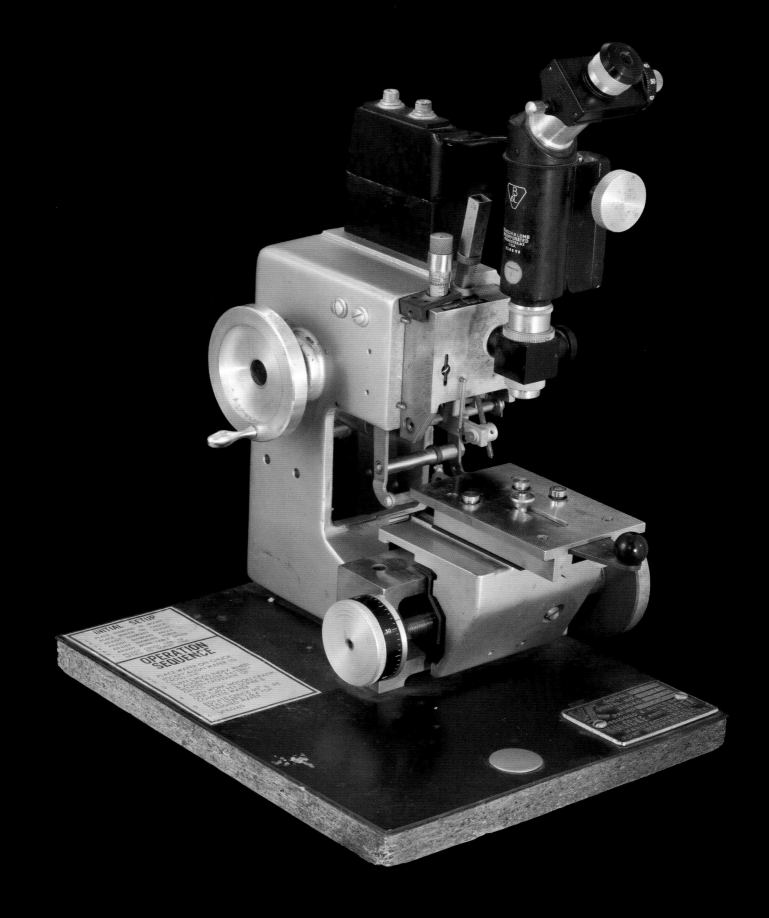

SCRIBES & AWLS

AWLS ARE USED FOR scratching and scoring across or poking through material, including wood, leather, plastic, and metal. Simple round, pointed awls can be used to scratch a line along a straight edge or to mark a point where a hole will be drilled. In soft or thin materials an awl can be used to poke a hole all the way through. Sewing awls, often used on leather, have a hole near the end that pulls a thread through the hole being made by the awl.

Awls have smooth, rounded handles meant to be held in the hand, not hammered like a chisel's. Those meant primarily for poking, rather than scratching, will have a broad end that fits in your palm and gives you a wide surface area to push against.

The machine on the left is one of the most precise awls imaginable. OK, it's not technically an awl, but functionally it's what you get if you imagine crossing an awl with a small milling machine. This obscure device is a silicon microchip wafer scribing tool. It has a very fine diamond-tipped scribe (this is the awl-like part) mounted on a spring-loaded arm. The rest of the machine is dedicated to very precisely aligning the scribe with the divisions between individual chips on a wafer, and then dragging it in a very straight line between two columns of chips. This leaves a scratch that then lets you snap the chips apart. It's basically the world's most accurate glass cutter.

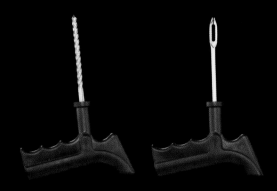

▲ This pair of tools is used to repair puncture holes in tires. The rat-tail awl is used first to clean out and rough up the inside surface of the hole. The second tool, similar to a leather awl, is used to pull a rubber plug down into the hole and leave it there.

◄ The microscope eyepiece on this silicon wafer scribing tool has a movable reticle (scale) with index marks on the adjusting knob spaced at 1/8,000 of an inch (0.003 mm). Why 1/8,000 and not 1/10,000 like any sane measuring tool? Maybe 1/1,000 of 1/8 inch? Life is full of mysteries I'm too lazy to google.

▼ This lovely array of awls are for scribing, marking, and poking holes.

▶ This tool starts as an awl at the tip, then has a section of gimlet drill, followed by a section of rat-tail file. It's generally useful for making and enlarging holes in wood or leather.

▲ This is a modern leather sewing awl, but it's functionally no different from one you could have found thousands of years ago.

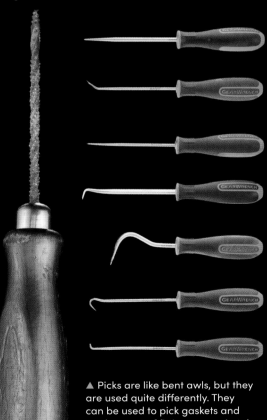

▲ Picks are like bent awls, but they are used quite differently. They can be used to pick gaskets and washers out of fittings, press in tabs to separate connectors, hook onto wires you can't otherwise reach, poke your eye out, and so on.

ROUTERS

ROUTERS AND MILLING machines are similar in operation, but different in scale. Both have a motor connected to a collet that holds a cutting bit. Both differ from drills in that they are designed to support strong sideways forces on the bit, so they can cut in all directions, not just straight down.

The difference is that a router is a hand-held tool meant for use on wood or plastic, and a milling machine is a large stationary tool meant for use on metal. This accounts for the typical thousandfold difference in weight and hundredfold difference in price. Even when a router is mounted on a computer-controlled frame so it can be moved automatically (called a CNC router), the machine is still much lighter than a milling machine of the same size.

A hand-held router is a versatile and essential tool in any wood shop. It rounds over edges; cuts slots (dados), mortises, and dovetails; and does a dozen other common operations. Because the bit is sharp and spins very fast, and wood is not very hard, the force needed to push one along is relatively small. Using a router is not an intensely physical activity: it's more about careful guidance and not letting it slip or drift off the template.

The motor in a router is fairly extreme: it has to be light and small enough to fit in a hand-held tool, yet typically ranges in power from one to three-and-a-half horsepower (¾ to 2 ½ kW). To achieve such power, all the electrical components are driven to the edge, and will eventually require some attention from electrical maintenance tools like those on the next page.

▶ Very large router bits are best used in combination with a router table, or in a more substantial tool called a shaper.

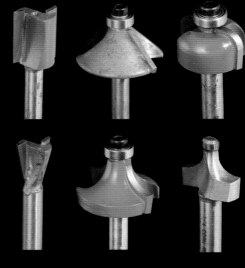

▼ The key to the versatility of routers is in the bits. There are countless shapes, from general-purpose rounding-over bits, to complex fancy-edge profiles, to specialized patterns for joint-making.

◀ Plunge routers are good at starting cuts in the middle of a board. I had one exactly like this stolen from my farm a few years back. Fortunately, what theft takes, auctions return. The slides, covered with bellows to protect them from dust, allow you to slide the body down to a predetermined depth while the baseplate remains firmly planted.

▼ Drywall routers spin very, very fast and use a small spiral-cutting bit to zip through plaster wallboard. This material is very soft (you can drill it with a screwdriver), so guiding the router is easy.

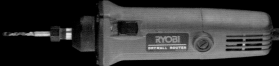

◀ A good basic router is little more than a motor with a bit on the end.

▶ As parents of toddlers can tell you, there is a particular brand of wooden toy train that is very nice, and very overpriced. You can make your own using this set of router bits, which cut the track and the ball-and-socket joints between segments of track.

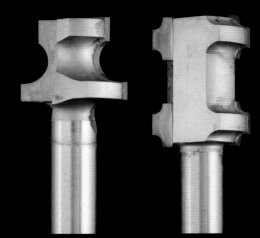

WIRE CUTTERS

THE SIMPLEST WIRE CUTTERS are like scissors, but with a larger ratio of handle to blade for more leverage. Wire cutters meant for electrical wiring should not be used to cut steel wire, because their blades are not hard enough and you'll end up leaving deep notches in the blades, which will never again close smoothly until you file or grind away the notched edge. (Someday I may learn this lesson, but so far not yet.) Cutters that you can use on steel cable (called aircraft cable if it's small and wire rope if it's bigger) have much thicker jaws made of hardened steel, and are much more expensive than regular wire cutters.

Wire cutters are usually made with one or more notches in their blades for gently stripping the plastic insulation to expose the wire underneath. The goal when stripping wire is to not damage the metal, which will cause the wire to either break or overheat at the point where it's been nicked. (I had an electric minicar where all the motor leads melted clean through, leaving blobs of copper on the ends of the wires, simply because they had been improperly stripped!)

▲ *Really* thick steel cable can be cut with this tool—and a sledgehammer to whack it with.

► Automatic wire strippers cut and pull off a measured amount of insulation. They can be fast, but also kind of annoying to navigate around the wire and clear of the stripped bits of insulation.

◄ Large-diameter, paper-insulated cables (which also have rubber insulation, not just paper) call for these unusually shaped pliers to strip the insulation off without damaging the wire inside.

◄ This model has discrete notches for each diameter of wire. It has forged blades and a high-quality machined lap joint. Using it on steel wire would be an expensive mistake.

▲ For cutting large-diameter wire rope (steel cable) being sold in a hardware store, this tool has a long handle and an interesting nautilus-like ratchet mechanism for variable leverage. Look at how thick the hardened steel jaws are!

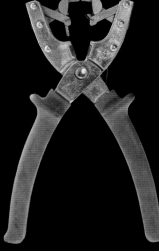

▲ This odd cutter is for non-metallic sheathed cable, known as Romex. The bent-over end strips the outer sheath, and the notches on the straight part strip the individual wires.

◄ This wire rope cutter is no bigger overall than a common wire cutter, but its superthick hardened steel jaws slice through ¼-inch (6 mm) steel aircraft cable like it was nothing.

▲ This lovely, somewhat enigmatic tool is a heavy-gauge electrical cable stripper. The end of the cable is threaded into the hole that matches its diameter. Twisting the tool like a corkscrew causes a small chisel blade inside to cut away the insulation in a spiral.

▲ The tool most like a wire cutter, that isn't a wire cutter, is a dog nail trimmer.

LOPPERS

SCISSORS, SNIPS, wire cutters, and nippers tend to have two similar blades, both of the same thickness, sharpness, and general shape. There's another group of cutters, which I refer to as loppers, which have one sharp blade that cuts against something more like a block or anvil. The blade either passes by the block, which is called a bypass lopper, or dead-ends into it, an anvil lopper.

Garden loppers of the bypass variety often have one narrow but thick, dull blade that can slip between branches, and then a deep, sharp blade that does the actual cutting. It's important to keep the sharp blade toward the live part of the plant, to avoid crushing it. For dead, dried-out branches, anvil loppers sometimes work better, because the blades tend not to twist and separate.

If you put a bunch of bypass loppers all in a row, you have what's called a sickle bar. Sickle bars are anywhere from a fraction of an inch (1 cm or less) wide, such as a nose hair trimmer, to several yards (meters) wide, as in a tractor-mounted brush mower.

▲ These "miter shears" (which are actually anvil loppers) cut soft sheet, rod, or bar material at a moderately accurate angle.

◄ I think Hollywood has missed a trick in not using this tool in a slasher movie. It's a garden lopper, but the blade is a chainsaw! Imagine the possibilities!

◄ Anvil-style garden loppers should not be used on live plants because they crush the branch while cutting it.

▼ We're so used to electric hair and beard trimmers that it's quite surprising, at least to me, to find the mechanism in a completely mechanical version.

▲ Bypass loppers are good for pruning live branches.

▼ If you own a hobby farm, as I do, a gas-powered sickle bar "hair trimmer" is a very handy tool. The blade can tilt left and right to easily go over uneven ground, and it will cut anything up to about an inch thick without missing a beat—which is why you should not use it when there are toddlers around.

▶ Here's an unusual anvil lopper. Instead of a blade, it has a long, thin heating element. It simultaneously cuts and seals plastic bags or the filling stems of mylar helium balloons.

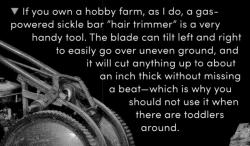

PIPE CUTTERS

PIPES CAN BE CUT like you would cut a solid bar, using a hacksaw. But for copper or iron pipe the job is done better using a clever tool that cuts the pipe from the outside in. The tool starts by making a shallow cut all the way around the outside of the pipe, then slowly deepens the cut until it reaches the full thickness of the pipe wall, at which point the pipe falls in half. This leaves a smooth cut, and by the nature of the tool the cut will always be perfectly square to the end of the pipe. (If the tool isn't going around a circle that's exactly perpendicular to the length of the pipe, then it will spiral its way down the pipe instead of cutting deeper along the same line—which is very annoying when it happens.)

Pipe cutters typically have a single hardened steel or tungsten carbide cutting disk on one side and a pair of smooth rollers on the opposite side. The pipe is trapped between the two sides, which slowly tighten as you turn the handle and rotate the tool around the pipe, deepening the cut with each turn.

The tool shown on the left is unusual in having four cutting wheels, and a wedge mechanism that pushes them all together at the same time. It's used to cut car exhaust pipe, which has very thin walls compared to its diameter. (A single-disk pipe cutter would tend to distort it more than cut it.)

Cast-iron drainpipe, on the other hand, is so hard, but also so brittle, that it can be cut with a tool that doesn't cut at all: it simply squeezes the pipe at multiple points around its diameter until it suddenly cracks apart.

◀ This exhaust pipe cutter is delicate compared to a normal pipe cutter and has four times as many cutting disks, which dig into the pipe from all sides when the jaws are clamped around it.

▼ This pipe cutter works like a bypass lopper. It's used on plastic water pipe, hoses, rubber tubes, and other round things measuring an inch or two in diameter and reasonably easy to cut.

◀ This cutter for large-diameter (4-6-inch, 100-150 mm) steel pipe has four cutting wheels and a frame that allows it to exert tremendous pressure.

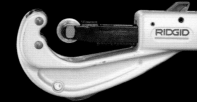

▲ The long bar of this cutter adjusts more quickly than the standard design, but means the tool is only strong enough for plastic or thin-walled metal pipe.

▶ Why use a power tool for a job you can do more quickly by hand? Because you have to cut pipe manually a hundred times in a row and your hand will get tired.

▶ Add some carbide cutting disks to a chain wrench and you have a tool designed for cutting cast-iron drainpipes, but also used in rock shops to break open geodes.

▲ This tiny pipe cutter is great for small-diameter copper pipes, and for working in areas where there is very little space around the pipe (which is common since pipes are often run next to each other, through holes in studs that keep them close to a wall surface).

▶ I got this heavy-duty pipe cutter for a really good price: the online auction listing did not mention that it was autographed by Tony Stewart, a famous race car driver sponsored by The Home Depot.

◀ You never know what's inside a geode until it's cracked open. Look for one that seems light for its size: an interesting hollow rock naturally weighs less than a boring solid one.

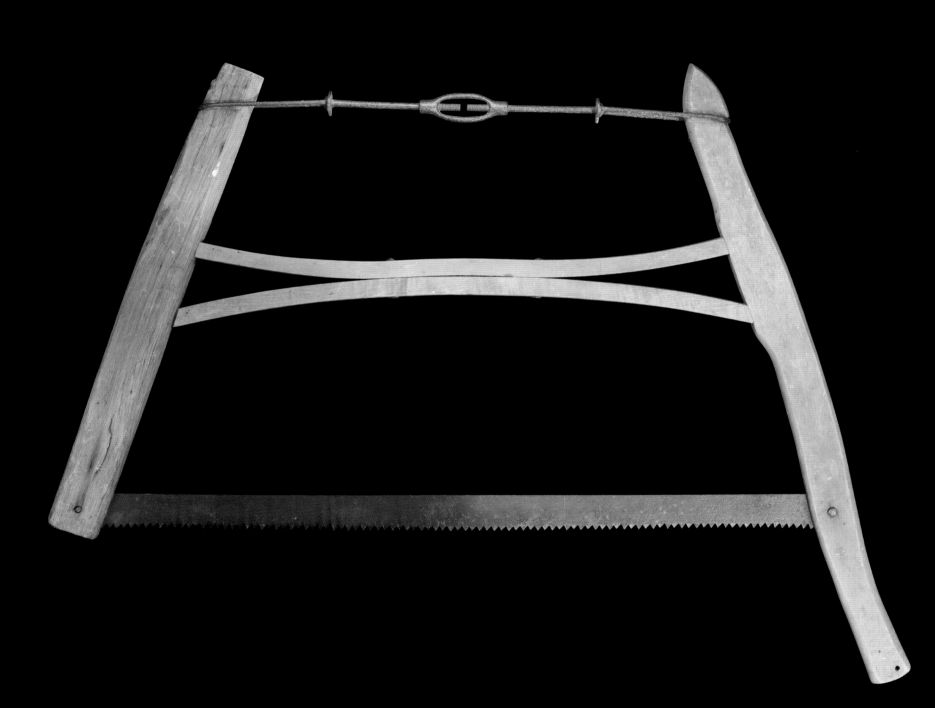

BOW SAWS

BUCKSAWS TYPICALLY have large teeth designed to cut in both directions. They are crude saws for crude work, like cutting up firewood or trimming trees. They are also distressingly common in antiques shops and tool collections. If I had a bucksaw for every time I saw a bucksaw for sale . . . I would have even more than the six or so I already have, only one of which I bought on purpose. (The rest just came with other stuff I wanted at auctions where I was bidding on the contents of a pile, or everything hanging on a given wall.)

What accounts for the popularity of this design? There is an inherent conflict in the construction of saw blades. They should be thin, because the thicker they are, the more material you have to remove to make room for them in the cut. But they also want to be thick so they are stiff enough to do their job. One way around this dilemma is to put the blade under tension with some sort of stretching frame. Anything, even a rope, is stiff if it's being pulled tight enough, so a stretched saw blade can be as thin as the tensile strength of the blade material allows.

The hacksaws we saw earlier are other examples of this idea, as are coping saws and fret saws, which have very thin blades with many small teeth. They cut on the pull stroke for better control and are used to cut curves in thin material, or to "cope" molding. (Look up a video to see how this is done: it's fascinating, but too complicated to explain here.)

Stretched saws all have one flaw: you can't cut farther into a piece of wood than the depth of the frame. For that you need a jigsaw.

▶ Add a motor to a coping saw and you have a primitive scroll saw.

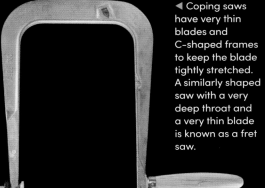

◀ Coping saws have very thin blades and C-shaped frames to keep the blade tightly stretched. A similarly shaped saw with a very deep throat and a very thin blade is known as a fret saw.

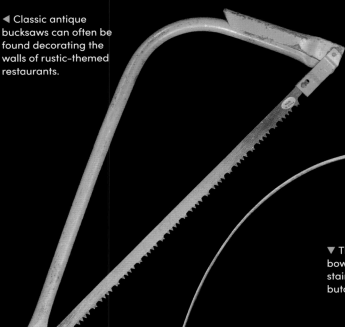

◀ Classic antique bucksaws can often be found decorating the walls of rustic-themed restaurants.

◀ This modern bow saw is used for yardwork and cutting branches off trees and shrubs. It's very light for its size.

▶ Make a hand-held, powered coping saw and you have this oddity, which includes an optional table that turns it into more of a scroll saw.

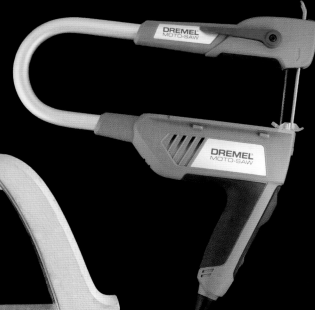

▼ This elegantly curved bow saw is made of stainless steel: it's a butcher saw.

JIGSAWS

JIGSAWS ARE ONE OF the most popular categories of power tool. Discount models are inexpensive and there are many options for shape, weight, and features. Fancy models come with a speed control dial and a knob to select whether the blade oscillates front to back while it's going up and down. Jigsaws are used to cut simple or complicated curves, and can be quite gentle if handled properly. Or they can bind in the cut and rattle alarmingly.

The key to using a jigsaw is to keep steady downward pressure on the plate, so the blade never has a chance to lift the tool off the surface and become twisted. Most jigsaw blades cut on the upstroke, which helps keep the tool in contact with the work. The downside of this action is that when cutting wood, the top surface of the grain is easily damaged with the upward stroke of the saw. A simple solution is to cut the wood upside-down, but if that's not possible, reverse blades, which cut on the downstroke, are available. They require you to use even more downward force to keep them in contact with the work . . . and of course they ruin the bottom side of the wood.

I used to use jigsaws a lot more than I do now, and there's one simple reason: I bought a big laser cutter. For wood or plastic ½ inch (12 mm) or less thick there is simply no better tool for making complicated curved shapes. The same goes for coping saws, scroll saws, and bandsaws. Each of these tools still has its occasional uses for me, but the laser cutter covers a lot of the saws' territory.

Jigsaws are good at cutting curves. For cutting a straight line, you need a circular saw.

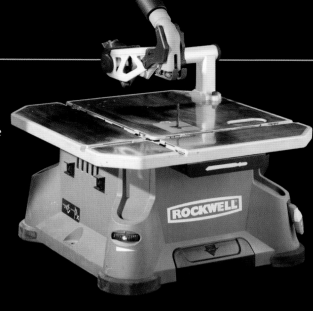

▲ At first glance, this looks like a table saw or a scroll saw, but close examination reveals that it is actually an upside-down jigsaw with an oversized base plate. It takes standard jigsaw blades, which stick up from below.

▲ Miniature jigsaws are for model building and art projects.

◀ This doesn't look like a fancy jigsaw, and it's not. But it runs smoothly and precisely, making it a joy to use.

▼ Battery-powered jigsaws are great for ad-hoc cutting in and around the house. They don't use as much power compared to other kinds of power saws, so the batteries tend to last and last.

▲ This model has a silly knob that lets you select the material and type of cut you want to make, and automatically sets the type of blade movement. So instead of just setting the movement you know will work, you have to reverse engineer the mind of the person who designed the tool to figure out what kind of material they thought would call for the motion you want.

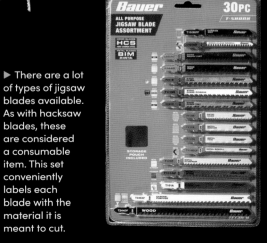

▶ There are a lot of types of jigsaw blades available. As with hacksaw blades, these are considered a consumable item. This set conveniently labels each blade with the material it is meant to cut.

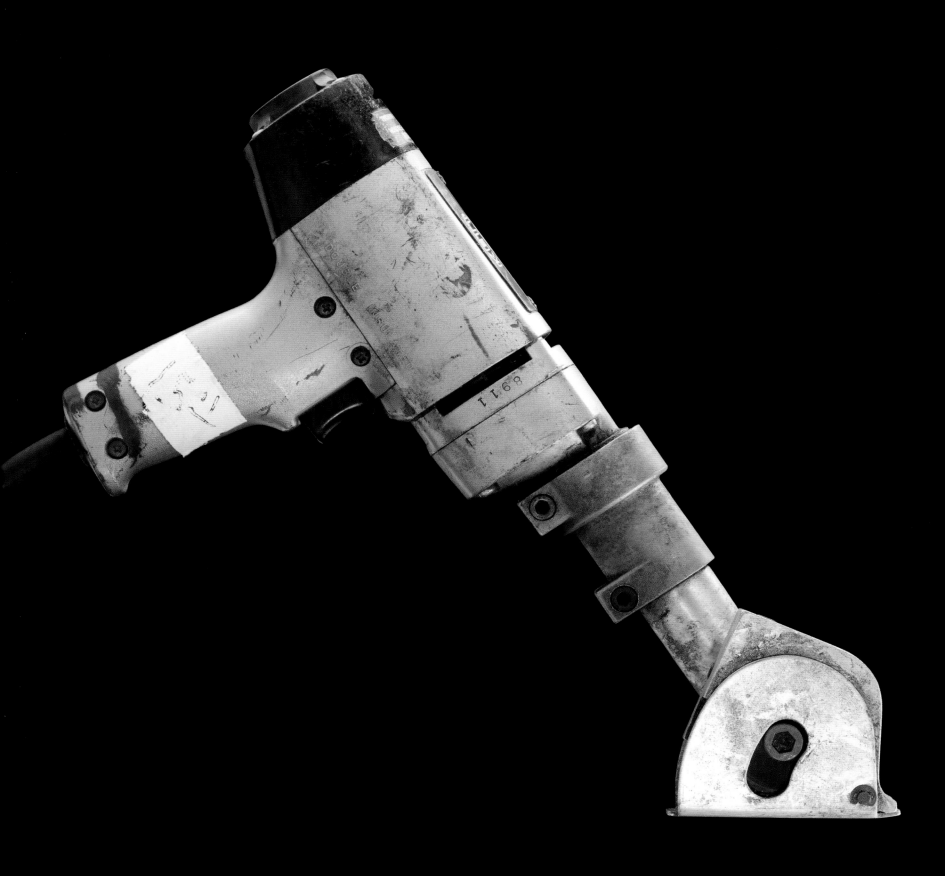

CIRCULAR SAWS

A CIRCULAR SAW IS exactly what the name implies: an ordinary saw wrapped into a circle. Circular saws have the inherent and significant advantage of a blade that keeps going in the same direction all the time. There is no jerking back and forth, which makes them easier to control and smoother in action.

The tooth configurations that exist with handsaws also apply to circular saws: big teeth for fast, rough cutting, lots of small teeth for smooth, precision cutting, and abrasive or diamond powder teeth for cutting bricks, tiles, and concrete. But the conditions are much harder for circular saw teeth, because they operate at a much higher speed than a handsaw and tend to be used for

a much longer periods of time to cut through much more material.

Steel circular saw blades are available, but you really want to get one with tungsten carbide teeth. They will last much longer than plain steel, and can be sharpened with a diamond hone, or by taking the blade to a sharpening service. A carbide blade is happy to cut through any kind of wood, as well as aluminum or brass. There are even heavy-duty carbide blades that can cut through steel rebar (which is more commonly cut with an abrasive wheel in a cutoff saw).

A circular saw is a basic tool for anyone doing nearly any sort of woodworking or construction and should be among the first power tools you buy.

◀ Large gas-powered circular saws are known as demolition saws. This one is used by my local fire department to rapidly cut their way into a burning building or rescue someone trapped in a car.

◀ This odd little tool is a long-reach, miniature circular saw. It came from the estate of a famous race car builder, where it was most likely used to cut sheet metal panels to be formed into the shell of a car.

▶ Small circular saws are handy for cutting plywood panels, because they are light enough to be comfortable even when reaching to the far side of a full sheet, and you don't need a large blade to cut thin material.

▼ This has been my workhorse circular saw for decades. Most recently I used it to cut the tops off dozens of 4 by 4-inch (100 cm square) fence posts after they had been set in concrete.

▲ Battery-powered circular saws are surprisingly powerful these days. Even inexpensive ones are very effective. Just don't expect them to work all day without having to replace the battery.

◀ This style gives you some extra reach.

SAWS FOR JOINTING

YES, THERE IS A serious tool called a wobble dado, and if you mess with one, it will be only too happy to tear your hand off. But first some background on dados.

A dado is a slot cut into a piece of wood that's just the right width for the edge of another board to fit into. You see these a lot on bookcases, drawers, boxes, cabinets, and so on. The fastest, most accurate way to cut a dado is with a table saw or shaper that has a blade the exact width of the slot you want. In factory production situations that is exactly how it's done: they have a separate blade or bit for each width of slot they need to make.

In a home shop it's a lot more practical to use a "stacked dado" set, which has two full-sized circular saw blades and several two-toothed "chippers" stacked between

them. You can add as many chippers as you need to increase the width, and you can fine-tune the width with thin metal shims that add tiny bits of space between the chippers. These sets are not overly expensive, and they are relatively safe and reasonably convenient to use. But what if you want something even more convenient, and don't care if it's safe? That's when you reach for the wobble dado.

Wobble dados have a single set of teeth that, as the name implies, wobble back and forth to cut a slot wider than the blade itself. They are no longer made, but you can find one easily at auctions and garage sales. Which is not to say you should find one. There's a reason they don't make them anymore: the potential for grabbing and throwing the wood is high.

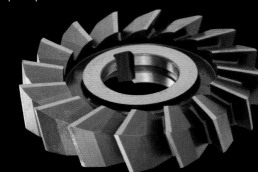

▶ The high-dollar solution to cutting dados is a separate solid blade for every width of slot. These are extra-tough versions for cutting slots in steel using a horizontal milling machine, but the principle is the same.

◀ This fancy—for its time—wobble dado has big, chunky carbide teeth. The dial lets you adjust the degree of wobble, and thus the width of the slot.

◀ Stacked dado sets are safe—to the extent that any rapidly spinning knife edges can be called safe—and effective tools for cutting slots.

▼ A shaper blade is like a fancy dado blade. Mounted in a table saw it will cut a variety of interesting profiles into wood (or a finger) passed over the top. Save your fingers and use a router or shaper instead.

◀ How long before one of the teeth on this wobble dado breaks off and flies into your eye?

▲ Tragically, people used to have to cut dados by hand using specialized dado saws like this.

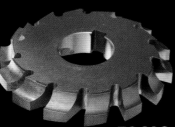

▶ The serious way of saw-cutting profiles is an expensive set of solid cutters for every shape.

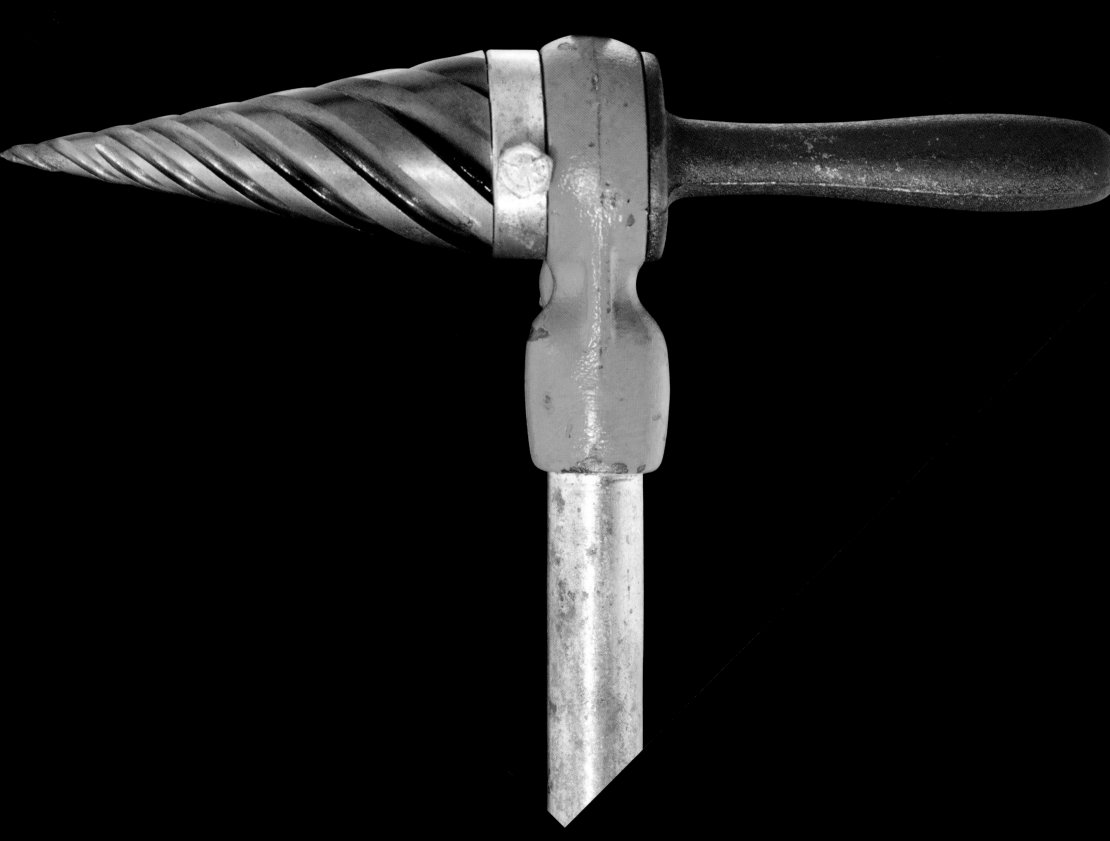

REAMERS

REAMERS ARE TOOLS that take an existing hole and enlarge or reshape it to its final dimensions. They are essential tools because creating accurate shapes and removing a lot of material are two very different tasks that are difficult to accomplish at the same time. Drill bits are great for rapidly removing a bulk quantity of material from a hole, but they are inherently not very accurate, and the large chips they create leave the sides of the hole rough.

Reamers have cutting edges designed to work more slowly but more accurately. They take an existing hole and remove just a bit more material from the side, leaving behind a silky-smooth surface.

A reamer can also be designed to create a tapered (cone-shaped) hole, or one with a more complicated profile. For example, I have several bone reamers designed to hollow out a femur (upper leg) bone and create a very specific tapered shape of hole that receives the end of an artificial hip joint implant.

Pipe reamers, on the other hand, just trim off burrs left from when a pipe was cut, leaving the end of the pipe with smooth, slightly beveled edges ready to be threaded with the tools on the next page.

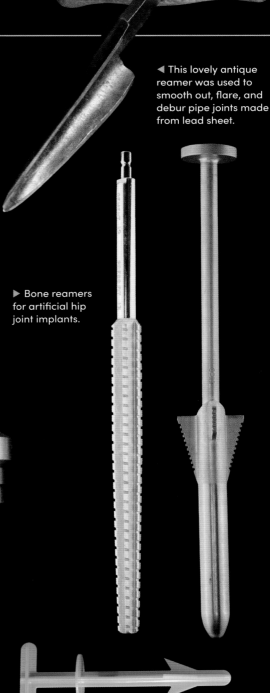

◀ This lovely antique reamer was used to smooth out, flare, and debur pipe joints made from lead sheet.

▶ Bone reamers for artificial hip joint implants.

◀ Believe it or not, this is *not* a ratchet-action spiral brain spike for zombies. It is instead a ratchet-action spiral pipe reamer for pipes up to 2 inches or 50 mm in diameter.

▼ Used in a milling machine, a reamer like this can true-up a previously drilled hole to an exact diameter and leave it with very smooth sides.

▲ Hand-held reamers are less about ultimate precision and more about simply enlarging existing holes, or cleaning them up by removing burrs and rough spots.

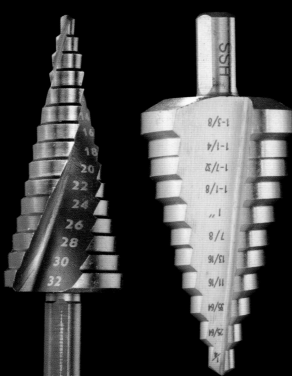

▲ These reamers, known as step drills, work only on thin sheet metal. They are great because one drill can make a dozen different diameters of hole, up to quite large. The spiral versions look cool, but don't work any better than the straight ones.

▲ This is hands-down, without question, the most disgusting reamer I have ever had the misfortune to encounter. I'll just tell you that it's called the Butt Out 2, and it's used by deer hunters. Sorry.

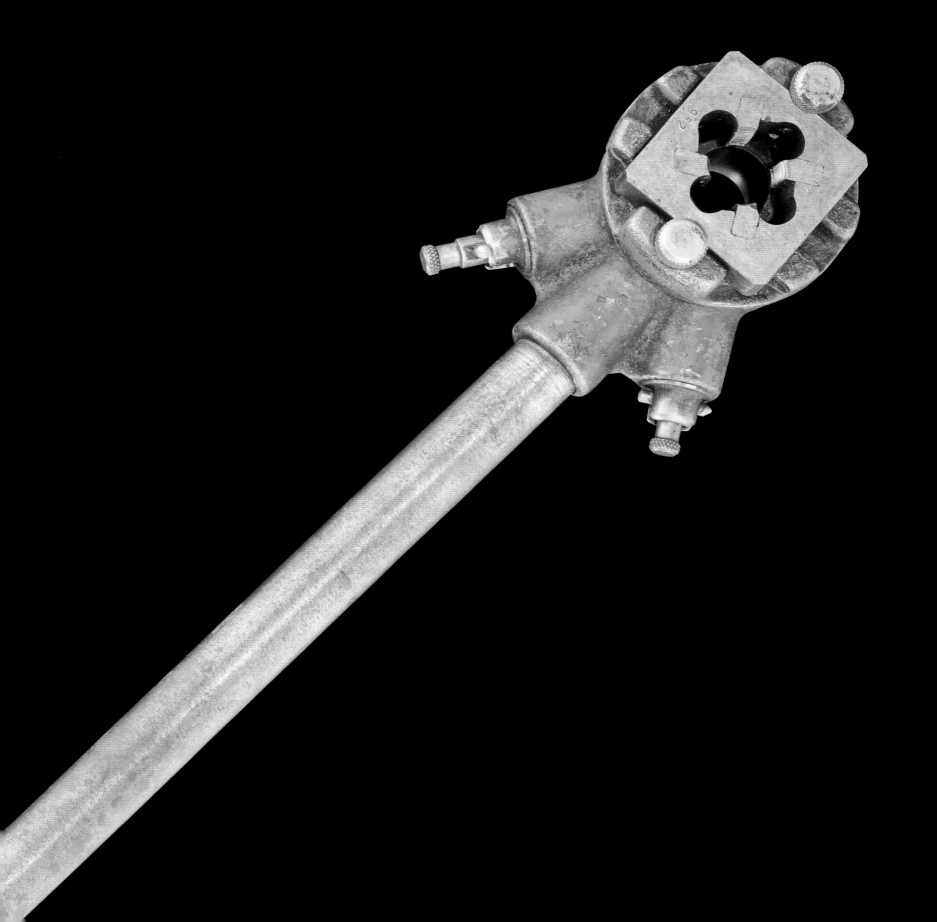

THREADING TOOLS

ONE OF THE HEADLINE reasons for drilling holes in metal is so you can tap them, which means cutting threads in the hole to receive a screw. This is done using a tap that matches the diameter and pitch (spacing) of the threads you want to make.

After drilling a hole with the correct size drill bit (which you look up in a table), you screw the tap down into the hole. When you reverse it back out again, you're left with a threaded hole. It's important to get the tap started exactly straight, or you'll end up with "drunken threads" that wander in the wrong direction. You're also likely to break the tap if you keep going after starting it wrong, or if you don't use good cutting fluid and back it up every few turns to clear chips.

Taps start with very small teeth, which get slowly bigger over about half a dozen threads before reaching their full diameter. If you need to thread all the way to the bottom of a blind hole (one that doesn't come out the other side), you have to tap it with a regular tap first, then follow up with a bottoming tap, which cuts full diameter all the way to the end (but can't start threading in a fresh hole).

The complement of tapping is threading: making the external threads on a rod to turn it into a screw, or on a pipe to allow it to be screwed into a pipe fitting. This is done with a threading die and a handle that lets you turn the die with a lot of force.

▶ A manual tapping machine helps keep the tap straight in the hole.

◀ Pipe threading dies are slightly tapered so the threads end up smaller at the end and larger as you go back along the pipe. That way, when you screw the pipe into a fitting it gets tighter and tighter until eventually you can't turn it anymore, and there is a (hopefully) watertight seal.

▶ Tap wrenches come in many sizes and styles.

◀ Regular taps start slow and build up to the full diameter of the threads.

◀ Bottoming taps cut full-diameter threads right to the bottom of a blind hole.

◀ Pipe taps, used to thread the inside of pipe fittings, are tapered just like the dies used to thread pipe.

◀ This is Spiral Tap.

◀▶ Die wrenches, like tap wrenches, come in many sizes, including the large one on the left, used on pipes.

CORDLESS DRILLS

WHEN THEY FIRST CAME into existence, battery-powered drills were heavy and weak. The old nickel-cadmium (Ni-Cd) batteries didn't hold much energy, and the brushed electric motors were large and had trouble developing enough torque to match even a low-end AC-powered drill. But that's all in the past now.

Lithium-ion batteries, of the kind found in cell phones and laptops, are light and hold enough energy to keep a drill going for hours of heavy use, or days of light work. Brushless motors with ultra-strong neodymium magnets are similarly light and powerful. (This is the same pair of technologies that makes quadcopter drones and electric cars possible.)

Today, even an inexpensive cordless drill is powerful enough for most common uses, up to and including home construction. More expensive models buy you everything from more power to longer battery life, more accurate torque clutches, a hammer drill feature, fancy keyless chucks that read your mind, and other such luxury features. Given the convenience of not needing a power cord, there is very little reason, other than cost, to use an AC-powered drill (outside of factory production or seriously heavy-duty drilling situations).

What's more, any cordless drill also works as a power screwdriver. Many have two or three speeds, fast for drilling and slow for screwdriving (or drilling large-diameter holes). These tools are usually sold as "drill/drivers" because they are good for both. The best can even do a credible job turning nuts and bolts.

◄ When I first started using cordless drills seriously, DeWalt was the undisputed leader. These were the cream of the crop in the nineties. (A statement that would have gotten me ripped apart on Twitter, if it had existed back then, because sadly there have always been people who are wrong, even before the internet.)

▶ I bought these two drills around the same time, the less expensive one because I needed a drill to keep at my girlfriend's house, and the more expensive one because I needed a drill *right now* in a town with no discount hardware store. I like the less pricey one better overall.

▶ Collections of power tools are typically a sea of one color, representing the brand their owner is married to. Not so with my motley crew, which I assembled to show the variety out there.

◄ The bane of every longtime cordless tool user: a mess of incompatible batteries and chargers.

TOOLS 115

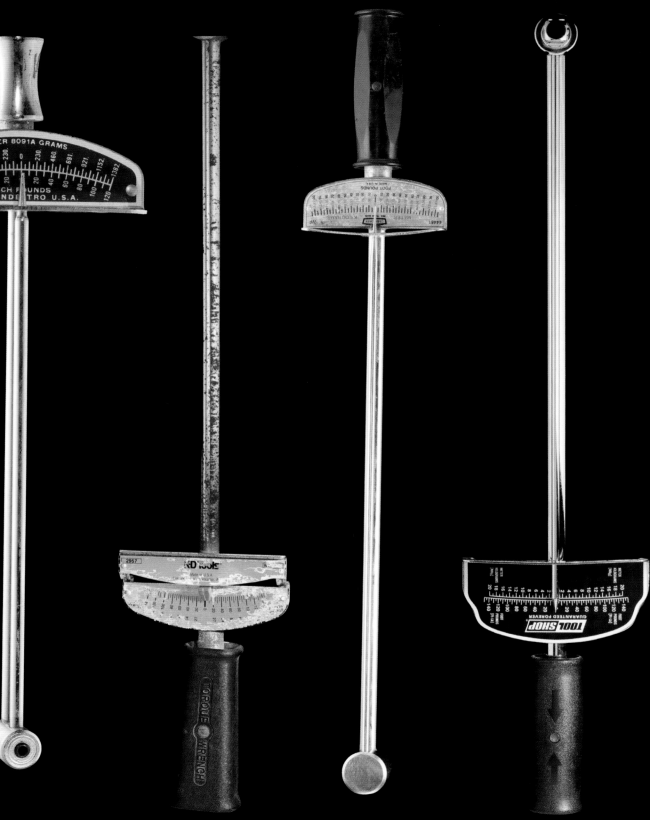

TORQUE WRENCHES

TIGHTENING A NUT or bolt can usually be accomplished by feel. Does it feel tight enough? Great, you're done. But sometimes the degree of tightness matters. The tightness of a bolt is measured by torque, which is measured in units of force times distance. The distance is the length of the wrench handle you're using (how much leverage is applied), and the force is a measure of how hard you are pushing sideways on the end of the handle.

In imperial units, torque is measured in foot-pounds. For example, if you have a 1-foot-long handle, and you push it sideways with a force of 10 pounds, you will be exerting a torque of 10 foot-pounds. You can get the same amount of torque using a longer handle and less force: if your wrench is 2 feet long, you only need to push with 5 pounds of force to get the same 10 foot-pounds of torque (2 feet x 5 pounds = 10 foot-pounds).

I hesitate to mention it, but you should know that measuring torque in foot-pounds gets some people upset. For reasons that make no sense, they believe that torque should be measured in pound-feet, even though foot-pounds has been the accepted convention for centuries. Mathematically it makes no difference: you are multiplying the units, and multiplication is commutative (meaning the order makes no difference).

I have decided to always use foot-pounds when referring to torque, not because there's anything wrong with using pound-feet, but because it's wrong to care. If this discussion seems pointless. . .well, that's exactly my point. It is pointless.

▶ This very large torque wrench looks fancy with its dial indicator, but inside it's no different than the ones on the opposite page: torque is measured by the flexing of the tool head itself, magnified by a gear-driven dial.

▶ This digital torque gauge can turn any wrench into a torque wrench, or it can be used to check the accuracy of a torque wrench (though you won't know which one is wrong when they inevitably disagree).

◀ This style of torque wrench uses the bending of the handle itself to measure how hard it is being twisted. A thinner rod with a pointer on the end is not under stress, so it remains straight as it points at the scale.

▶ This elegant miniature torque wrench uses the bending of a thin rod to measure the tiny torque needed to seat a dental implant into a jawbone. That's one set of threads you do *not* want to strip!

▲ Assembly instructions will sometimes say "tighten nuts finger-tight, and then ½ turn beyond." This gauge lets you get that exactly right, by measuring rotation from a starting point. In bridge construction, for example, bolts are tightened to contact, and then a specified number of one-sixth turns more, which is easy to mark and inspect by the six flats on the bolt head. The greatest danger is overtightening, which can lead to the threads stripping, or the bolts snapping years later. The other greatest danger is under-tightening, which can lead to the bolts loosening with vibration and temperature changes.

▲ This torque wrench has a screw adjustment that presets a desired amount of torque. You don't have to look at a scale when tightening a series of bolts to the same torque. Instead, when you reach the prescribed torque, the handle gives a little snap, like knuckles cracking, and you know you've reached the limit.

▼ Digital torque wrenches can be set to beep when you reach a preset torque, but of course they don't work when the battery is dead, which is invariably when you need them most.

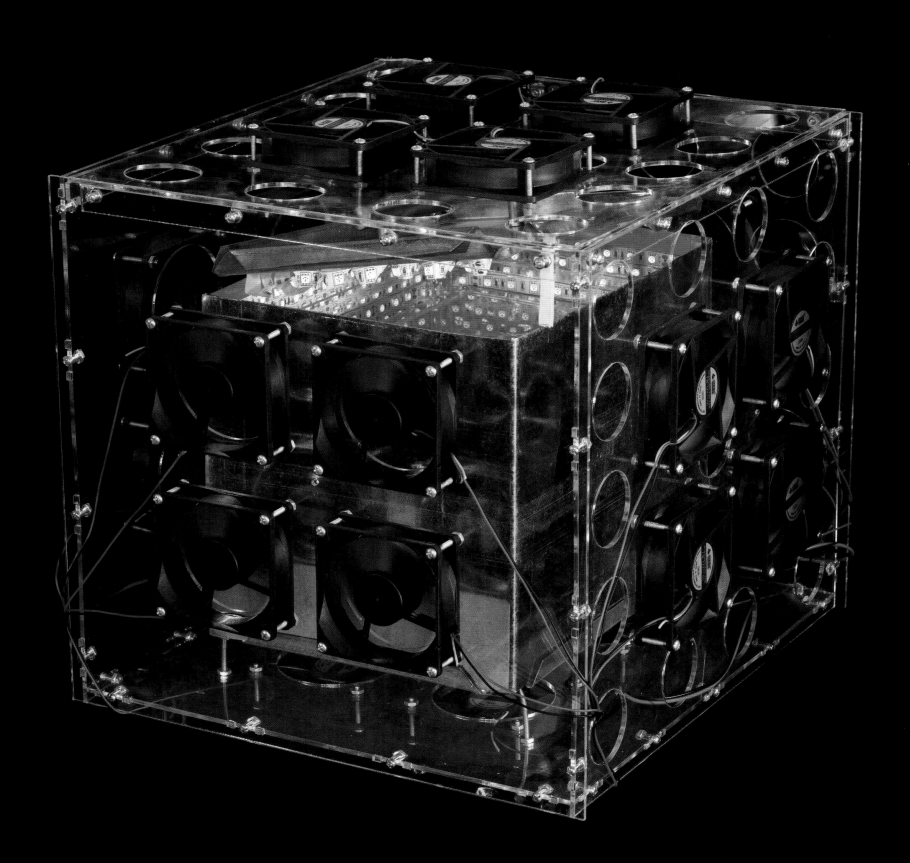

MAKER TOOLS

THE "MAKER" MOVEMENT, like many craft movements, is defined by its tools. Woodworkers have their planes and routers, quilters have their sewing machines, and makers have 3D printers and laser cutters. Of the two, only one currently earns my love.

Filament (FDM) 3D printers are, I am sad to say, not on my list of favorite tools. I have one, and never use it. Someday maybe I'll have a sintered metal 3D printer, but in the meantime I'm reasonably satisfied with my stereolithographic (SLA) resin printer. It makes parts that are solid and smooth, reasonably strong, and good-looking. But like all 3D printers it is incredibly slow. Hours and hours later, you have maybe half a part finished.

But then there's my laser cutter. Hoo-wee do I love this machine! I've had it for years and never tire of watching it zip through acrylic, creating crystal-clear parts with beautiful flame-polished edges. It's fast, powerful, precise, and versatile. OK, it only makes 2D shapes, but the parts are as strong and cheap as the bulk materials they are made from.

And it's very, very fast. This machine can create thousands of parts a day, or dozens of iterations of a single part as you refine the design. Having a design-make-test cycle that is literally under five minutes is life-changing.

From a tool that is my favorite because it works so well, we will move next to ones that I love just because they are nifty, if not always ideal for the job.

▶ This is my low-end resin printer, which is very affordable: some models are under $200. It makes strong, almost clear parts with smooth, attractive surfaces, unlike the printer itself, which is terminally ugly due to partially hardened resin that can't be cleaned off.

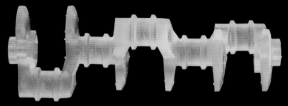

▲ A few of my kits include resin 3D printed parts, like this crankshaft used in several car and engine models. Crankshafts are fundamentally three-dimensional objects, so there's no way to laser-cut one.

◀ Resin printed parts need to be cured in an "oven" that exposes them to lots of 405 nm (almost UV) light for fifteen to thirty minutes. I made my own with strings of LEDs and a lot of fans to keep them cool.

▼ Here it is. This is it, my absolute favorite tool of all time, a GU Eagle 130W CO2 laser cutter with a 51- by 35-inch (1,300 x 900 mm) working area. I accidentally bought one that's far larger than I'd intended, but now I am so happy I didn't get the small desktop model I had originally planned.

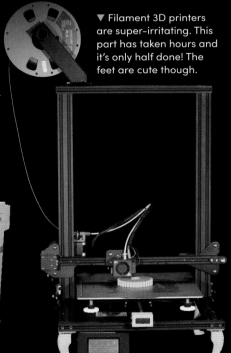

▼ Filament 3D printers are super-irritating. This part has taken hours and it's only half done! The feet are cute though.

▶ I use my laser cutter to make what I call "Mechanical GIFs." You can buy them in kit form from my website, and each part included in the kit is cut with this very laser cutter. I'm pleased with the complex shapes it makes out of entirely flat laser-cut acrylic.

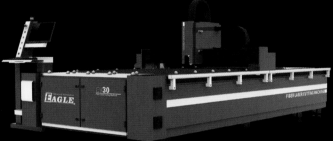

▲ There are few tools I covet as much as this one: a GU Eagle 3-kilowatt fiber laser cutting table. I've watched this machine cut ⅛-inch (3 mm) thick stainless steel much faster than my laser cutter can cut the same thickness of mere acrylic. Sadly I was watching it at the company's warehouse, not in my shop.

SWISS ARMY DRIVERS

THE DIFFERENCE BETWEEN a Swiss Army knife and a regular folding pocketknife is that the Swiss version has lots of blades, and some non-blade tools as well. The concept of a single pocketknife that also hides lots of pop-up little tools inside is so powerful that it's been adapted to all kinds of situations.

Swiss Army hex (Allen) wrenches are very common. I must have a dozen of them. There are also sets with regular screwdrivers, Torx bits, ball-end hex wrenches, and most exotically, nut drivers.

These tools are great. They work reasonably well, you're much less likely to lose the individual bits like you do with a loose set, and they fit nicely in a tool bag. But clearance can be an issue, since you have to swing the whole set around with every turn. And once one of the hex wrenches gets rounded over, as they are wont to do, it's impossible to replace just the one wrench.

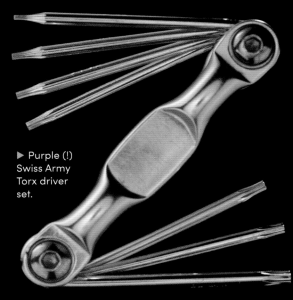

▶ Purple (!) Swiss Army Torx driver set.

◀ You've seen a Swiss Army knife, but have you seen a Swiss Army nut driver?

◀ Slightly upscale Swiss Army hex wrench set with ball ends (for driving at an angle).

5/64" 3/32" 7/64" 1/8"
9/64" 5/32" 3/16" 7/32" 1/4"

▶ Two antique metal Swiss Army hex wrench sets.

▲ Dime-a-dozen Swiss Army hex wrench set.

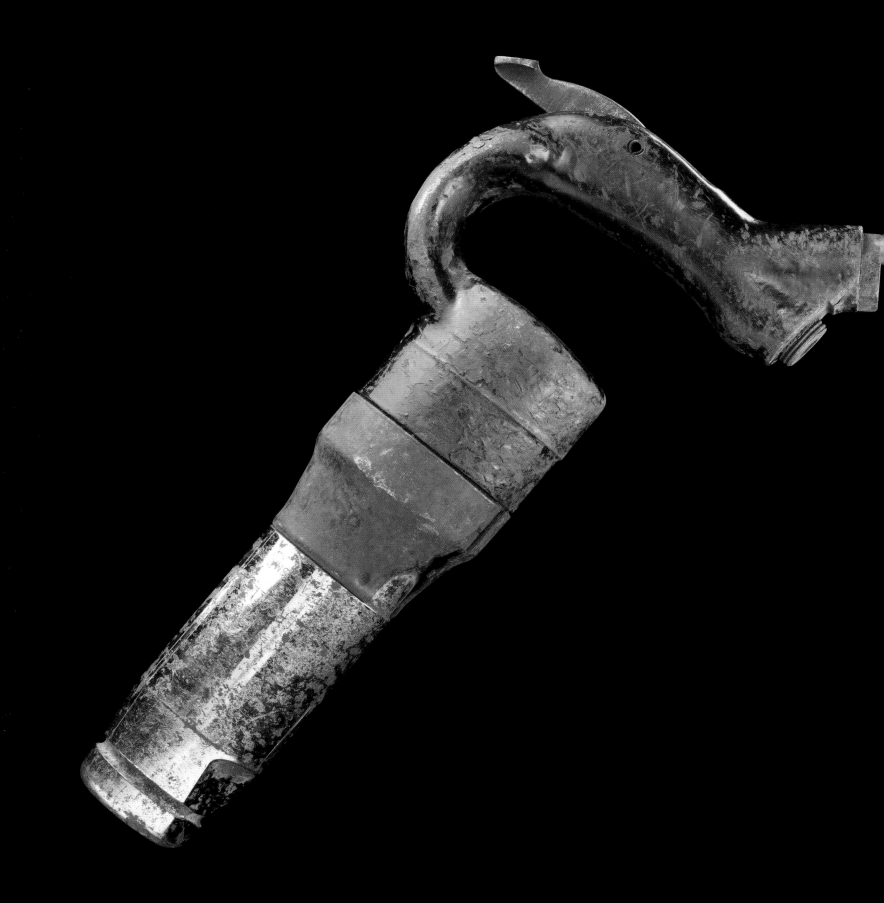

POWER HAMMERS

RIVETS HOLD a special place in the iconography of industry. Old black-and-white films set in factories and construction sites always seem to feature people riveting. Not to mention that iconic hero of the war effort, Rosie the Riveter. Today bolts and welding have largely replaced hot rivets, but while rivets and rivet hammers have settled into specialized niches, power hammers in general are alive and kicking. Because kicking is their job!

On the spectrum of power tools there is a progression from drills (turning only, for drilling and screwing) to hammer drills (turning *and* hammering, for drilling concrete) to air hammers (hammering only, for chipping stone or brick) to jackhammers (again hammering only, but more so). At each step the tool gets heavier and louder, the bits get duller, and rotation becomes less important, while hammering becomes more important.

To be effective, jackhammers need to be big and heavy, because their job is to break up slabs of concrete early in the morning when everyone is meant to be asleep. (Seriously, you can't make this stuff up: I finished writing this page around midnight on a Sunday night. I was woken up at dawn *the next morning* by a jackhammer being used to install a new water main half a block down the road.)

▶ Big jackhammers use a *lot* of compressed air. I don't actually own a compressor large enough to run any of my jackhammers, so I keep them just for show

◀ Hot riveting is done using a pneumatic hammer with a cup-shaped end that forges the head of the rivet. I don't know why more hammering tools don't have handles like this one, located directly behind the head. It's the optimal arrangement for a tool whose only purpose is to hammer.

◀ *Really* big jackhammers are mounted on the end of a backhoe or excavator's hydraulic arm. Powered directly by the machine's hydraulic system, they can destroy roadways, sidewalks, walls, bridges, and the sanity of anyone living within a five-block radius. This is the one that woke me up.

▶ Air chisels are like baby jackhammers. They can be used for stone carving, splitting bricks, or chipping rust and scale off metal parts.

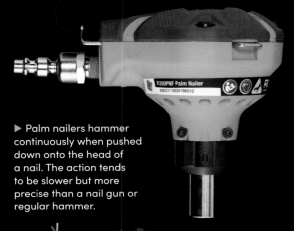

▶ Palm nailers hammer continuously when pushed down onto the head of a nail. The action tends to be slower but more precise than a nail gun or regular hammer.

R350PNF Palm Nailer

AIRLESS JACKHAMMER

▼ I'm convinced the main use of this tool is to give it to the new hire as a joke. You pull the heavy handle up and then slam it down, which gives a kick to the standard jackhammer bit. Talk about backbreaking work!

▲ There are many different styles of air hammer bits, including this "bushing" bit. It's like a meat tenderizer that mounts to a power hammer, for when you need to seriously pound your concrete to level it or rough up the surface to prepare it for coating.

EXTREME NAILERS

USUALLY THE WORD "gun" in a tool's name is more metaphorical than literal. A glue gun has very little in common with a pistol other than its shape. But the explosive-powered concrete nailers on this page really are guns in nearly every sense. They use .22 (5.6 mm) or .27 (6.9 mm) caliber black powder cartridges ignited by a primer charge set off by a firing pin. The explosive force of the gunpowder propels a projectile out the barrel. Some of them are even made by Remington, a well-known gun manufacturer.

The only difference is that the projectile is a nail instead of a bullet, and there's a safety interlock that prevents the tool from firing unless it's being pressed hard against a surface. The manufacturers of these tools are very eager for you to know that this safety interlock means the tool is not a weapon and most definitely *can't be used as a gun*. OK, if you say so. Eye and ear protection are essential: these things are *loud*.

If you venture into slightly more specialized nailing arenas, you will find some fascinating variations in form and function. Roof shingles, for example, require nails with large plastic heads over an inch (25 mm) in diameter. There's no good way to make a compact strip of these, so some roofing nailers are equipped with both a spool of nails with fairly large (⅜-inch/9 mm) heads and a spool with even larger plastic heads, which are combined as they are driven.

On the next page we're going to move on from all this pounding and study the gentle art of scraping things with rough stones.

▲▼ Full-head nailers are fed with coils of nails with large heads spaced out along a pair of wires.

◄ This beautiful retro-futuristic art deco ray gun complete with plasma shield is actually an example of a gunpowder-actuated nailer. It's made by Bostitch, a company best known for making pneumatic nailers.

▶ This beautifully complicated tool drives full-head nails from a coil through the center of plastic disks drawn from a second coil.

▶ I don't have a lot of enemies, but I learned this trick from one of them: coiled roofing nails, which are held together by a pair of thin wires, can be cut into groups of three or four and twisted into a pyramid to make a quick and easy tire-puncturing trap.

▲ Remington is well-known as a maker of guns, but this explosive nailsetter, according to the marketing literature, is absolutely not a gun.

▲ This butane-powered framing nailer has been through a lot with me. It's powerful, reliable, and an absolute joy to use. It's cordless, but not battery-powered. Instead, when you push the nose down onto the board, a puff of butane gas is injected into the cylinder. A spark plug ignites the fuel-air mixture, setting off an explosion that drives the nail. (I lied, there is a battery, but it's used only to power the spark plug and the mixing fan.)

▲ These cartridges for nailers, color-coded by the amount of gunpowder they contain, are indistinguishable from rifle blanks of the same caliber. They lack only a bullet, and even come in strips for semiautomatic, er, tools.

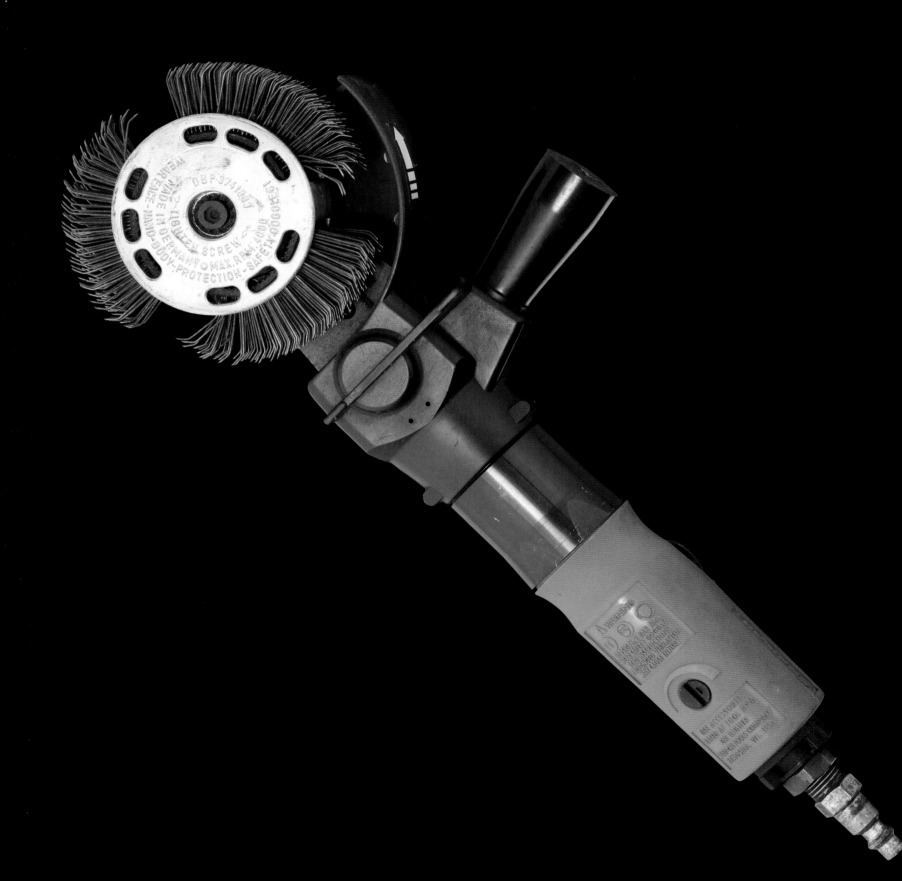

HAND GRINDERS

HAND-HELD ANGLE GRINDERS are versatile tools, good for anything from actual grinding to polishing, buffing, sanding, scraping, sawing, and carving, depending on what kind of disk you attach. Instead of a chuck, hand grinders have a threaded stud, similar to a circular saw, onto which you can screw any one of a hundred different attachments (including circular saw blades, if you don't mind the occasional missing finger).

Angle grinders are big and turn relatively slowly. Die grinders and Dremel tools are smaller and faster (up to 20,000 revolutions per minute, compared to around 3,000 for an angle grinder). Dentist drills are a particularly high-speed form of die grinder: their turbine motors spin up to 180,000 revolutions per minute.

Die grinders are typically used with a very small grinding wheel to clean up rough edges or do detailed carving (on models or teeth, your choice). There are many shapes of grinding wheel for die grinders, as well as diamond burs, sanding cylinders, and tiny circular saw blades. Tiny wire brushes, lapping wheels, and specialized bits are available in large assortments.

Pneumatic (air-powered) die grinders are light and powerful. They also run cold, because air cools as it expands in the tool. Electric die grinders, the tools generically known as Dremel tools, are heavier, but more convenient because you don't need an air compressor to run the motor.

▲ Dremel tools are electric die grinders popularized by the company of the same name.

◄ Die grinders are commonly sold for use on nails (human, dog, and construction).

▼ So many choices! The best die grinder bits are made of solid tungsten carbide, and the many variations available make for extraordinary versatility.

◄ This tool is specialized for scraping off rust or paint from metal surfaces, or, with a rubber eraser wheel in place of the wire brush, for rubbing stickers off painted surfaces without damaging the paint.

◄ This monster angle grinder is so heavy it's exhausting just to hold. But with a grinding wheel or "tiger paw" flap wheel it can clean rust off sheet metal, smooth welds, or round over edges like nothing else. The side handles are easy to lose, but standard bolts or pipes work as replacements.

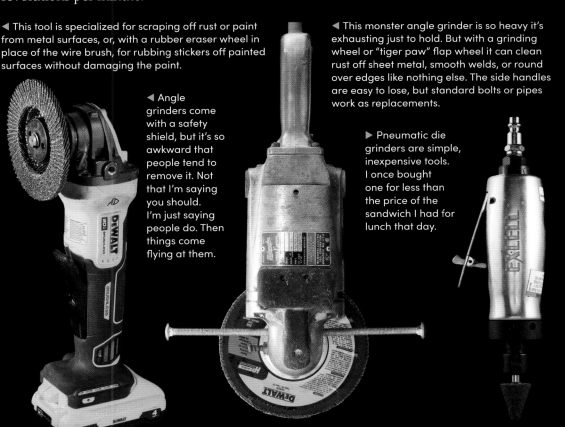

◄ Angle grinders come with a safety shield, but it's so awkward that people tend to remove it. Not that I'm saying you should. I'm just saying people do. Then things come flying at them.

▶ Pneumatic die grinders are simple, inexpensive tools. I once bought one for less than the price of the sandwich I had for lunch that day.

SANDERS

THERE ARE THREE fundamental types of power sanders, defined by the direction in which their sandpaper moves: in one direction for belt and drum sanders, back and forth for linear and oscillating sanders, or randomly in all directions for random orbit sanders.

Equipped with a coarse grit belt, a powerful belt sander like the one on the left can remove material almost as fast as a power plane. They are excellent for roughly cutting down high spots, shaping curves, rounding over edges (a lot), and other crude work.

Compared to belt sanders, linear sanders remove material less rapidly, and therefore are better suited to smoothing surfaces rather than removing material.

Finally, random orbit sanders are the tool of choice for getting a fine finish on quality wood. Normally the rule is that you should always sand along the direction of the grain, never across it, but the random nature of the sander's motion means that any cross-grain scratches are magically averaged out.

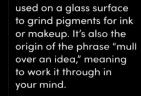

▲ Several of my favorite tools, including the Bosch random order sander I used to sand all the floors in my house, have been stolen over the years. The Bosch had sentimental value, but I replaced it with this pneumatic version, which is lighter and more comfortable to hold.

▶ This is a muller. It's used on a glass surface to grind pigments for ink or makeup. It's also the origin of the phrase "mull over an idea," meaning to work it through in your mind.

◀ This is my pride-and-joy belt sander. It weighs a ton. I use it, for example, when I need to remove some material from the bottom of a door and can't find my power plane.

◀ This miniature "bandfile" is handy for reaching into tight spots. It's only ½ inch (12 mm) wide.

▼ Electric and pneumatic linear sanders use standard sheets of sandpaper cut into different proportions depending on their size.

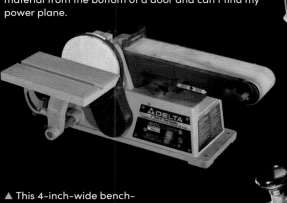

▲ This 4-inch-wide bench-mounted belt and disk sander has been my friend for decades. Commercial models can be several feet (over a meter) in width. I use the disk on the side only rarely.

▼ This extra-wide drum sander is for large, gently curved surfaces. For example, sanding down car body panels before painting.

▲ Disposable razor blades aren't meant to be sharpened (hence the name), but they used to be. This lapping wheel automatically flips the blade over periodically as you turn the handle, sharpening both sides.

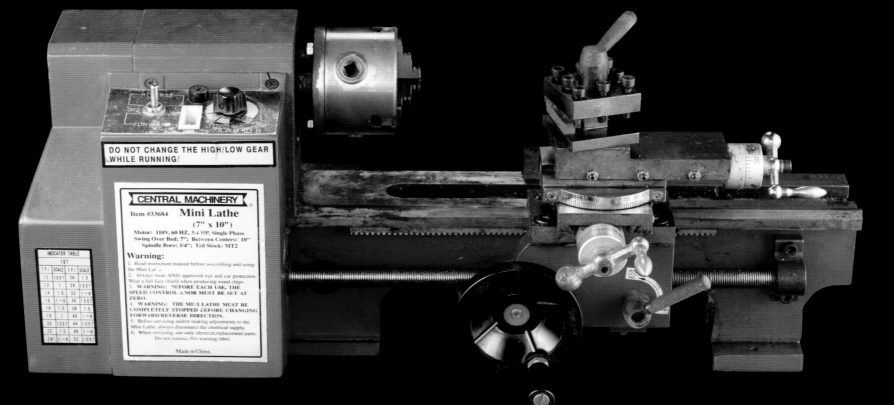

LATHES

USING A LATHE is like an advanced form of chiseling. The lathe spins the material while you apply the chisel. With the right technique, chips fly as you gracefully shape the material into the desired profile. With the wrong technique, the lathe grabs the chisel and throws it across the room.

Woodworking lathes have an adjustable bar, called the tool rest, which you brace the bit against while holding onto the handle of the chisel and guiding it against the workpiece. Metalworking lathes, where the cutting force is far greater, have a tool post that firmly clamps the chisel (called a lathe tool in this case) and a set of lead screws that guide the chisel tip precisely against the work.

Once the shape of the material is established with a chisel, you can hold a strip of sandpaper against the piece to smooth the surface. While doing this you will be reaching over the spinning workpiece, so it's *super-important* not to be wearing loose clothes that can get caught in the lathe.

Full-sized engine lathes are outside the range of tools reasonably found in a home shop, but the smaller, tabletop versions are very nice to have, and not overly expensive.

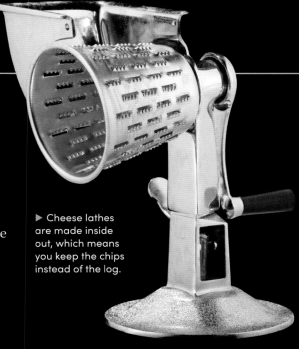

▶ Cheese lathes are made inside out, which means you keep the chips instead of the log.

◀ I've always wanted a big engine lathe, but the logistics of moving, leveling, and truing one are just too daunting. Instead, I own this baby lathe, which is small enough for me to lift and handy for making small metal parts. It even has a lead screw for cutting screw threads.

◀ I bought this small tabletop wood lathe about fifteen years ago, literally because I was feeling bad and needed something to cheer me up.

▲ When I was a kid, I had this exact type of plastic toy lathe. What time takes, eBay returns. Despite it being a toy, I was able to use it to make many small wooden toys, furniture handles, and candlesticks.

◀ Apple lathes are used to remove the bark from the fruit.

▲ This modern mini-lathe is proof that not everything gets more plasticky over time. It's about the same overall size as, and no more expensive than, my plastic toy lathe, but it is a hugely superior, all-metal toy lathe. So good in fact that I hesitate to call it a toy.

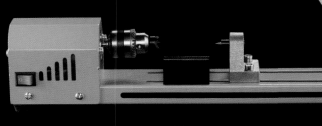

◀ This is the smallest lathe I know of. It's a 3D-printed soapbox derby wheel lathe, whose only job is to shave the outer rim of the small wooden wheels used in competitive toy car racing.

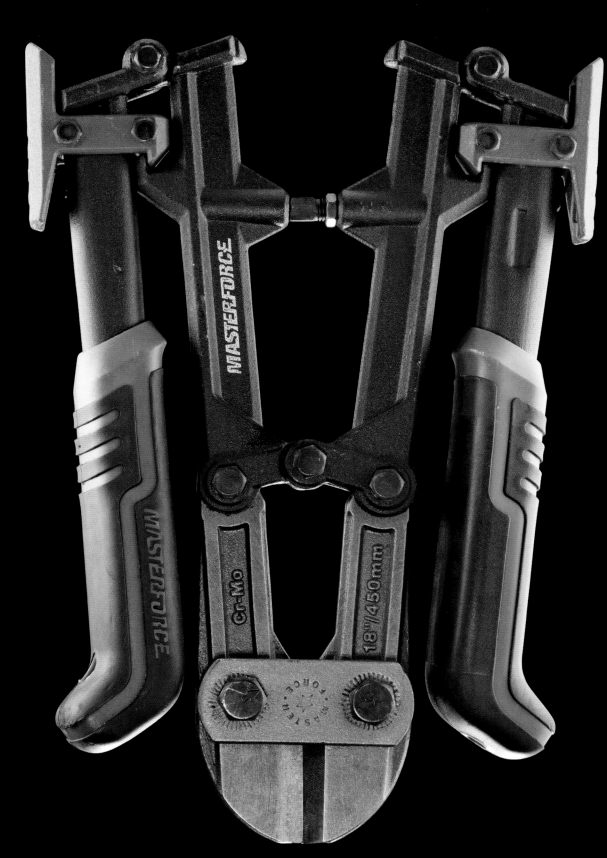

BOLT CUTTERS

BOLTS ARE NOTORIOUSLY difficult to cut. Any bolt with a diameter of more than ½ inch (12 mm) usually requires a hacksaw, angle grinder, or torch to sever it. Bolt cutters work on smaller bolts by using a *tremendous* amount of compound leverage to drive short, thick, hardened steel jaws (which shatter dramatically if overloaded).

You know what else bolt cutters can cut? Bicycle locks. A whole industry exists dedicated to making bicycle locks that can't be cut with bolt cutters, either because their solid bars are too thick and too hard, or because they are made with a steel cable. (If you try to cut a steel cable with bolt cutters, the cable will just squash down and become too flat for the blades to attack. Cutting those cables requires the sort of heavy-duty cable cutters we saw earlier on the wire cutters page.)

I've also included guillotine-style cutters here. These tools are used for cutting things much softer than bolts, and combine sharp jaws (which would dull instantly if used on a bolt) with a shearing mechanism (which would twist apart if used on anything as hard as a bolt). They include dehorners, which are large tools, alarming in appearance, that are used to cut the horns off cattle to prevent them injuring each other. Cigar cutters use the same idea: smaller, but equally suggestive.

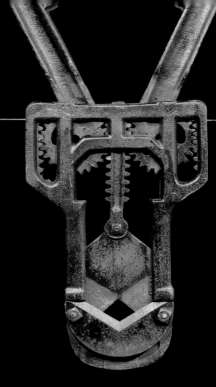

▲ We use this tool for cutting bully sticks in half for our dog. And no, that's not what it's designed for: it's actually a cattle dehorner.

◄ The handles on this bolt cutter fold up. This is absolutely not so you can carry it more stealthily under your bicycle-stealing trench coat. Definitely not.

▼ The red handles on these bolt cutters provide the first stage of leverage. They move the smaller black inner "handles" a much shorter distance. The black handles in turn move the jaws by an even smaller amount. Swinging the red handles wide open moves the jaws barely enough to fit around a bolt. This fifty-to-one ratio of movements turns into an equal increase in the amount of force transmitted to the jaws.

▶ The hooks on this military bolt cutter are so you can reach into a tangle of barbed wire and pull out strands to cut. The handles are insulated in case said barbed wire is also electrified.

▼ Chains cut a lot like bolts. This thing with its massively deep hardened steel jaws was mounted to a shelf full of chains for sale in a hardware store.

▶ Sometimes a cigar cutter is just a cigar cutter.

▲ Bolt cutters come in a wide range of sizes. The smaller sizes are perhaps best thought of as heavy-duty wire cutters that work on steel wire, screws, and very small bolts.

▲ Not a cigar cutter. It's a pickle slicer and it cuts the other way, lengthwise.

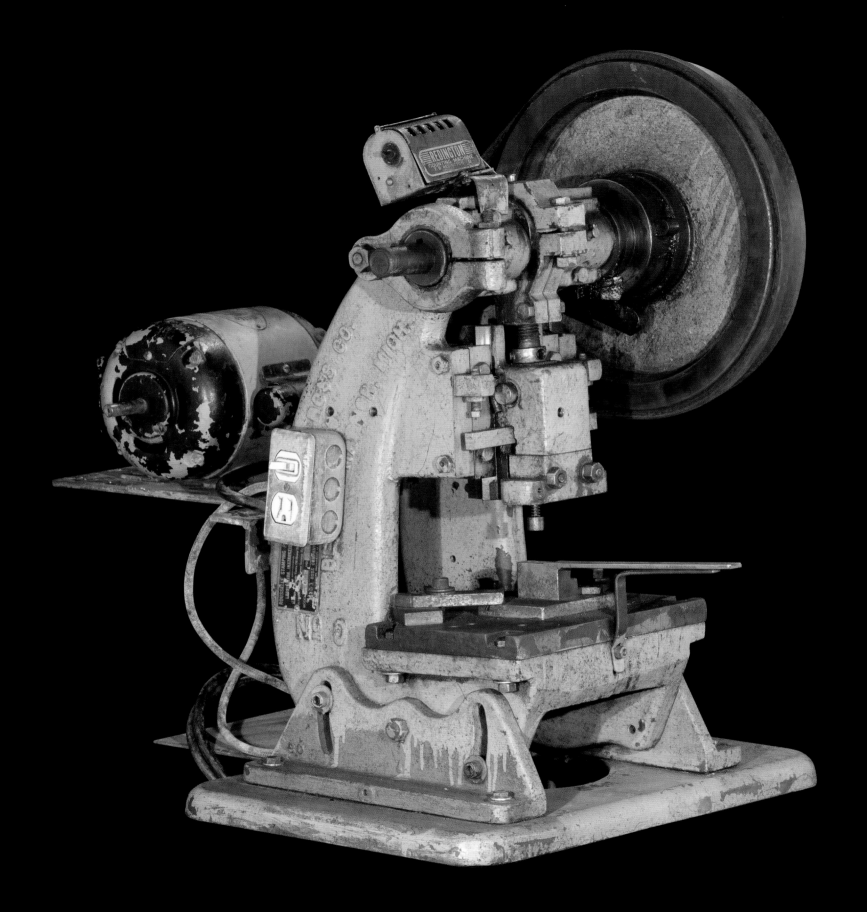

PUNCHES & DIES

PUNCH AND DIE SETS can be anything from hand-held plastic tools to some of the largest machine tools in the world. Some material (wood, steel, fabric, paper) is placed between a punch and a matching die, then a force (manual or motorized) squeezes the punch into the die and leaves a correspondingly shaped hole in the material.

An old train conductor's ticket punch is an example. At the other end of the spectrum, large stamping presses, which can be several stories tall, effortlessly cut through steel as thick as your finger. (By effortlessly I mean it looks effortless when there's a 100-horsepower motor and a multi-ton flywheel behind the punch.) These presses are well beyond the scope of a home shop, but I happened to get a few medium-sized punch and die sets from a machine shop auction, so I can show you what they look like inside.

More practical for home use are a range of hand-held or desktop punch tools. Craft stores sell dozens of shapes for paper crafts, and similar but much sturdier versions can punch holes in thin sheet metal, leather, rubber, or cardboard.

◄ This is the most darling tiny baby stamping press you'll ever meet. But don't be fooled by its fetching appearance: *do not reach into the press.* The heavy flywheel stores up energy from an electric motor. When you step on the foot pedal, it engages a catch that hooks onto the flywheel for one revolution, driving a punch through whatever is in the jaws of the beast. The electric motor itself is not strong enough to drive the punch, but the stored-up energy in the flywheel powers through.

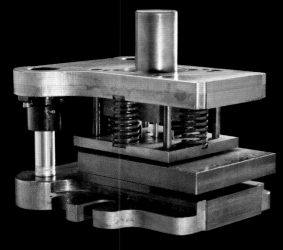

▲ This surplus bit from a medium-sized (about 12-foot-tall) stamping press is alarmingly solid. The top and bottom are literally 2-inch-thick (50 mm) solid steel plates. Between them a custom arrangement of punches and dies cuts holes into sheet metal about ⅛ inch (3 mm) thick.

▶ The classic train conductor's hole punch has long since been replaced everywhere, except in a few third-world countries such as Long Island, by a barcode scanner.

▲ This is what a train conductor's hole punch would look like if train tickets were made of metal.

▶ This livestock ear punch makes V-shaped notches in pigs' ears, which are used to record the litter number (right ear) and pig number within the litter (left ear) using a base-3 numbering system. Pity pig 26 in litter 242.

▲ Punches can get very complicated! This one cuts a snowflake shape into paper, for scrapbooking.

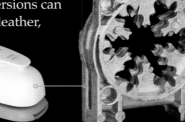

▶ Large-diameter holes in the sheet steel used to make electrical junction boxes can be cut using this multi-piece punch and die set. A punch and matching die are squeezed together using the large, fine-thread screw fitted through a pilot hole and turned with a wrench.

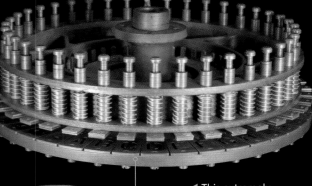

◄ This extremely elaborate tool has a separate punch and die for each letter of the alphabet and numbers 0–9. The big wheel on top rotates the punches to select the one you want. Oiled stencil board is advanced automatically with each punch. These days a laser cutter would be used instead.

AIR PRESSURE TOOLS

MANY TOOLS IN THIS book operate on compressed air (they are known as pneumatic tools). For them air is just a means to an end. Here we're going to look at tools where the air itself is the point.

The obvious example of this kind of tool is an air compressor, whose job is to supply compressed air to all the pneumatic tools. Every workshop should have at least a small portable air compressor, which can be used for inflating tires, blowing dust off things, and running small pneumatic tools for short periods of time. Larger tools require a larger, stationary air compressor to supply enough air continuously.

What distinguishes air compressors isn't the pressure they deliver: most pneumatic tools operate at a maximum of about 100 psi (pounds per square inch, or about 700 kPa). What you're paying for in a more powerful compressor is the greater *volume* of air it can deliver at that pressure.

Sometimes it's negative pressure that's required. Vacuum cleaners and dust collectors work by creating less-than-atmospheric pressure, as do suction cups, vacuum formers, and vacuum hold-down plates.

Other times the situation is less about pressure and more about temperature. If a job requires a lot of hot air, and there's no politician on the payroll, a heat gun is what's needed. Heat guns resemble hair dryers, but do not dry your hair with one! They operate at *much* higher temperatures—some can even be used to melt metal, as we saw back with the soldering irons.

▲ This automatic balloon inflator has two modes: the nozzle on the left delivers a consistent, adjustable volume of air with each activation, and the nozzle on the right delivers helium up to a fixed, very low pressure, to perfectly inflate metallized Mylar balloons.

◀ Mini air compressors take a long time to inflate a single car tire, but are very handy in a roadside emergency, unless they are back in your photo studio waiting to be photographed for a book project when you get a flat tire.

▶ Hair dryers don't go above about 140°F (60°C) lest they burn your scalp. Heat guns can't even go that low and can reach 1,000°F (540°C) or even higher for specialized versions.

◀ This heat gun has a special head designed to shrink heat-shrink tubing from all sides at the same time.

◀ A vacuum forming machine takes a sheet of plastic, heats it until it's soft, then sucks it down onto a shaped mold. This is how they make the annoying plastic packaging you can't get open.

▲ Small air compressors are really loud. They typically have a bellows that opens and closes rapidly, pushing air under pressure into a small storage tank.

▲ Large air compressors are also loud, but hopefully don't have to run as often because they save up a lot of air in their large tanks. Instead of bellows these models have pistons, which last longer and can deliver far more air.

▲ A vacuum is the opposite of compressed air: it's decompressed air at lower than atmospheric pressure. Large suction cups, which create a strong vacuum when you flip their handles, can be used to pull out dents in car panels or remove screens from computer monitors.

CRAZY SAWS

ALL OF THE SAWS on this page would make excellent props in a horror movie. Regular buzz and chain saws are popular tools of the genre, but I think filmmakers could branch out to some of these less-known varieties. "If you liked *The Texas Chain Saw Massacre*, you'll love the *Oklahoma Circle Saw of Death*!" Or *The Wright Blade Saw Bloodbath*!

Most of the larger tools featured here are intended to cut logs, in much the same way you would use a chain saw. They exist only because they predate the invention of the chain saw. As soon as that superior solution was perfected, these tools quickly fell out of use. Chain saws are just better: lighter, faster, safer (sort of), cheaper, more portable, more reliable. So we are left with an eBay and auction legacy of bizarre and scary tools that generally no longer operate and should probably best be left in that condition.

These saws did evolve into modern, sensible tools. Buzz saws and circle saws morphed into table saws, miter saws, and hand-held circular saws. Even the Wright blade saw evolved into the smaller electric reciprocating saws you can read about on the next page.

▲ Buzz saws are used to cut logs with a bit more precision than a chain saw. The L-shaped table in front tilts back as the cut progresses. They no doubt also work to cut heads off bodies, but that would be considered a misuse of the tool.

◀ This "circle saw" is perhaps the most insane tool I've ever seen. It's powered by a small gasoline engine that sits on the ground. A flexible shaft transfers the power to a rubber drive wheel that spins a ring-shaped saw blade (just like a circular saw, but with the center of the blade missing).

▼ The Wright blade saw is a gas-powered handsaw with huge teeth. Thankfully the engine on this one is in terrible shape and it will probably never run again.

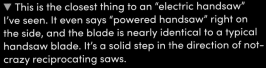

▼ This is the closest thing to an "electric handsaw" I've seen. It even says "powered handsaw" right on the side, and the blade is nearly identical to a typical handsaw blade. It's a solid step in the direction of not-crazy reciprocating saws.

▼ Exactly the same thing exists for butchering, just made of stainless steel and much more expensive. It's *literally made for cutting meat*. Wes Craven, are you listening?

RECIPROCATING SAWS

THE "POWER HANDSAWS" we saw on the last page evolved over time into the modern reciprocating saw, a popular and powerful tool of destruction.

Reciprocating saws are similar in many ways to jigsaws, and in theory you can use them to do similar jobs, but in practice they are very different in flavor. Whereas jigsaws are gentle and controlled, reciprocating saws are rough and sometimes on the edge of insanity. The blades are bigger, thicker, and longer, the motor more powerful, and the grip optimized for reach rather than control. And, as you might expect, these saws tend to be rather jerky in operation. They shake the material back and forth,

sometimes quite violently if the blade binds in the cut. I do not like using these saws, but I do like the fact that they will make short work of any job requiring the immediate severing of something in a ruthless manner.

Much of the versatility of reciprocating saws comes from the range of blades you can get for them. A properly chosen blade will cut wood, metal, plastic, insulation, glass, tile, bread, turkey, and so on. (The bread and turkey blades are for use with the type of reciprocating saw known as an electric knife for kitchen use.)

I will use one of these tools if I have to, but I very much prefer those on the next page.

▶ Battery-powered reciprocating saws avoid the not insignificant danger of sawing through the power cord.

◀ Early model reciprocating saws resemble early power handsaws, but with more body and less blade. Reciprocating saws today are common, inexpensive tools. You can get blades for these tools up to about 12 inches (30 cm) long, but they have a tendency to get bent very quickly.

▼ As with any saw, select blades with smaller teeth for thinner material, carbide for durability, diamond for stone.

▼ Reciprocating saws are often used in wet locations, for example cutting pipe in the bottom of a trench while it's raining. For maximum electrical safety, this one is powered by compressed air.

▼ Knife edge

▼ Thick metal

THE TORCH
METAL CUTTING   14 TPI   BI-METAL   USA

▲ Thin metal

SUPER SAWZALL
WOOD WITH NAILS   BI-METAL   USA

▲ Rough wood
▼ Abrasive materials

HERCULES
CARBIDE TEETH

▼ Stone

DIAMOND

▶ This specialized saw for cutting insulation is remarkably similar to a powered kitchen knife.

MITER SAWS

ONE OF THE MOST versatile woodworking tools at any price is a compound sliding miter saw. It is basically a circular saw mounted on a sliding rail that typically allows it to travel 10–12 inches (250–300 mm) in the direction of the cut.

What makes this tool so versatile is that the rail can be rotated by a little over 45 degrees to the left or right, and the saw can also be tilted by a little over 45 degrees in either direction. This mobility allows the tool to make pretty much any kind of angled cut you could want as easily as a straight cut. And because the blade slides, it can cut boards over 12 inches (300 mm) wide and 4 inches (100 mm) thick.

If you are building a house, a fence, a chicken coop, a toy box, or really, just about anything made of wood, you will be very happy to have a quality saw of this type. I've even used mine to cut aluminum extrusions, which is perhaps a slight misuse of the tool, but it works great even with a (carbide tooth) wood blade.

My DeWalt model, which I keep at my farm, is fairly high-end. For in-town use I have a much cheaper version, but it's fine. Maybe not quite as accurate, and maybe it won't last the same twenty-five plus years, but really good for the price. Less expensive versions do away with the slide rails, which limits the size of wood they can cut. And the cheapest only allow the blade to swing left and right without tilting. But even those models are useful, as are the even more satisfying saws on the next page.

◄ A battery-powered miter saw? Yes.

▼ This miter shear is for trimming off paper-thin slices from the ends of picture frame or molding pieces that have been cut with a miter saw, to get them to a perfect fit.

◄ I've probably spent more time using this sliding compound miter saw than any other power tool in my shop (with the possible exception of the laser cutter on page 119).

◄ This miniature chop saw looks almost like a toy, but it's actually quite a useful tool. I use it for cutting acrylic rods and polystyrene square tube for the mechanical models I sell.

▼ This fancy manual miter box holds a saw firmly at an adjustable angle, allowing it to make the same kinds of cuts as a powered miter saw, but more slowly.

▼ Miter boxes are also available for cutting bread, but these generally cut only at 90 degrees to the loaf and are more about spacing than angles.

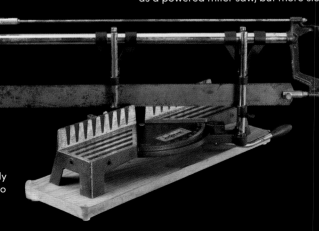

◄ Chop saws look similar to miter saws, but they do only one thing: tilt straight down. They are commonly fitted with an abrasive cutting wheel and are used to cut steel bars, angle iron, and square tube.

BANDSAWS

NOTHING BEATS A BANDSAW for smooth, gentle, precise cutting. It's like a scroll saw except the blade always moves in the same direction (down). There is absolutely no jerkiness to the motion, just smooth, continuous cutting.

Bandsaw blades come in a large range of sizes. Wide blades make long, straight cuts, almost like a table saw. Narrow ones are for curves and intricate pattern cutting. At the extreme end of the spectrum, some sawmills use immense bandsaws to cut up entire tree trunks.

To build my house I bought a lot of wood from an old sawmill in Paris, Illinois (pronounced pay-riss, ill-in-oi). The great bandsaw at the T. A. Foley lumber company had been in operation for 115 years before it was switched off

for the last time in the mid 1990s. The immense blades will never again face off against an ancient log in the belly of a great machine. I got my hands on a few and keep them, slowly rusting, in hopes that maybe someday they will find a place somewhere, perhaps in a work of art, or perhaps as the world's most painful stair railing.

Normally bandsaws have two large wheels, and the depth (throat) of the saw is determined by the diameter of the wheels. Compact models have three smaller wheels to give them a deeper throat without needing the extra height for large-diameter wheels. The first bandsaw was introduced just less than two hundred years ago, which makes this a very young tool compared to those on the next page.

▲ Bandsaws for cutting metal are often mounted horizontally on a hinge. Their own weight pulls them down slowly, cutting through thick steel bars, rods, and pipes. A switch at the bottom automatically shuts the saw off when it finishes the cut.

◀ This brand-new micro-mini battery-powered bandsaw has stolen my heart. It's just about the cutest little saw I've ever seen. Isn't it adorable?

▼ This hand-held bandsaw has been a favorite of mine for decades. The blade is exactly like a manual hacksaw blade, but the continuous circular motion makes this saw an absolute joy to use. Almost as much of a joy as the even smaller one on the left.

◀ This old wood-cutting bandsaw came from an auction. Works great, nothing fancy.

▶ Compact saws bend the blade more sharply around smaller wheels.

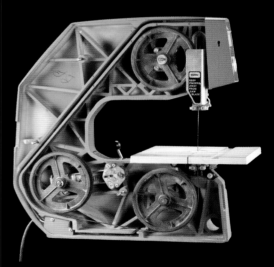

▶ The T. A. Foley blades are 37 feet (11.3 m) long and a foot (300 mm) wide. Cat for scale.

AUGERS

THE MARVELOUS FORSTNER bits we learned about earlier have no flutes for pulling chips up out of the hole. Auger bits, which are actually a much older design than the Forstner, have a tip similar to self-feeding Forstner bits, but also have spiral flutes that pull debris out of the material as you drill. This makes them suitable for drilling deep holes, for example in the huge beams used to build barns or fancy post-and-beam roofs in ski chalets.

Although auger bits date back hundreds of years, they are still used today in largely unchanged form. The key to auger bits is torque, not speed: they cut a lot of material with every revolution. In the past you would have used a manual brace drill (page 77) to turn your auger bit, but today you're more likely to use a large "hole-shooter" style power drill (page 189) or a drill press (page 187).

You can think of spade bits as un-twisted augers. They are simple, cheap, don't lift chips out, and don't make very smooth holes. Did I mention they are cheap? That's really their only advantage, along with being able to drill holes that aren't straight, because nothing keeps the shaft centered in the hole. They can be used with cheaper, less powerful drivers because they chip away a little at a time, instead of forcefully carving out the hole like an auger.

Augers and spades, like other drill bits, are typically held by the contraptions on the next page.

◀ This is certainly the most beautiful drill I've ever seen. It's a hand auger meant to be turned with a handle stuck through the tube at the top. But it's not sold with a handle, because you're meant to use a stick you find lying on the ground: this is a camping auger, for which portability is key.

▼ Auger bits [top] are quite complex to manufacture, so a set can be expensive. Spade bits [bottom] are *much* cheaper, but inferior in nearly every way.

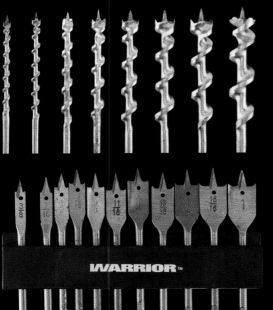

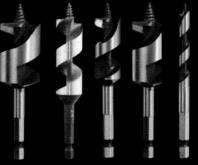

◀ This spade bit is adjustable. I got it and never used it, because why use an adjustable bit when a full set of fixed bits costs less?

▲ Short, stubby auger bits can be used on the end of looooong extension rods to drill holes through walls and floors.

▶ Because spade bits are so cheap and easy to make, even very long versions don't cost much.

▲ Augers work for dirt and ice as well. The point on this earth auger [left] is odd: I've never seen another like it. We use the ice auger [right] to test the ice on my lake: if it's 6 inches (150 mm) thick in six places, it's safe for skating.

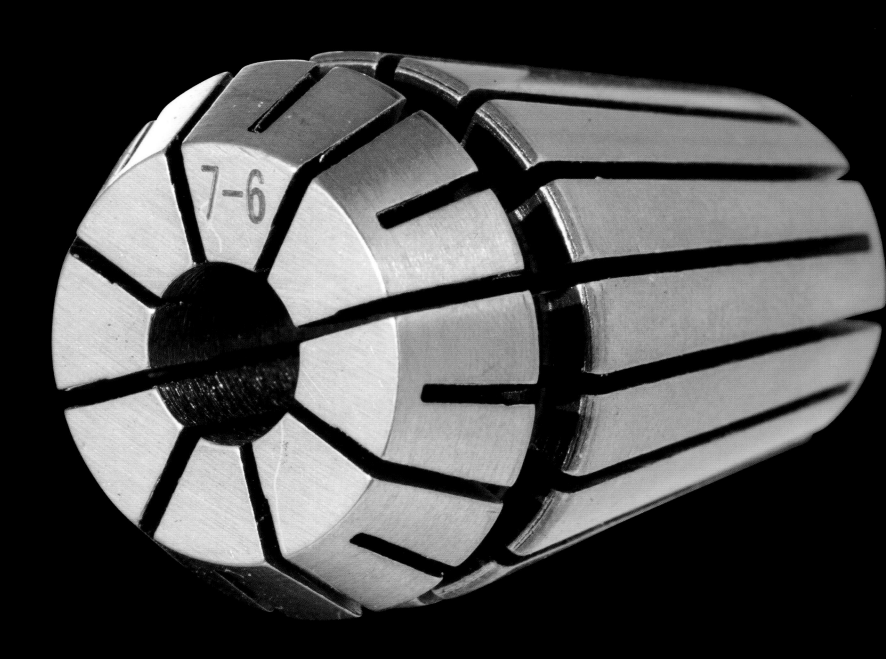

CHUCKS

CHUCKS ARE USED to hold a workpiece or cutting bit in place with a set of jaws that clamp down tightly. The vast majority of chucks in the world have three jaws and mostly hold drill bits. Every hand-held drill and every drill press comes by default with a three-jaw, automatically centering scroll chuck.

The other common type of chuck has four jaws and is usually found holding workpieces to be spun in a lathe. The important difference is not the number of jaws but the fact that each jaw moves independently, which allows you to center the workpiece in them more precisely. The downside to four independent jaws is that you have to manually center the workpiece by adjusting all four jaws separately, one at a time. Four-jaw chucks are far less convenient, but more flexible than their three-jaw cousins.

An alternative to a chuck is a collet. A collet is made specifically for a single diameter of bit (or a small range of diameters), and it grips the shaft of the bit either continuously around or at least at a large number of contact points spread evenly around the shaft. Collets are significantly more accurate than three-jaw chucks, and they resist sideways forces much better than any kind of chuck with jaws.

The relative advantages and disadvantages of chucks and collets mean that you will almost always find three-jaw chucks in drill presses meant for drilling holes straight down, while in milling machines, where there is likely to be much more sideways force on the bit, you will almost always find collets. Similarly, routers and die grinders use collets, while the drills on the next page use chucks.

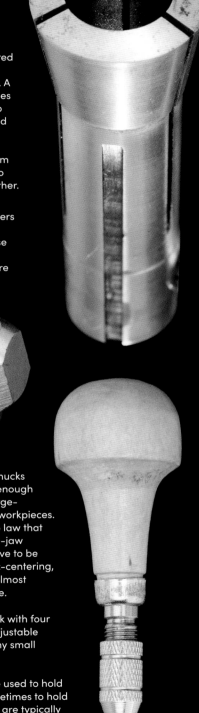

▶ A collet has a tapered outside, which exactly matches the tapered hole in the milling machine's spindle. A threaded rod comes down from the top of the machine and pulls the collet up into the spindle, compressing it from all sides as the two tapers come together.

▼ Hand-held routers for woodworking use collets because they spin quickly and have to endure a lot of sideways force.

◀ This mini collet works with a 1 mm range of shaft diameter (e.g., from 6 mm to 7 mm), so my set can accommodate any diameter of shaft from 1 to 12 mm.

◀ A good chuck is a thing of beauty.

▼ Drill chucks have relatively long, thin jaws that grip the shaft of a drill bit. The jaws are moved in and out by a threaded ring that turns with the body of the chuck.

◀ Lathe chucks are wide enough to hold large-diameter workpieces. There's no law that says three-jaw chucks have to be automatic-centering, but they almost always are.

◀ This small chuck with four independently adjustable jaws came with my small metal lathe.

▶ Collet vises are used to hold small bits, or sometimes to hold workpieces. They are typically used in jewelry making.

ANGLE DRILLS

PISTOL-SHAPED DRILLS are popular because they're comfortable, well balanced, and fairly easy to control using arm strength to apply direct pressure to the bit. But sometimes you need to drill a hole in a tight space, and a pistol-shaped drill just doesn't give you any flexibility, literally. Instead, what you need is a drill that drives the bit from the side, at an angle. Enter the angle drill.

Instead of having their motor directly in line with the drill bit, angle drills insert a set of beveled gears that turn the motion somewhere between 45 and 180 degrees. This robs the drill of some power, but the angle means you have better leverage to resist the turning force of the bit: the Hole-Hawg line of angle drills are some of the most powerful available.

One of the first "serious" tools I bought was a heavy-duty Milwaukee plug-in right angle drill. It's sturdy and powerful. But as right angle drills go, it's not all that compact behind the bit. The version I really fell in love with is the angled one shown on the left. It's elegant, effective, expensive, and durable. It's even got two triggers, so you can operate it comfortably in different positions. I love it, but the angle means it's still not as compact as possible.

In search of the least-tool-behind-the-chuck design, I found two Makitas that move the chuck progressively farther back. The most compact is right about at the limit of what you can do and still have a drill chuck for holding arbitrary diameters of bits. If you just want a hex driver or socket wrench drive, you can make the whole thing even more compact, but then it's actually one of the tools on the next page.

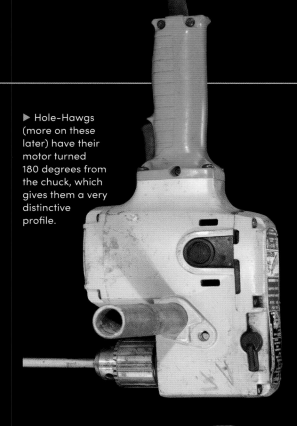

► Hole-Hawgs (more on these later) have their motor turned 180 degrees from the chuck, which gives them a very distinctive profile.

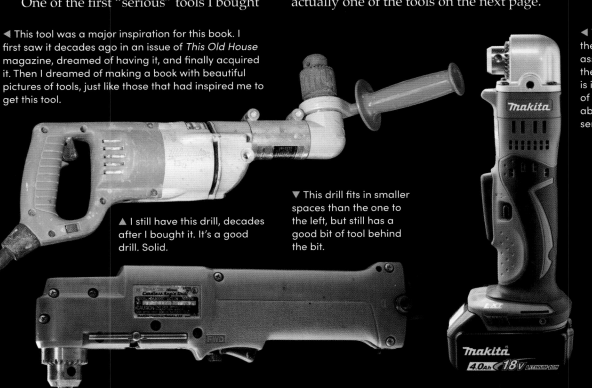

◄ This tool was a major inspiration for this book. I first saw it decades ago in an issue of *This Old House* magazine, dreamed of having it, and finally acquired it. Then I dreamed of making a book with beautiful pictures of tools, just like those that had inspired me to get this tool.

▲ I still have this drill, decades after I bought it. It's a good drill. Solid.

▼ This drill fits in smaller spaces than the one to the left, but still has a good bit of tool behind the bit.

◄ This drill compresses the chuck and gear assembly so much that the bottom of the chuck is in line with the bottom of the body, which is about as far as it makes sense to be.

► If you can't justify buying a whole new right-angle drill, an adapter like this lets you use your ordinary drill in a new way.

IMPACT WRENCHES

TAKING THE WHEELS off a car typically requires removing twenty lug nuts, five on each wheel. It can be done with a manual wrench, but if you've ever been to a tire shop, you know the sound of the preferred tool: an air-powered impact wrench. This wrench makes two sounds: a rapid hammering noise followed by a scream, which means the wheel is being taken off. Or a scream followed by rapid hammering, which means the wheel is being put on.

Air-powered wrenches are used in shops because, compared to electric models, they are lighter, more powerful, cheaper, faster, and they last nearly forever. Because air cools when it expands, they can't burn out. The tool actually gets colder the longer you use it. Electric, and even battery-powered, impact wrenches have become quite effective in recent

years, and can be amazingly useful if you need to change wheels on a truck or camper by the side of the road. But they are quite a bit heavier, and they eventually break, which air tools generally do not.

It's important to note that impact wrenches are *not* the same thing as hammer drills. They both turn and hit at the same time, but hammer drills hit straight down the shaft of the tool, like you would hit a chisel. Impact wrenches hit *sideways*, in the rotational direction, as if you were hammering on the end of a wrench, trying to knock the nut loose, which is exactly what this tool is doing.

And impact wrenches, unlike drills, do not insist that the bit turn. They simply hit it repeatedly until it sees the wisdom of turning. That means these tools, even very large ones, don't need long side-handles, and will never try to twist your arm off.

▶ An electric impact wrench is heavier and less reliable than an equally powerful pneumatic version.

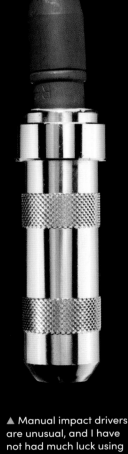

◀ This brutally powerful air impact wrench weighs almost 30 pounds (13 kg). It's far too large to use on a car and would be more at home working on large trucks or factory machines.

◀ A typical hand-held pneumatic impact wrench is light, loud, and strong. It should be used only with impact-rated sockets (typically black, for some reason).

▶ Angle adapters exist for impact wrenches but can't allow much range due to the extreme forces involved.

▲ This is an air-powered wrench, but not an impact wrench. To get a lot of turning force you have to move the handle just like a manual wrench.

▲ Manual impact drivers are unusual, and I have not had much luck using this one. The idea is that an internal wedge shape translates a hammer blow to the back of the tool into a twisting motion of the bit.

OPTICAL INSTRUMENTS

THE CLASSIC MICROSCOPE typically found in science classrooms—or lab scenes in low-effort movies—is not very useful in the shop. They work only for very thin, transparent things, and generally the magnification is too high. Inspection microscopes, on the other hand, are built to observe three-dimensional objects, and can be very handy in the workshop. Fancy models zoom and give a stereo 3D view. I especially like my video inspection microscope because it has a nice big screen allowing several people to observe at once, and you can connect it to a computer to record images or video.

Pro tip: if you want a kid to get excited about looking at things under a microscope, get them a zoomable inspection microscope, preferably video. Lab-style microscopes are frustrating for young people.

So what can you do with an inspection microscope in a shop? Aside from reading

vernier scales, they can also be used together with microscope slides that have measuring scales etched on them. This is often the best way to accurately measure a dimension if you can't get a caliper or micrometer accurately registered to the part (and you don't have a much larger instrument called an optical comparator).

For example, when we were making masks during the recent pandemic, I used an etched glass slide with major divisions every 1 mm and minor divisions every $\frac{1}{10}$ mm to document the thread spacing of all our fabric choices (so customers could see how tightly woven a mask they were ordering). These slides are available with markings spaced as closely as 1 μm ($\frac{1}{1,000}$ mm), which is barely larger than the wavelength of visible light, and certainly impossible to see without serious magnification.

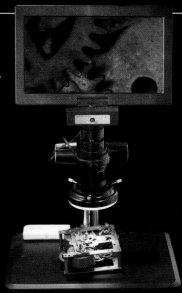

▶ My favorite, which I use almost exclusively, is this zoomable video inspection microscope. You won't regret having one.

▼ A glass slide with 0.1 mm divisions is lying on top of this piece of mask fabric. Thread count is the sum of the number of threads per inch in each direction, 60 + 60 = 120 in this case.

▼ The same slide laid over silk fabric shows just how astonishingly fine silk threads are. What looks like one thread is actually dozens of fibers bundled together.

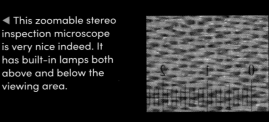

◀ This zoomable stereo inspection microscope is very nice indeed. It has built-in lamps both above and below the viewing area.

▼ An inspection microscope is a good choice for the workshop.

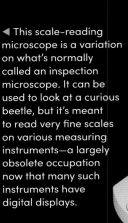

◀ This scale-reading microscope is a variation on what's normally called an inspection microscope. It can be used to look at a curious beetle, but it's meant to read very fine scales on various measuring instruments—a largely obsolete occupation now that many such instruments have digital displays.

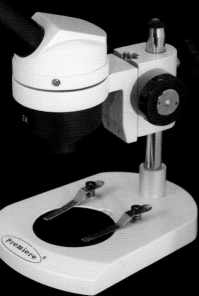

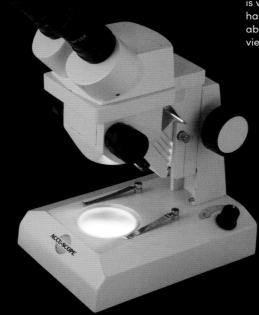

◀ This is my most specialized microscope. It mounts in the spindle of a milling machine and positions a crosshair at the center of revolution of the spindle.

SCREW GUNS

THE SINGLE MOST universally useful hand-held power tool is a combination drill/driver—which I have arbitrarily categorized with drills on an earlier page. A modern lithium battery–powered drill/driver can do a very good job of both drilling holes and driving screws.

On the other hand, the tools here, known as screw guns, are dedicated screwdrivers only. In a pinch they can be used to drill (using hex-shank drills that fit the screwdriver bit socket), but they turn too slowly to be good at it. They can also be used as a very light wrench with a socket adapter (but lack the torque of a proper impact wrench).

The big advantage of the screw gun is that it's small and light. Instead of a bulky chuck able to hold bits of any diameter, they have a universally standardized ¼-inch hexagonal socket, into which you can fit a huge range of screwdriver bits, extensions, angle adapters, and so on.

Personally, I never use screw guns, though I have acquired plenty thinking they look useful. I do all my screwing with a larger drill/driver, because that's what I always have with me. We take it for granted that anything you can screw you can also unscrew, but on the next page we will meet a whole category of tools designed to deal with the fact that this is not true of other kinds of fasteners.

▲ This is the most elaborate quick-change tool I've fallen for. It tries to solve the very real problem of wanting to alternately drill pilot holes and drive screws into them.

◄ The tools on this page are generically known as screw guns, but few take the name as literally as this one. Unlike the gunpowder-activated nail guns on page 125 this tool doesn't actually *work* like a gun.

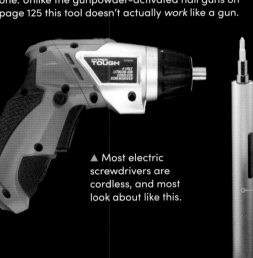

▲ Most electric screwdrivers are cordless, and most look about like this.

► There is clearly a strong Apple influence in the design of this super-premium miniature precision electric screwdriver, the Wowstick 1F+. It's held like a pencil, and since the screws it works on are so tiny, torque is not an issue.

▲ Here's a reliable way to make money: invent a new design of quick-change screw gun and show it to me. I won't use it, but I will definitely buy it.

► Yankee spiral screwdrivers were used almost exclusively with slotted bits, which made them hateful things because the bit would constantly slip out of the slot while you were trying to jerk the stupid thing back and forth.

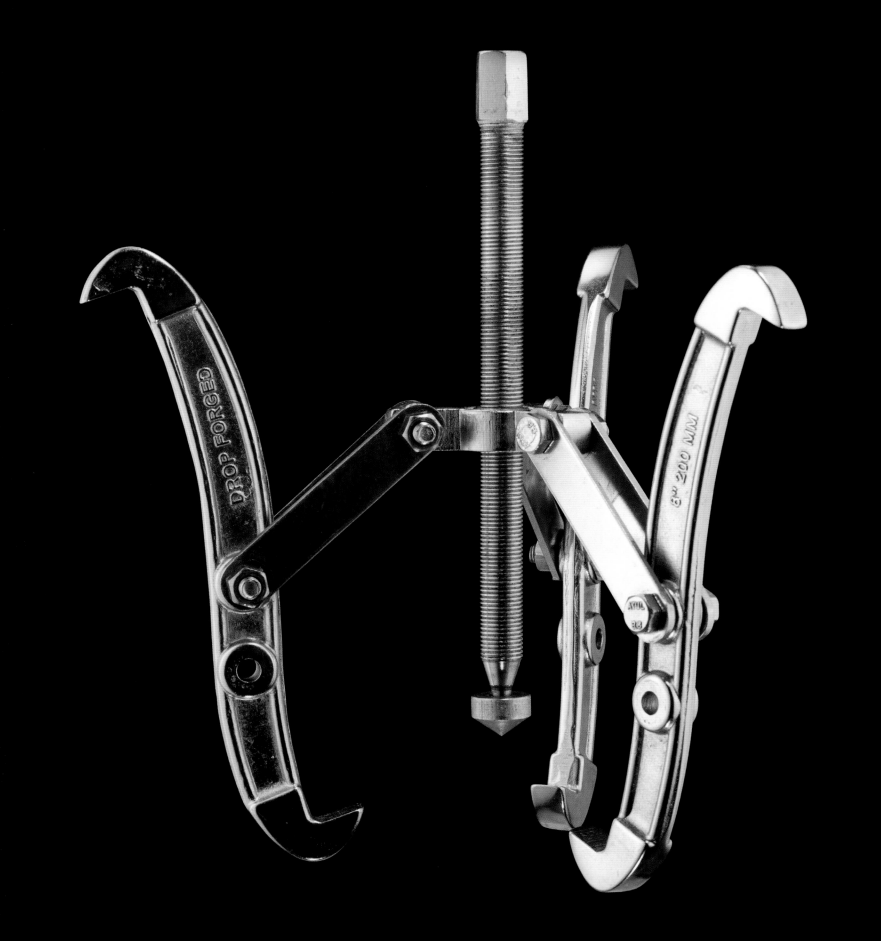

NAIL PULLERS

REMOVING NAILS FROM where they ought not to be is an irritating task. There is no perfect solution, despite the variety of nail pullers that have been designed over roughly the last two thousand years.

Assuming the nail has been properly seated, the head will be partially submerged under the surface of the material it's banged into. The only option to remove it is to displace at least some of the surrounding material in order to slide the nail puller under the head and extract the nail.

Cat's-paw nail pullers have a V-shaped fork that slides around the shaft of the nail just under the head, like a claw. Leverage allows you to pull out the nail, but first you have to dig the sides into the wood to get the fork around the shaft, unavoidably digging out some neighboring wood. Slide-hammer nail pullers have two pointed claws, and a built-in weight that slides up and down the handle, allowing you

to drive the two claws around the nail head by slamming the weight downward, compressing but not necessarily chewing up the surface of the surrounding material. The claws automatically grip tighter as you use the handle to lever out the nail.

There's another situation in which you may need to pull something forcefully toward you: removing a pulley, hub, or gear from the end of a shaft or axle. Gear pullers do this by gentle persuasion, with a screw that pushes against the shaft in the center while hooks pull on the gear. When that's not enough, the obvious temptation is to use a hammer, but there's a problem: you need to hammer the thing toward you, not away from you, and that's not possible with an ordinary hammer. A slide hammer solves the problem. You pull the captive weight rapidly toward yourself, sliding it along the handle until it slams into the stop at the end. This imparts a powerful shock in the pulling direction.

◄ This slide hammer has a weight that slides along a rod. A variety of adapter plates allow you to fasten the rod to whatever needs extracting, for example a wheel from a car axle, which gets a powerful tug when you smash the weight into the stop at the far end of the rod.

◄ To get a stubborn gear or pulley off its shaft, you can hook the three jaws of a gear puller around the outside of the gear, then tighten the rod in the center against the shaft until the gear pops off.

▼ Cat's-paw nail pullers range in material from stamped to forged to beautiful fully machined tools.

◄ This well-made little guy, with its comfortable wooden handle, is designed to pull small nails and tacks.

▶ This miniature gear puller is supposedly for lifting up the edges of an ingrown toenail and keeping them elevated. How you are supposed to do anything with this thing clamped to your toe I do not know.

▶ This elaborate nail puller combines a lever-action pincer to grab the head of the nail with a slide hammer to dig the claw down into the wood to reach it.

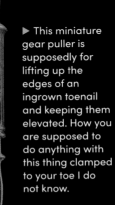

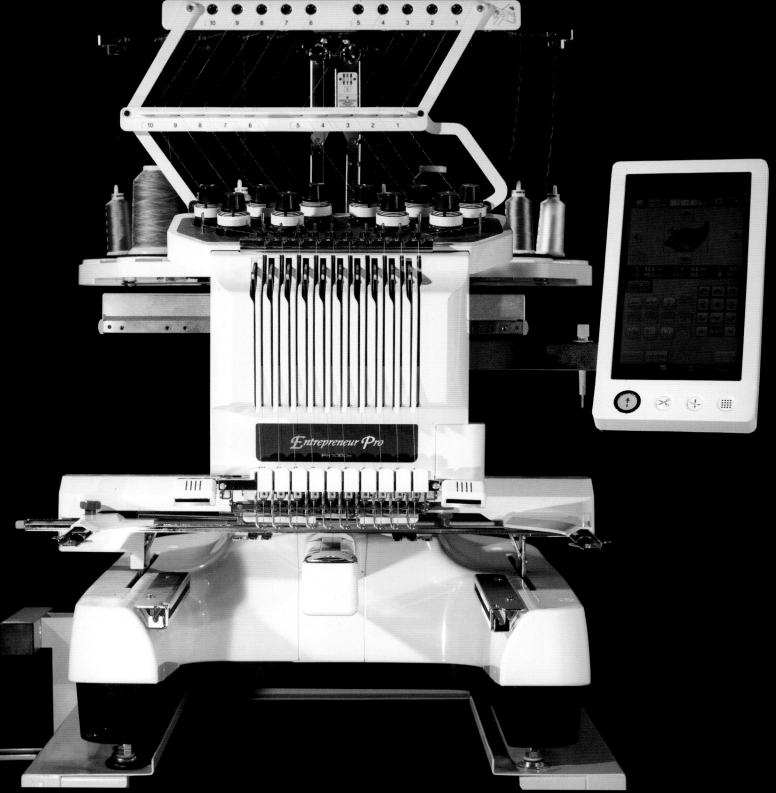

SEWING TOOLS

IT SEEMS WRONG to me that sewing machines, which are precision machine tools by any reasonable definition, aren't usually classified that way. At least many makerspaces do have computerized embroidery machines alongside their standard-issue 3D printers, laser cutters, and CNC routers, so apparently they get it.

My own shop houses two sewing machines that can't reasonably be called anything other than machine tools, and pretty big ones at that. The smaller one is a ten-needle embroidery machine, and the real beast is a massive full-frame quilting machine. I recently had to weigh the main beam of the quilter (the part that moves front to back across the stretched fabric) to be sure the dolly I had built would be strong enough to move it. It came in around 1,300 pounds (590 kg) or well over half a ton. And that's just the weight of the moving beam!

Sewing occupies an interesting niche in manufacturing technology. Nearly all large machine tools, with the exception of 3D printers, do "subtractive manufacturing"— you start with a block of something, then cut, carve, drill, grind, burn, or chip away at it until you have the shape you want. 3D printers on the other hand are "additive" because they start with nothing and add material until the desired shape is formed.

Sewing and embroidery machines are like 3D printers because they add material—thread—to build up a finished product, but they also start from a substrate—fabric, batting, and stabilizer— which they modify and form into its final shape. (Knitting machines, on the other hand, are pure 3D printer. They turn a spool of filament—i.e., yarn—into a sweater, which is just one very elaborate knot.)

I think these "soft" machines deserve full credit as shop tools, but if you have an axe to grind with that, I can help you on the next page.

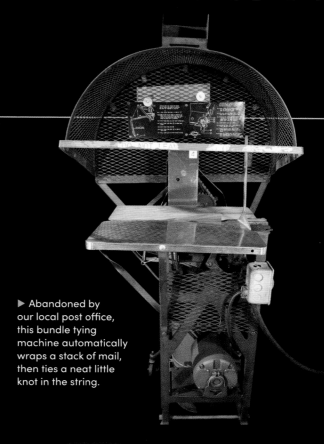

▶ Abandoned by our local post office, this bundle tying machine automatically wraps a stack of mail, then ties a neat little knot in the string.

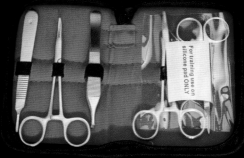

◀ This beautiful CNC (computer numerical control) machine tool stitches patterns in up to ten different thread colors automatically. It's about the size of a dorm fridge.

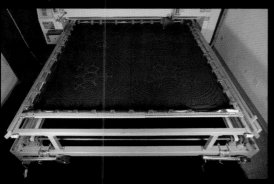

▲ This quilting machine is like an XY pen plotter, except instead of a pen it has a sewing machine, which it moves freely across an 8-foot (2.4 m) square working area. At around the size of two midsized sedans, it is the largest sewing machine I have.

▲ This machine can stitch up to three hundred embroidered patches simultaneously, making tens of thousands on a single roll of ultra-wide fabric. At 45 feet (14 m) long, it is about the size and weight of a Greyhound bus.

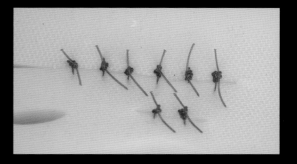

▲ At the other end of the sewing size spectrum, I recently wanted to cut out a small mole I have and suture the incision myself. You know, for science. I practiced suturing on a silicone practice pad until I was reasonably good at it, but fortunately came to my senses before actually slicing myself open.

BENCH GRINDERS

GRINDING IS LIKE the opposite of what happens with concrete drills and jackhammers: steel meets stone, but this time the stone wins. I think it's fascinating that a steel chisel can be sharpened by holding it against a spinning grinding wheel, but if you put the same chisel against the side of the same grinding wheel and hit it with a hammer, you will break the wheel in half. It's all about exploiting the relative degrees of hardness, brittleness, and toughness. When the stone has a chance to scrape the metal away a bit at a time, its superior hardness wins. When a blunt end of steel meets stone head-on in an impact, the steel's superior toughness wins.

Grinding wheels in good condition can sharpen just about anything, but even old wheels worn with grooves can reshape bolt heads, sharpen sticks for toy arrows (a favorite of my kids when they were little), grind notches and curves into bits of metal for whatever reason, debur and round over edges of cutoff bars and rods, and so on.

At an industrial level, grinding is used in various high-precision machining processes, including surface grinding (which can produce a flatter, more accurate surface than milling), centerless grinding (which can produce accurately round shapes rapidly and repeatedly), and cylindrical grinding (used in manufacturing crankshafts and the like). But in the home shop, grinding is usually more of a hand-held job: either the grinding tool or the workpiece is held by hand and manipulated by feel. We saw hand-held grinders earlier; on this page we're looking at stationary bench grinders that you hold the workpiece against.

A typical bench grinder has a motor in the middle and a wheel on each side. The wheels can be mixed and matched: a fine and a coarse grinding wheel, a grinding wheel and a buffing wheel, a grinding wheel and a wire wheel, etc. Safety glasses and preferably a leather coat and face shield are *strongly* advised when using a grinding wheel. Sparks fly! I always instinctively stand away from the wheel's trajectory when first switching it on. You never know if it's going to fly apart.

▲ If you have an axe to grind, boy have I got the tool for you! This pedal-powered grinding wheel is like a bicycle for wreaking vengeance on your enemies with sharp-edged tools. The stone is quite soft and doesn't actually work very well for sharpening, but that's OK because most of my axe grinding is metaphorical.

◀ When grinding wheels inevitably develop grooves, or get clogged up, a wheel dressing tool can be used to clean them. This one is made with hardened steel-toothed wheels that turn with the grinding wheel, chipping away at it without rubbing (which would grind away the steel).

◀ This bench grinder came with my farm, on a post literally embedded in the concrete floor of the workshop. It's not uncommon to find them this way because they're most useful when mounted away from any obstructions.

▶ I have several miniature bench grinders, both at home and in my shops. They are relatively weak as grinders go, but that makes them relatively safe. I use one of them to debur the ends of tiny #2 threaded rods in the kits we sell. A bigger tool would be pure overkill.

▲ This is the boxiest grinder I've ever seen.

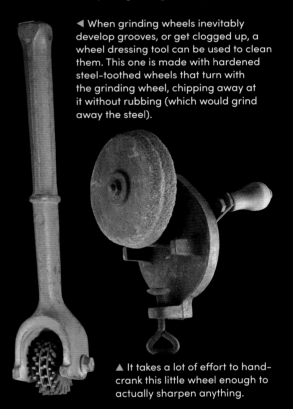

▲ It takes a lot of effort to hand-crank this little wheel enough to actually sharpen anything.

◀ This chunky old belt-driven grinding wheel was used to sharpen the teeth on large sickle bar mowers.

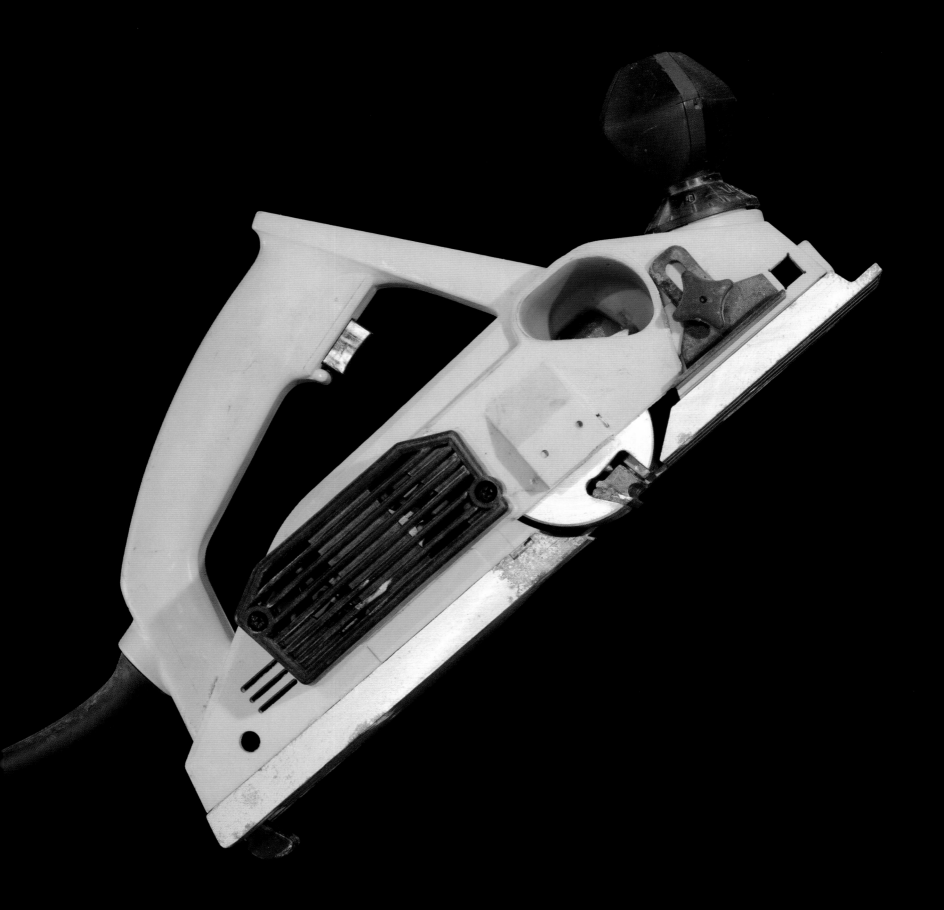

PLANES

Planes, particularly antique block planes, are perhaps the single most controversial subject in the tool world. Feelings run deep and extend far beyond brand loyalty. In Japan they hold national competitions to see who can create the longest, thinnest curl of wood by dragging a huge block plane along a perfectly smooth beam.

Personally, I have no use for them. I have never encountered a task that could not be done faster and better with a jointer, thickness planer, power plane, thickness sander, belt sander, or random orbit sander than with a block plane.

I know there are people who will at this point write me off as a hopeless dolt who knows nothing about tools and should be sent to some kind of reeducation camp. To them I would reply that there is a such a camp right nearby in Arthur, Illinois: the Amish community. And they don't use block planes. They run diesel engines to drive hydraulic pumps and air compressors, which in turn run their jointers, thickness planers, power planes, thickness sanders, and all the other power tools that these highly traditional, old-school, electricity-shunning people use instead of block planes.

▲ There are a *lot* of different special-purpose planes for making dados, mortises, profiles, and other things that are more easily made with a router.

◀ This hand-held power plane is one of my favorite tools that I rarely use. But when I do, it never fails to delight me with its speed and clean cutting action.

▼ Some block planes, both old and new, are made of steel.

◀ Despite everything I've said about block planes, this *particular* variety—a chamfer plane—is actually very useful. It quickly rounds over the sharp edge of a board to give it a pleasing, splinter-free feel without having to drag out a whole router.

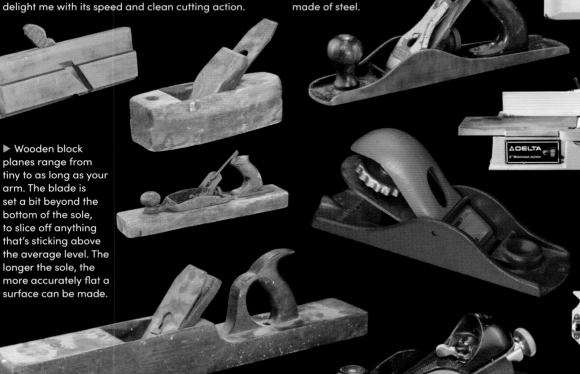

▶ Wooden block planes range from tiny to as long as your arm. The blade is set a bit beyond the bottom of the sole, to slice off anything that's sticking above the average level. The longer the sole, the more accurately flat a surface can be made.

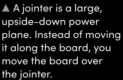

▲ A jointer is a large, upside-down power plane. Instead of moving it along the board, you move the board over the jointer.

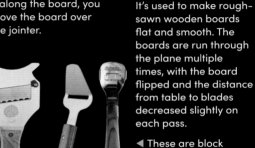

▲ A thickness planer is a power plane with a flat table underneath. It's used to make rough-sawn wooden boards flat and smooth. The boards are run through the plane multiple times, with the board flipped and the distance from table to blades decreased slightly on each pass.

◀ These are block planes for shaving strips off truffles, cheese, and feet, respectively.

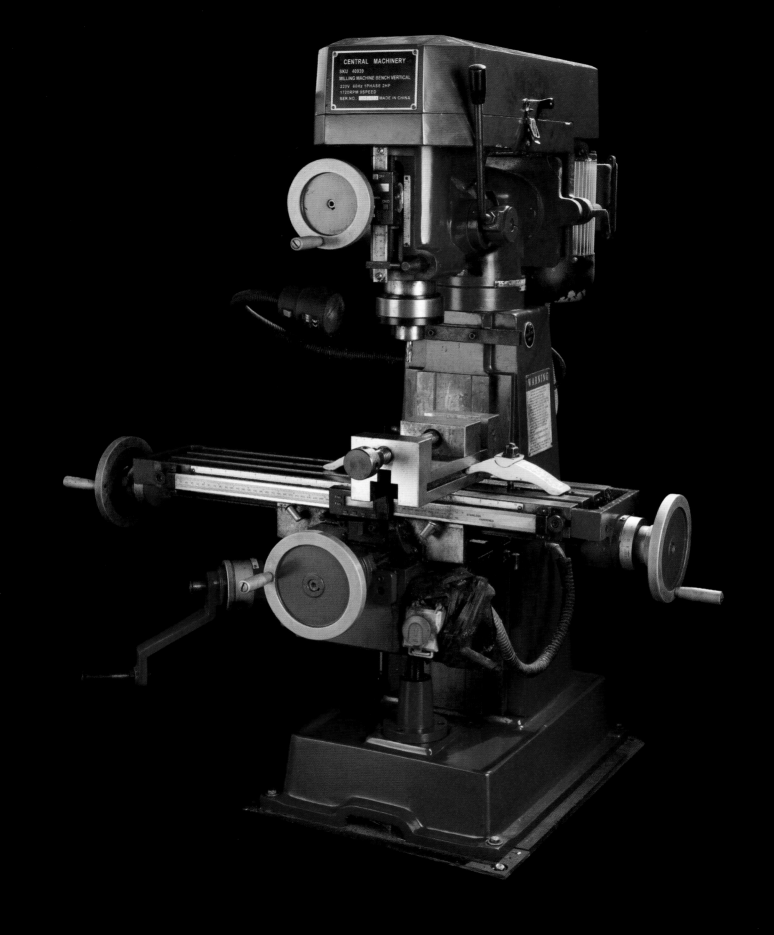

MILLING MACHINES

USING A ROUTER on an aluminum or steel workpiece will get you nowhere. Cutting metal requires *much* more pressure. A milling machine is like a router where the bit and workpiece are both held very rigidly on a common frame. Lead screws control their movement with very little room for deviation. The machines are made of great hulking masses of cast iron with sliding tables that run on machined "ways," and vises that alone weigh 100 pounds (50 kg) or more. There is something deeply satisfying, as well as deeply inconvenient, about just how monstrously heavy these tools can be.

Cast iron is the material of choice because it's cheap, easy to cast (hence the name), and easy to machine. More importantly, it's wear-resistant and tends to absorb vibrations, both because of its sheer weight and because of the metal's internal structure. The fact that cast iron is not very strong is easily overcome simply by making the parts thicker, which also helps with vibrations. That's how milling machines end up with parts that are as thick as anyone could imagine them needing to be, then doubled in thickness, because why not.

All of this strength and solidity of the machine is in service to the bit, which cuts with a sharp edge pushing against the workpiece. The stiffness of the machine resists the cutting force and keeps the alignment between bit and workpiece within the required accuracy of the cut, typically $\frac{1}{1,000}$ of an inch (0.02 mm) or better.

A full-sized milling machine of the old school weighs 2 tons. Lifting one is impossible without equipment. This, however, is a miniature benchtop milling machine. I still couldn't lift it, but I could tip it, which allowed me to slowly build up a pedestal underneath it until it was at a convenient height.

Milling machines use bits that look somewhat like drill bits, but with flat or rounded ends. Instead of drilling down, they cut sideways, removing far more material than a drill of the same size.

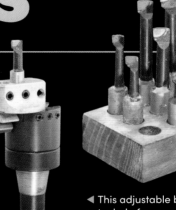

◄ This adjustable boring tool will cut a hole far more accurately than a drill bit, but can only be used in a milling machine (note the taper mount).

▼ The best milling machine bits are made of solid tungsten carbide.

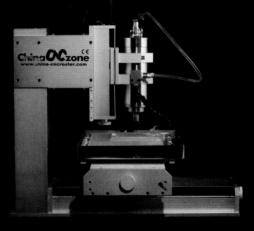

▲ Everyone should learn to use a manual milling machine for making simple, one-off parts, but these days most mills are computer controlled. I have a small CNC model I use to cut small brass parts for the engine kits I sell.

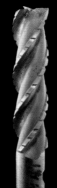

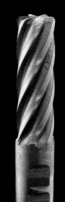

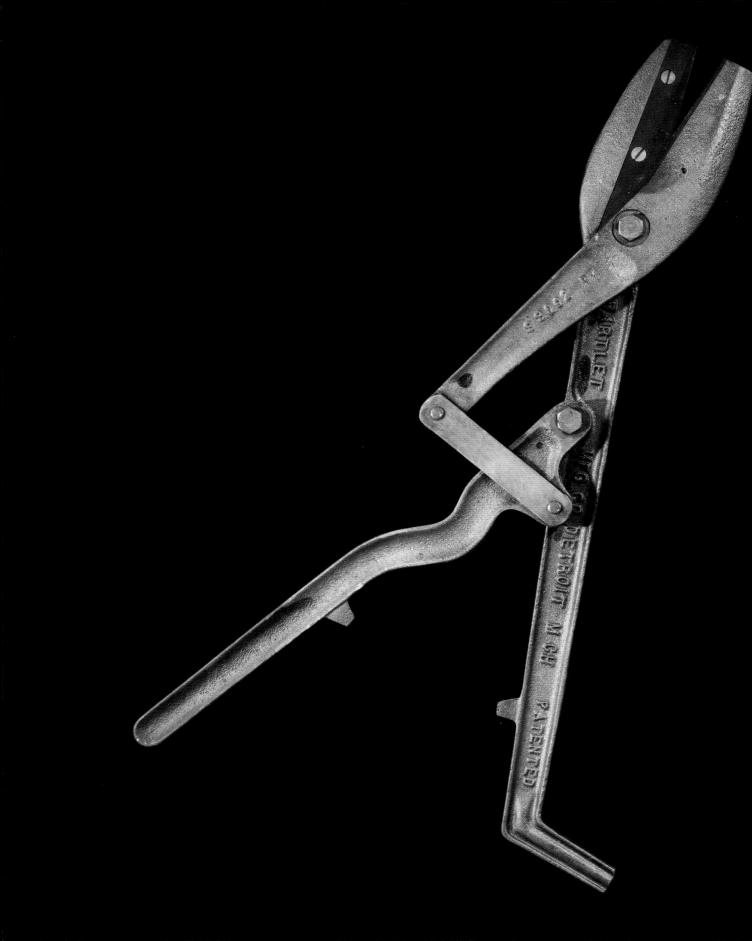

THIN SHEET METAL can be cut with tin snips, but more substantial material usually requires a bench-mounted shear. Some of these industrial-strength jaws look and work like a big pair of scissors. Others have more of a table-and-blade configuration, with a sharp blade that passes by a square-edged platform or table.

The classic paper cutter, for example, is a type of shear. The same tool applied to sheet metal is huge in comparison but similar in operation. The blades on both are designed to begin the cut on one end of the material and cut progressively to the other, fighting only a small part of the material at a time instead of trying to cut it all at once.

Other shears, for example those for linoleum and antique asbestos tiles, cut across the whole width simultaneously, to avoid the material splitting off in the wrong direction.

Shears are generally only able to cut straight lines, or gentle curves in the case of the more scissor-like models. On the next page we see a tool specifically designed to make the most complex of curves.

◄ Thi
for to
leave.

◄ These large metal shears are beyond tin snips. They combine compound leverage and size to cut thick metal. Well, thick*er* metal.

◄ There are specialized shears for many specific materials. This one is for cheese.

◄ This one is for cutting the lead slugs created by Linotype machines.

▲ This cutter/slitter remains a mystery to me: please tell me if you know what it is. No, it's not an asbestos tile cutter.

▲ These so-called "jaws of life" are powered by a gasoline engine running a hydraulic pump. They are used to cut through car doors to extract people trapped inside.

▶ This imitation Beverly shear (generically called a throatless shear) can cut heavy sheet metal, like an oversized pair of tin snips. The "throatless"

▶ This baby combination press brake, shear, and slip roll can cut sheet metal up to 30 inches (760 mm) wide. The blade near the bottom of the machine is not level so it doesn't have to cut the whole width at the same time. Instead it cuts a bit at a time from right to left. Larger versions of this machine

PANTOGRAPHS

I PURCHASED THE pantograph milling machine on the left at the estate auction in Kansas City of a recently deceased music producer, whose assets included three buildings spread over a lovely property with a creek running through it. I have absolutely no idea why a music producer with no other significant machine tools would have owned this beast.

A pantograph is the manual precursor to today's CNC (computer numerical control) milling and engraving machines, or laser cutters. A stylus (pointer) traces over the outlines of a drawing, or through the grooves of a template, and a clever arrangement of bars and pivot points duplicates its movement in the motion of a cutting bit. Often the machine is set to shrink the movement of the stylus by as much as ten-to-one: a large template can be

used to delicately engrave tiny letters on a ring or intricate designs on a watch face.

The templates can be quite beautiful in their own right. I used a lovely set of brass letter templates to engrave the wooden tiles in my periodic table table, using a 2-to-1 reduction ratio to create 1-inch (25 mm) high letters from 2-inch (50 mm) templates. These templates were themselves engraved, probably with a machine similar to the one on the left, using even larger templates that, at some point, had to be hand-made.

There's not much call for these machines today. A smaller, lighter CNC engraving machine can do the same job just as well, and it's not limited to following physical patterns. Running from a program file, which is just a list of coordinates, a CNC machine can create any design from scratch.

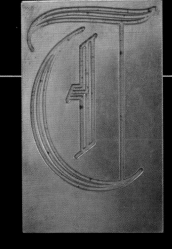

▶ A manual pantograph requires templates to run the stylus through. These beautiful old brass letters contain a complete alphabet in Gothic script.

▲ The lettering on each tile is engraved with a V-shaped groove traced out with the pantograph shown above.

◀ This is the second-heaviest tool I own, a pantograph milling machine of the old school. It's monstrously heavy and deeply obsolete and I probably shouldn't have bought it.

▼ This is a much more reasonable pantograph engraving machine, meant for engraving wood or bi-color plastic signs. I spent many, many hours using this machine to engrave all the wooden tiles in my periodic table table. The router is really nothing more than a small electric motor with a collet chuck on the end of the shaft.

▲ Pantographs can be used to scale a drawing up or down, depending on where along each bar the pivot points are placed.

▲ This table is what got me started writing books. I made it as a joke, and because I needed a table for my office. I had no idea how completely it would change my life.

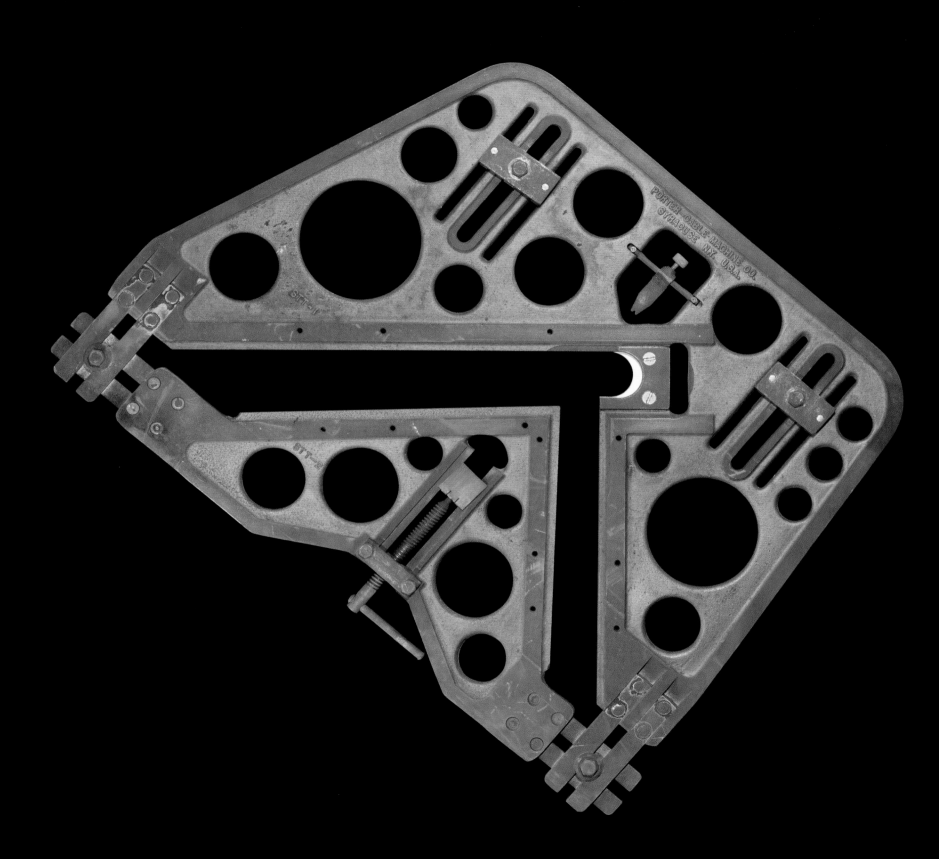

JIGS

JIGS, FIXTURES, STORY poles, and standards are tools that replace more general-purpose measuring tools. Some are adaptable to a variety of uses, but often the best thing to do is to make a custom jig for a particular job, with the required dimensions built in. Over the years I have made many such custom jigs, but I've only kept a few, because after the job is done, the jig generally gets thrown away or disassembled and the parts used again for something else.

For example, I recently built a fence for our new dog. After setting the posts in concrete, I needed to cut each one to the right height, and bevel one side so it would look pretty. I could have done this by making two measurements at different heights (one on each side of the post) and using a clamp-on saw guide twice. Instead, I made a jig that fit over the post and temporarily screwed it in place, providing two edges to run the saw along, exactly the right offset from each other.

A more elaborate example is the jig I made to cut slots in the roof of a pergola my son designed. The slats are set at a precise angle that allows sunlight to enter in the winter but blocks it in the summer. We had to cut about 150 slots in the beams that hold the slats, each with just the right angle and depth. The jig made the job go fast, with perfect consistency in every slot.

▲ I have a little business selling acrylic kits that can be assembled into mechanical models. One acrylic piece needs to be bent after it's laser cut. This jig holds it in the right shape as it's cooling.

◀ This very heavy cast-iron router jig is designed to cut blind pockets in stair stringers (the two long boards that run along either side of a stairway and hold up the treads). Many little adjustments on the jig let you set the size and spacing of the treads.

◀ Fence post cutting jig.

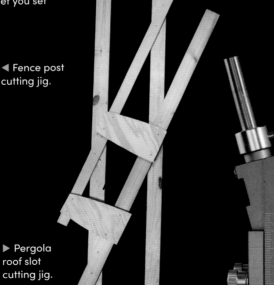

▶ Pergola roof slot cutting jig.

▶ This jig automatically aligns a drill bit with the center of the board.

◀ This pocket hole jig aligns a bit to drill a hole at a steep angle at the edge of a board.

▲ There are many times I wish I had known this tool existed. Imagine you have two overlapping sheets of some material, and you need to drill a hole in the upper one in exactly the same place as an existing hole in the lower one. This hole duplicator slips in between the sheets and the pin goes into the existing hole, which positions the bushing on top in exactly the same place, allowing you to drill a perfectly positioned hole through it.

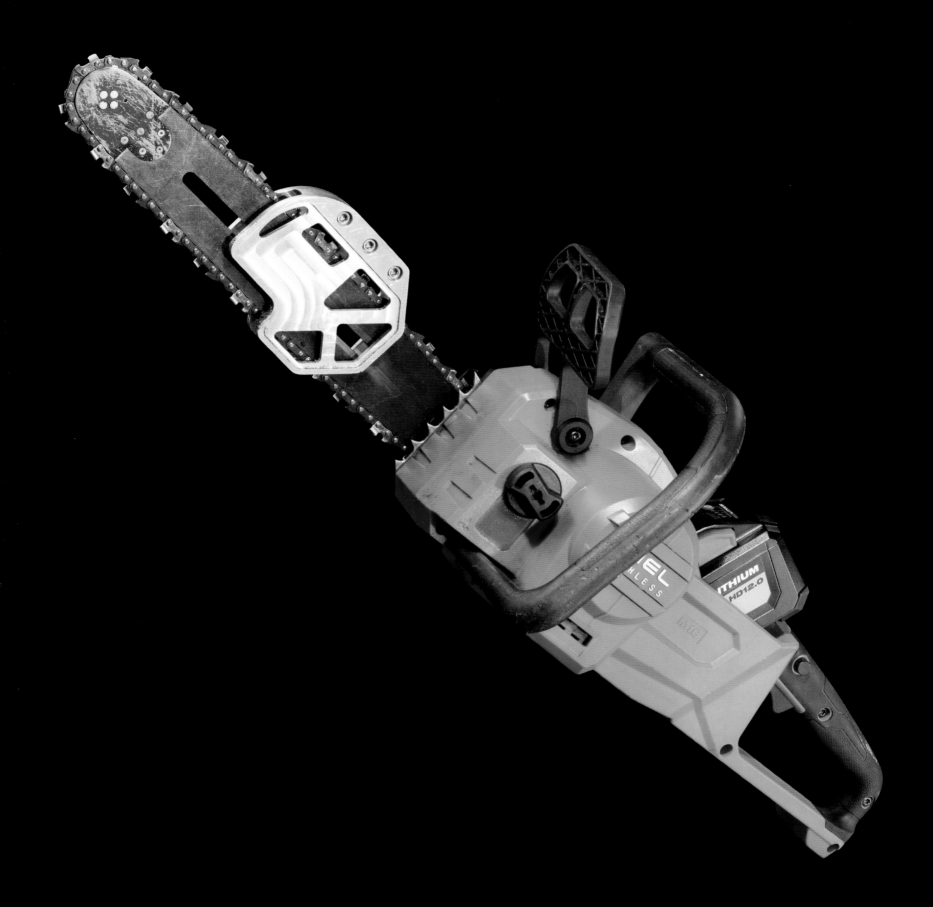

CHAIN SAWS

CHAIN SAWS ARE amazingly effective tools for cutting down trees, and for cutting them up once they are down. They are also famously dangerous. All powerful tools are risky, especially if they are stronger than you are. A drill that's stronger than you can send you to the hospital with a broken wrist. A chain saw that's stronger than you can send you to the hospital in several pieces. That's why in many cases I'm a fan of using the least powerful tool that can get the job done. An experienced lumberjack can use a massive chain saw safely, but I use one maybe once every two years, and I do not want it to be able to overpower me!

My favorite chain saw is a cheap AC-powered electric model I got from a discount hardware chain. It is not particularly well made, but I could buy ten of them for the price of one proper model (so far I have only had to buy two).

Even this badly made saw effortlessly cut through an oak tree a solid foot (300 mm) in diameter. With a sharp blade, it's ruthless. Where chain saws are ruthless, scroll saws are gentle, favoring serene precision over brute effectiveness.

◀ My local fire department keeps these battery-powered chain saws for cutting into burning buildings. I guess that's a pretty good recommendation! The strange thing clamped to the blade is a depth stop to prevent them cutting too deep into a wall or roof.

▼ This inexpensive electric chain saw wouldn't last a day in a logging camp, but that day might involve as much cutting as a suburban homeowner would do in a lifetime.

▼ A typical small, gas-powered chain saw is a great tool, except for the gas-powered part. That's hateful, because of course it won't start.

▲ I would choose a plug-in electric chain saw over any alternative. The gas-powered one won't start because it's been sitting for two years, and the battery-powered one won't start for the same reason. Either way I'd be out $100 for a mechanic or a new battery.

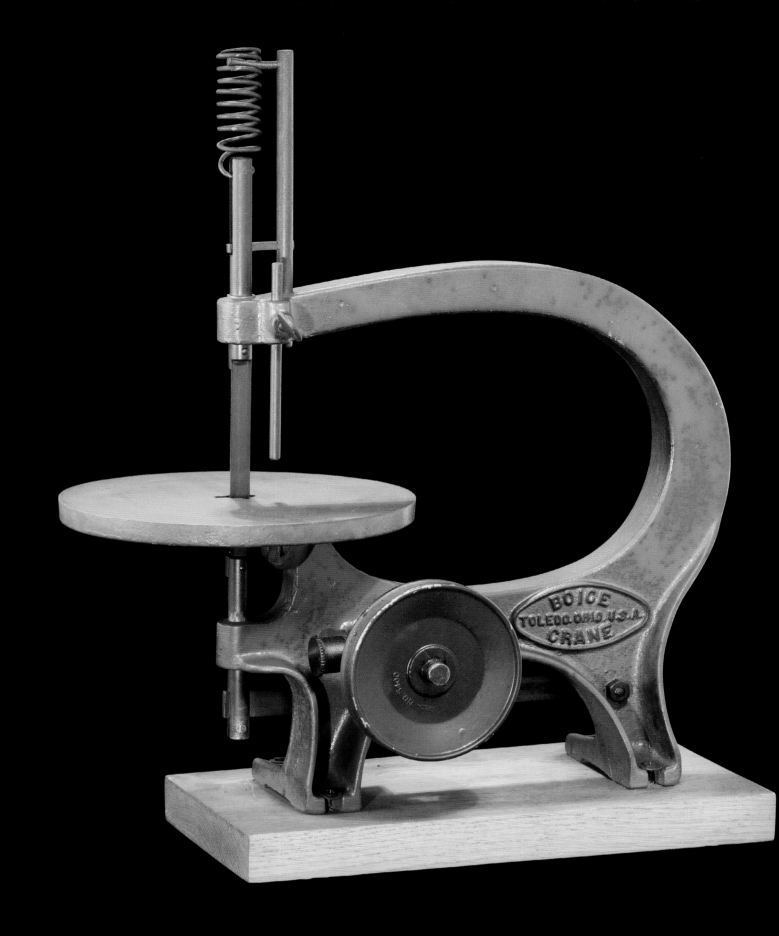

SCROLL SAWS

SCROLL SAWS ARE like bench-mounted power coping saws with a table. They have a very thin blade held at both ends and stretched hard enough to keep it straight. Because the blade is thin, it can make very sharp corners, as well as gentle curves and arcs. Because the tool is large and stationary, work can be guided through it very precisely. Short of a laser cutter or waterjet, a scroll saw is the best tool to use for cutting complex shapes for inlays, fretwork, etc. You can make some very beautiful things with a scroll saw, and I would probably use mine a lot more if I didn't have a laser cutter.

You might think a scroll saw would be jerky like a jigsaw or reciprocating saw, but scroll saws tend to be quite gentle, only surpassed in serene cutting by bandsaws. There are three design approaches to holding the blade taut under tension. The simplest has a motor on the bottom of the saw that pulls the blade down, while a spring on top pulls the blade up. The cutting is done on the downstroke. The next has a C-shaped arm that attaches to the top and bottom of the blade. The whole arm moves up and down, just as if it were a manual coping saw with the blade stretched in its frame.

The most common modern design has an arrangement of two levers, one above and one below the table, with a bar in the back connecting them. They pull the blade up and down while keeping the amount of frame in motion to a minimum.

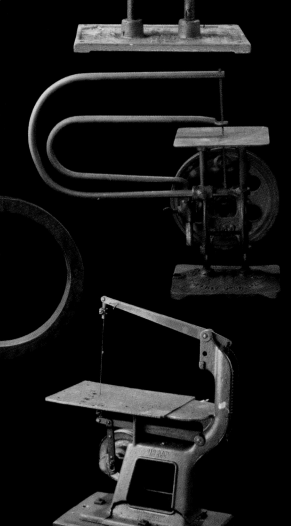

◀ This elegantly shaped scroll saw has a spring to pull up on the blade.

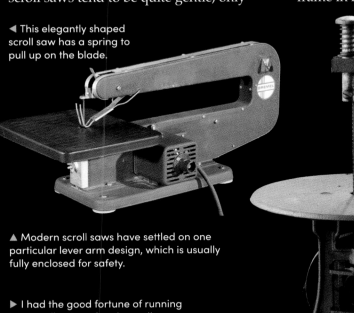

▲ Modern scroll saws have settled on one particular lever arm design, which is usually fully enclosed for safety.

▶ I had the good fortune of running into a collection of early scroll saws at an auction, so I can show you a pretty good spectrum of how these things evolved. Some have just a spring on top, some have a solid C-arm, like a powered coping saw, and others have a double-pivot lever design similar to modern scroll saws.

BIG SAWS

RADIAL ARM SAWS have a *terrible* reputation for safety. You will not find many in home shops these days, but in the fifties, sixties, and seventies they were promoted as the wonder tool for every woodworking enthusiast. They could do everything! Including cutting off a finger. While there are many things you *can* do safely with a radial arm saw, there are more you really *shouldn't* do. The main problem is that the blade is typically right out in the open with no guard, and if anything goes wrong, it can come leaping out at you, teeth bared and snarling.

A combination of modern tools—a sliding compound miter saw, a table saw, and a router or shaper—can do everything a radial arm saw can do, and each of these tools is better and safer at its job than the radial arm saw is at any of them. Operations best done on a table saw are some of the most dangerous to do with a radial arm saw.

The most useful thing a table saw can do is make long cuts in long pieces of wood (ripping a board to the correct width). But with the blade tilted it can make angled cuts, and used with a dado set it can cut slots much faster than a router. Two people using a table saw can cut up whole sheets of plywood. If you don't have a large space indoors to house a big table saw, consider getting a portable model to put out on the driveway when you need it. Along with a leaf blower, using a table saw in your driveway is one of the best ways to annoy your neighbors. They're pretty loud.

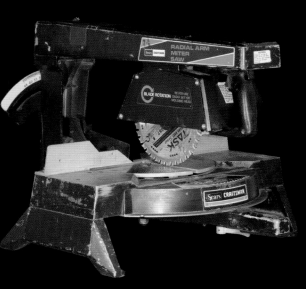

▲ A blade jamming in a modern miter saw is—unless you're being really careless—a minor thing that barely slows you down. Jamming a blade in this rare hybrid radial arm miter saw can ruin the wood, ruin the saw, ruin your day, and ruin your hand.

◀ This monster from the late 1950s or early 1960s is one of the original radial arm saw designs patented by Raymond DeWalt in 1925, with heavy cast-iron frame, column, arm, and yoke. Similar models are still made today for use in commercial shops, where they have a few safe applications. The table surface can be replaced periodically as it gets sawed into.

◀ This miniature table saw is not a toy; it's as expensive as some full-sized versions. The main uses are in model making and in sawing the lead or zinc "came" used in making stained glass windows.

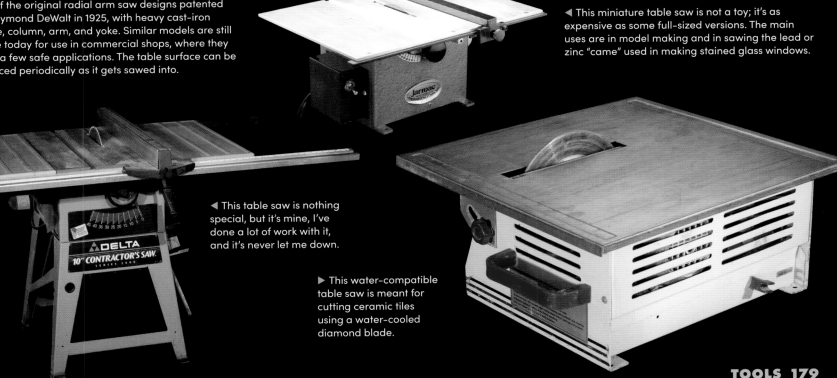

◀ This table saw is nothing special, but it's mine, I've done a lot of work with it, and it's never let me down.

▶ This water-compatible table saw is meant for cutting ceramic tiles using a water-cooled diamond blade.

OTHER TOOLS

YOU MIGHT THINK that 118 categories of tools is a lot, but even sticking with common shop tools there are many categories that just didn't make the cut. On this page I've tried to give you a taste of what's not in the rest of the book.

One thing that might not immediately seem like a tool category is chemical tools: glue, paint, oil, solvents, etc. But if you think about it these are often some of the most useful things to have in the shop. A drop of oil can do wonders. Having a dry chemical fire extinguisher in my shop has only saved my house from burning to the ground once, but that's enough times to qualify it as essential.

Electrical tools are another example. Learning to use a volt-ohm-amp meter will help you with wiring outlets and fixing lamps or car battery problems, and a couple of electrical safety tools that together cost less than lunch can save your life even if you're not the one who screwed up the wiring.

Masonry tools, drafting tools, automotive tools, gardening tools, that category you're going to tell me I forgot but actually I just didn't have room for, the other category I actually did forget, and all the categories I've never heard of. And beyond that an endless array of highly specialized tools. Really I can't even begin to scratch the surface, so I've just included a magnetic sweeper that I enjoy running over the shop floor after some heavy grinding. The *click-clack-plink-ping* sound of it picking up bits of iron, nails, and iron filings is so satisfying.

▲ You will often hear that there is no more important tool than a pair of safety glasses. In my case I think my eyes are OK only because I'm so nearsighted that I am forced to wear glasses all the time, whether I think of the danger or not.

▶ Outlets that have been wired with reversed hot and neutral lines can be deadly, especially in a kitchen or bathroom. A dirt cheap tool can save your life simply by plugging it into every outlet in your house to find the offenders (this fancy version also tells you the voltage you're getting).

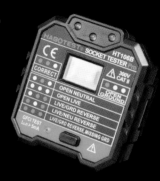

◀ Concrete and masonry work is underrepresented in the rest of this book, so please accept this gorgeous solid brass parting tool as compensation. It is used to make the grooves you see every few feet in concrete sidewalks (which are there so that when the concrete unavoidably, inevitably cracks, the crack will be in the bottom of a groove where it's less visible).

▲ What is this witchcraft? This clever caulk gun inches down the tube, and has a sharp knife edge that slits the tube as it's going along, so there's no need for a long plunger. The whole thing is less than half as long as the tube!

▲ A contactless voltage detector should always be used before opening up an outlet or rewiring a light fixture. You may think you switched off the right breaker, but did you really? The blinking light on this very inexpensive tool reveals the danger.

▶ An electronic stud finder is absolutely useless for finding studs (wooden boards) behind walls, but it works great for making dad jokes: point it at yourself and there's a good chance it will beep (proving again how bad it is at locating studs).

▶ This universal pair of tools solves all problems. If it's supposed to move and it doesn't, WD-40. If it moves and it shouldn't, duct tape.

▶ I used to host sodium parties wherein we would throw blocks of sodium into my lake (because they catch fire and then explode). This controlled dropping tool let me take videos of the process under more controlled conditions: when you pull on the string from a distance, the bowl flips over, dropping its contents into a bucket below.

▶ After working with metal, your shop or driveway will be covered with shards, chips, and filings, all of which are attracted to the magnets in the body of this magnetic sweeper. When you pull the handle on top, the magnets are lifted within the non-magnetic body, releasing all the collected material.

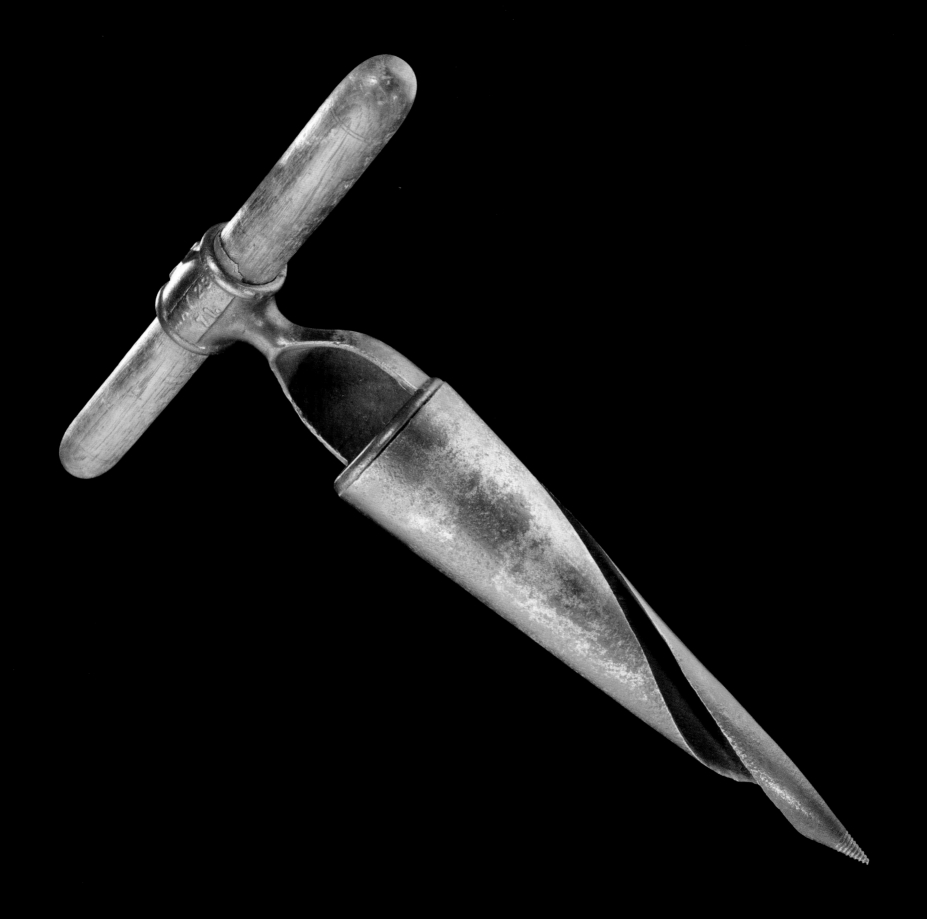

ANTIQUE AUGERS

THE DRILL IS ONE of the oldest of hand tools. Simple spoon bits and awls date back thousands of years. The modern drill bit started taking shape in the 1500s, and the same basic style is still in use today. Hundred-year-old drill bits are still relatively easy to find. There must be something about their heft and the obvious care with which they were made that prevents them from being discarded.

In rough historical order, the first drill bits were spoon bits, which have a very simple shape and no point, which allows them to change direction while drilling, and drill *almost* to the other side of a piece of wood without poking through, a feature that gives them a few modern applications.

Next are gimlet drills, which are like slightly twisted spoon bits, but instead of making a hole to its final diameter right from the start, they slowly enlarge the hole as the bit drills deeper, cutting on the sides instead of just the bottom.

Finally, auger bits are closest to modern twist drills (and still very widely used today). They cut at the tip and have twisted flutes to carry the chips up and out of the hole.

▶ This uncomfortable-looking bunghole auger has several functional zones. The lead screw pulls the auger into the wood to get it started. The auger enlarges the hole. Finally, the shaving edge reams out the hole to the desired diameter and taper.

◀ This tool, known as a spiral bunghole reamer, is used to bore out a bunghole in the side or top of a wooden barrel. After the barrel is filled through the hole, it's plugged by hammering a wooden peg into it. Similar to a gimlet drill, this reamer shaves the sides of the hole progressively larger the deeper it goes.

▲ Spoon bits are among the oldest design of drill bit.

▲ Gimlet drills are another very old style. I wish I had one of the largest, which were used to bore out the centers of entire tree trunks to make wooden water pipes.

▼▶ An auger bit set like this would have been a highly valued possession of a woodworker of any century.

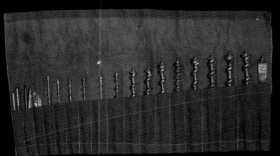

▶ Wooden bungs are hammered into bungholes to plug them up. To get them out you knock them loose with a mallet blow to the side.

▶ This beautiful old depth stop fits an auger bit.

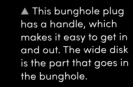

▲ This bunghole plug has a handle, which makes it easy to get in and out. The wide disk is the part that goes in the bunghole.

▼ This may look like an auger bit, but it's not. Notice there are no sharp cutting edges: this is a corkscrew for opening wine bottles.

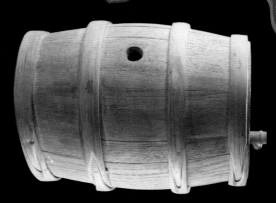

▲ In case you were wondering, this is a bunghole.

DRILL PRESSES

A DRILL PRESS IS the second stationary power tool the average home shop should have, after a sliding compound miter saw. Within the limits of the machine, the drill and clamping table can't move relative to each other, which allows for a lot more force to be applied, with a lot more precision, than with a hand-held power drill.

Forstner bits, for example, can only be used in a drill press because they exert a lot of sideways force at the start of the hole. While a hand-held drill just gets knocked off center, a drill press will keep the bit in line until it's into the hole and starts supporting itself. Drilling holes more than about ½ inch (12 mm) into thick steel is difficult with a hand-held drill, but easy with a drill press.

There are advantages to using a drill press even if you are holding the work by hand as opposed to clamping it to the table (which is common and safe if the drill bit isn't too big, or the drill press has a motor that isn't too strong). The hole will always be drilled exactly straight down, and you can clamp guides to the table to, for example, drill a series of holes exactly the same distance from the edge of a board. Just be very careful that the workpiece doesn't get away from you. That's likely to break the bit and/or your finger.

What about really large pieces that are too big to fit under a drill press, but require the force one can provide? There's a tool for that. . . .

▶ This solid old machine has a foot pedal that lets you keep both hands on the work as you lower the drill, doubling the chances of accidentally drilling through your hand.

▼ Rather than an exotic dual-spindle drill press, I keep two of these inexpensive desktop drill presses configured with jigs for making particular parts for the mechanical kits I sell. Saves a lot of time compared to setting up fresh each time.

◀ Old drill presses let you see, and stick your fingers in, all the moving parts. This one came from a school with the stipulation that it never again be switched on within half a mile of school grounds.

◀ This is a typical mid-grade home shop drill press. I've had it for decades and use it nearly every time I'm making anything out at my farm.

▶ Multi-spindle drill presses can save a lot of time changing bits, if you need to repeatedly use two different bits. In factories these can be found with dozens of spindles.

▶ This model maker's drill press is toy-sized, but very precise.

▲ This old post-mounted drill press can be operated by a belt drive or by manually spinning the large flywheel. An automatic ratchet mechanism slowly lowers the spindle as it's turning, so you don't need an extra hand for that.

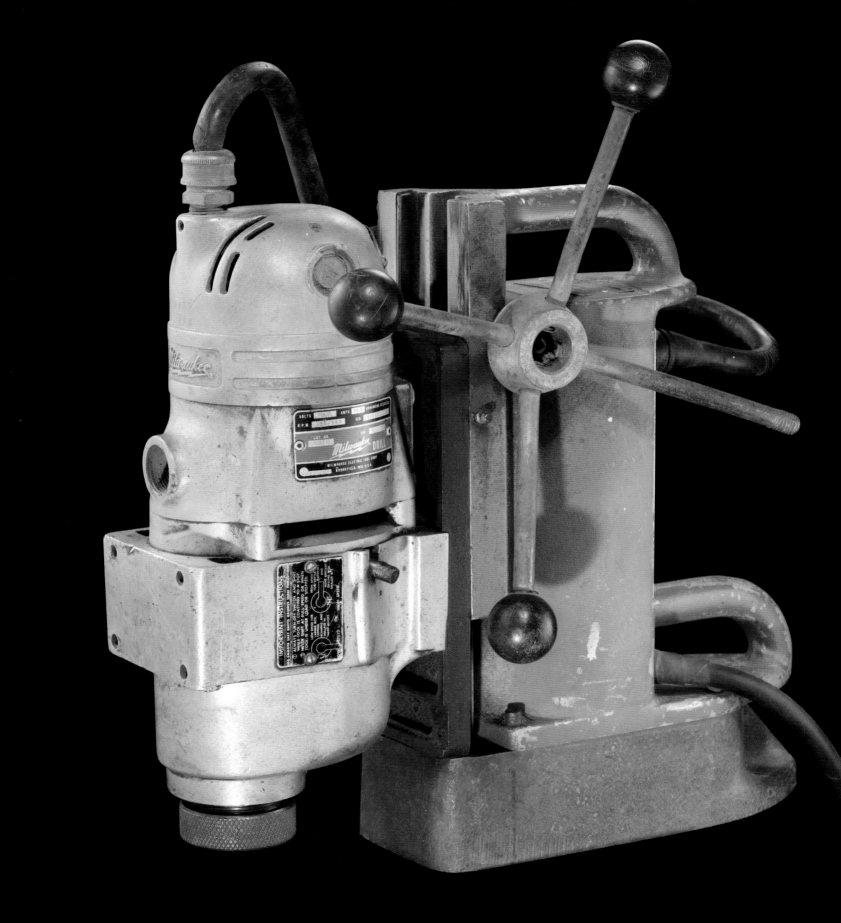

BIG DRILLS

THE BIG DRILLS on this page are so powerful that if the bit gets stuck, the drill will keep turning and there is not a single thing you can do about it until you have time to react, take your finger off the trigger, and wait for it to spin down. My favorite description is Neal Stephenson's: "the Hole Hawg rotated with the stupid consistency of a spinning planet."

Beam drills are a particular kind of big drill, a cross between a hand-held drill and a drill press. They are fastened to the thing they are drilling either magnetically, with bolts, or just by sitting on them. This forms a sort of in-situ drill press that can exert a lot more force than a hand-held drill.

The country version of a beam drill has a hand crank that turns a large auger bit, fastened to a platform that you sit on to hold it down on the face of a large wooden beam. Barns are the normal thing to build with this tool, but you might instead, just for example, build a scenic covered bridge, such as you can see in the 1995 movie *The Bridges of Madison County,* starring Clint Eastwood and Meryl Streep. I acquired such a drill in Parke County, Indiana, another place known for its covered bridges and annual covered bridge festival that has nothing to do with covered bridges. Until proven otherwise, I'm going to assume my drill was used to build one of those bridges.

◄ Not all monster drills are electric. This pneumatic beast requires a large-diameter, high-flow air hose and a huge air compressor. You twist the handle like the throttle on a motorcycle, one way or the other to make the drill run backward or reverse.

▼ Don't get me started on this thing. It's rusted to ruin and going to stay that way. Gasoline engines are *not* the way to power a drill! Don't get *me* started? Just try to get *this* thing started.

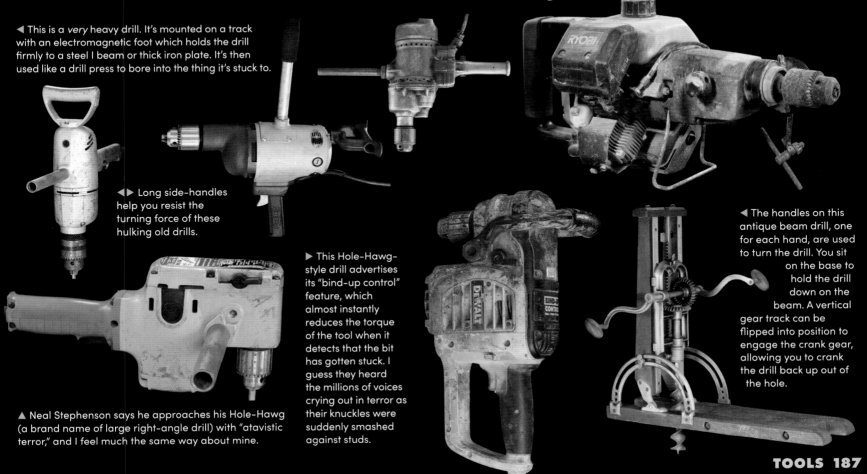

◄ This is a *very* heavy drill. It's mounted on a track with an electromagnetic foot which holds the drill firmly to a steel I beam or thick iron plate. It's then used like a drill press to bore into the thing it's stuck to.

◄► Long side-handles help you resist the turning force of these hulking old drills.

▲ Neal Stephenson says he approaches his Hole-Hawg (a brand name of large right-angle drill) with "atavistic terror," and I feel much the same way about mine.

► This Hole-Hawg-style drill advertises its "bind-up control" feature, which almost instantly reduces the torque of the tool when it detects that the bit has gotten stuck. I guess they heard the millions of voices crying out in terror as their knuckles were suddenly smashed against studs.

◄ The handles on this antique beam drill, one for each hand, are used to turn the drill. You sit on the base to hold the drill down on the beam. A vertical gear track can be flipped into position to engage the crank gear, allowing you to crank the drill back up out of the hole.

HAMMER DRILLS

THERE'S REALLY VERY little to recommend corded drills over the lovely cordless drill/drivers we met back on page 115, except in the most specialized circumstances; say in a factory where they will be used nonstop in one place. But it's a different story when it comes to the corded hammer drills featured on this page.

A lot of drills, corded and cordless, have a basic hammer feature, which is useful for drilling the occasional hole in concrete. But if you want to drill a lot of holes in stone or hard concrete, you will soon want the greater impact offered by a dedicated corded hammer drill, specialized in the gentle art of whacking stone hundreds of times per minute. In

fact, the larger ones are a good part of the way toward becoming jackhammers.

Dedicated hammer drills hold the bit loosely, allowing it to move (i.e., hammer) along its length without shaking the whole tool. This linear movement, not the rotation of the bit, does most of the drilling work. Special bit holders are required for this task, so these drills don't have a normal drill chuck and can't be used with ordinary drill bits.

A large hammer drill is actually less scary to use than a powerful regular drill, because it's unlikely to get ripped out of your hand by its own rotation. The bit does rotate, but not very fast, and masonry bits tend not to get stuck because they can't dig in and create a lot of torque.

► Oh boy, I remember this drill! Who could forget the color, even if the last time you used it was decades ago in high school?

◄ To the best of my knowledge, this is a hammer drill. I include it mainly because it's so weird-looking.

▼ The chuck on this larger hammer drill holds SDS-Max bits only. A lever adjustment gives the option for rotation with hammering or for hammering only, with no rotation.

◄ This hammer drill weighs almost as much as a small jackhammer. The chuck is specifically designed to allow the bit to move in and out as it's hammered.

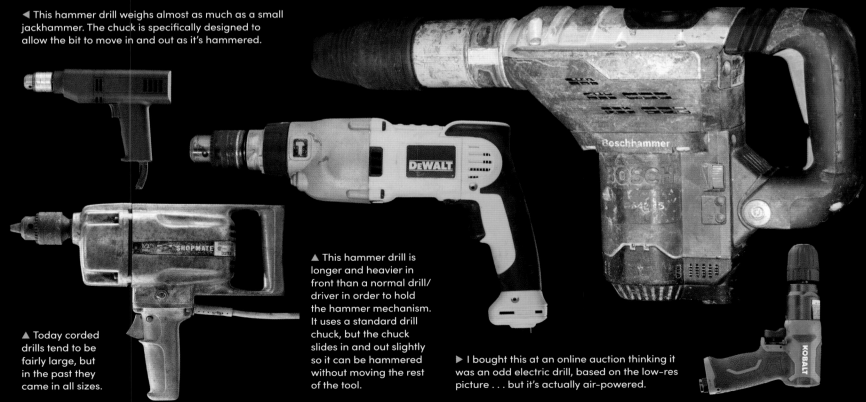

▲ Today corded drills tend to be fairly large, but in the past they came in all sizes.

▲ This hammer drill is longer and heavier in front than a normal drill/driver in order to hold the hammer mechanism. It uses a standard drill chuck, but the chuck slides in and out slightly so it can be hammered without moving the rest of the tool.

► I bought this at an online auction thinking it was an odd electric drill, based on the low-res picture . . . but it's actually air-powered.

TOY TOOLS

THE BEST MEASURE of what a culture values is how many toys there are of it. There are toy cars, toy stethoscopes, toy kitchens. And of course there are toy tools. Kids see their parents and others in their community spending the better part of their lives engaged with tools, and are naturally drawn to the subject.

The antique toy market is full of toy tools that are solid, but not always the safest things in the world. Surprisingly, even today you can get play sets intended for kids that have actual real tools able to cut wood, hammer thumbs, and otherwise injure their target market. I don't think this is a problem, in fact I see it more as a ray of sanity in an otherwise overly nerfed world.

Sure, an infant should probably be chewing on a plastic saw rather than a sharp steel one, and maybe chain saws are not the appropriate thing for six-year-olds to learn to juggle with. But kids can be careful and responsible when properly guided. When I was a kid, I mostly had real tools, used them extensively, and dreamed of the day when I could get more and better ones.

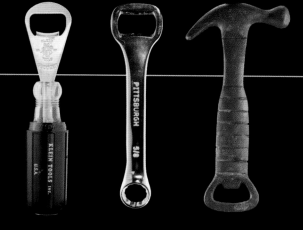

▲ Toy tools are not just for kids! Every major tool brand has a bottle opener done up in their trademark style.

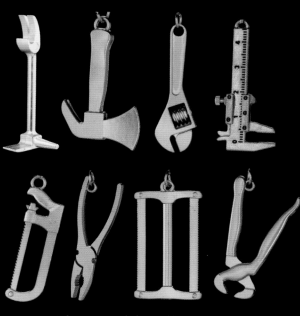

▲ So many tool-themed keychains!

◀ Chocolate tools! Is there really any need to continue the advancement of civilization beyond this point?

▼ Antique toy tools tended to be a bit more realistic than their modern plastic versions.

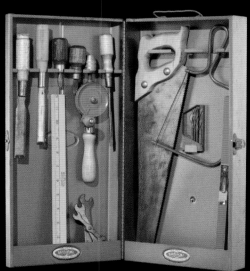

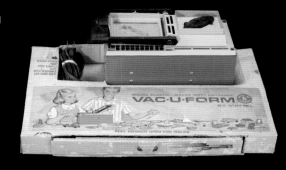

▲ I don't know how many kids dream of one day owning a vacuum forming machine, but I certainly would have, if I'd known what it was. (And now I have both the toy and the real thing.)

◀ This antique toy/ tool straddles the line. Safe enough for a reasonably coordinated young child, but not actually entirely safe.

▲ I like the idea behind these modern building sets: the tools are real, and you can use them to build something real.

▶ I suppose for infants these plastic tools are OK, but older kids should have tools that work.

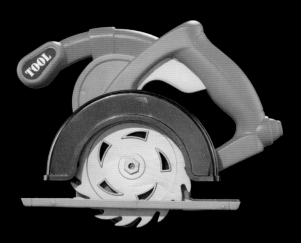

REPEATING DRIVERS

IN SOME TYPES of construction, for example building decks and fences or mounting drywall, nailing or screwing makes up the majority of the work. A nail gun can shoot nails as fast as you can pull the trigger, but rapidly installing screws requires more advanced technology.

As we've evolved from slotted screws to Phillips to square drive, and from manual screwdrivers to Yankee spiral drivers to electric screw guns, screws have slowly replaced nails in more and more situations. With the invention of automatic repeating screwdrivers, we've arrived at a point where screwing is almost as fast as nailing.

Lightweight impact drivers are another interesting development in recent years. Some say they work better than a drill/driver even for ordinary screwing jobs. These are not impact wrenches: they are nowhere near as strong. Instead, they are meant for driving ordinary screws by a combination of spinning in the ordinary way when the going is easy and hammering once resistance builds up. I have not used them much, so I can't say if this is as good an idea as some claim.

◀ The beauty of this repeating screwdriver cannot be overstated. I so very much wish I'd had one when I built all the decks and fences at my farm.

▲ If you can't justify buying a dedicated repeating screwdriver, this attachment will fit many standard drill/drivers.

▶ A battery-powered cordless automatic repeating screwdriver! I don't think I can take much more.

▲▶ Lightweight cordless impact drivers take standard screwdriver bits and work pretty much like an ordinary screw gun, until more force is needed to turn the screw, at which point they automatically start hammering.

RULERS

THE OLD SAYING "measure twice, cut once" puts measuring tools right at the center of the tool world. The most frequent measurement needed in the shop is length. Measuring length is so important that we're going to talk about it for the next fourteen sections, starting with rulers and rolling wheels.

If you want convenient, compatible measurements between projects, you need a standard unit of length, and you need rulers marked off in multiples and fractions of this standard. The oldest known standard of length, the Egyptian Royal Cubit, is divided into seven "palms," each palm divided into four "fingers," and each finger is divided into halves, thirds, fourths, fifths, etc., all the way up to sixteenths. The Imperial (English) system, based on yards, feet, inches, and fractions of inches, is nearly as confusing and inconvenient. Fortunately, nearly all rulers today are based on the metric system with its lovely multiples of ten all the way up and down the scale (except in Liberia, Myanmar, and, oh, that's right, the United States).

Rulers are good for short distances, but for longer distances you need measuring chains or tapes, which were not perfected until the 1700s. Before then, people used a clever alternative that's still used today: measuring wheels. My favorite thing about measuring wheels is that they are responsible for some people believing the great pyramids of Egypt were built by aliens.

You see, if you make a measuring wheel of a certain diameter, say one cubit, then roll it out a whole number of revolutions across a field, you will get a distance that is a multiple of π (3.141592 . . .) cubits, whether or not you know how to compute the value of π, or even what π means (which the ancients did not, until Archimedes worked it out around 250 BC, long after the pyramids were built).

So if you find a large ancient structure that has ratios of π in its major dimensions, there are two possibilities: either an advanced alien civilization helped build it, or some locals used a measuring wheel.

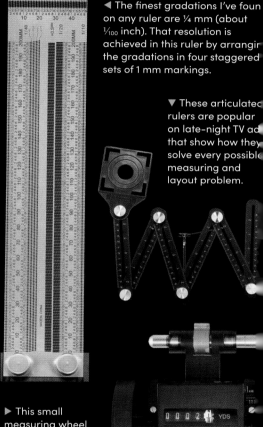

▲ The Egyptian Royal Cubit was 20¾ inches (526 mm) long. We know this because several wooden cubit rods have survived, and all are quite close in length.

◄ The finest gradations I've found on any ruler are ¼ mm (about ¹⁄₁₀₀ inch). That resolution is achieved in this ruler by arranging the gradations in four staggered sets of 1 mm markings.

▼ These articulated rulers are popular on late-night TV ads that show how they solve every possible measuring and layout problem.

Before tape measures there were folding rulers, and some people still prefer them. They are useful when you need to reach and poke to get the measurement, for example measuring to the bottom of a hole in the ground.

The shortest ruler I own is a 40 mm dentist's finger ring ruler. The longest is a 6-foot (1.8 m) carpenter's ruler. I've got rulers made of plastic, wood, steel, and aluminum, varying from quite expensive to free with an advertising message.

◄ Dentist's ruler at half actual size and to scale at left.

◄ I made a map of my entire farm property using just this measuring wheel.

► This small measuring wheel is used to measure cloth for the quilts my company makes.

◄ Before the internet we used miniature wheels to measure distances on maps.

2D RULERS

THE COORDINATOGRAPH (Koordinatograf in German) pictured below is a remarkable tool, like an iron giant from another age. It is a model 4416 made by the Hamburg-based Aristo-Werke of Dennert & Pape KG, founded in 1862. It is essentially a 2D ruler system able to position a marking pin to within an absolute accuracy of 0.1 mm (0.004 inch) anywhere within its 40 by 26-inch (1,000 x 650 mm) working area.

The historic factory building where it was made burned to the ground on the night of December 8, 2020. Although it's likely others exist, I like to think that maybe, just maybe, it is the last of its kind, an orphan to time and technology. If so, it is remarkable not only for its rarity but for its essentially perfect condition when it fell into my hands at an auction in Hendersonville, North Carolina. It may well never have been used. The previous owner was drag racing star Tom Hanna,

and if he ever used the device, it would have been to mark locations on pieces of sheet metal destined to become curved body panels, or perhaps to measure the locations of bolt holes on blueprints. This beautiful instrument is deeply obsolete: pen plotters, laser cutters, scanners, and digitizing tables can all do its various jobs far more conveniently.

The coordinatograph measures position within an area, but what if you want to measure area itself, as in how many square inches or cm² are enclosed by a given shape? Area is a two-dimensional property, yet mechanical planimeters measure it with only one rolling wheel. It seems self-evident that to measure a two-dimensional quantity you would need two wheels, one in each direction, but unfortunately for my intuition of the possible, the math checks out, and you can find YouTube videos that explain how these things work.

▲ It's common for precision instruments to come in fitted wooden boxes, and this one is no exception. But the coordinatograph box is *huge*, about 5 feet (1.5 m) wide and too heavy for me to lift. Every part has a carefully made, custom-shaped block or clamp to hold it in place, as in a fine violin case. Inside the big wooden box is a smaller box that holds individual vernier-scale heads, needle points, and some tiny, unopened bottles of neat's-foot oil. Even this mini-box is bigger than the box for any other precision instrument I own.

▼ This planimeter, with only one rolling wheel, measures area on maps simply by tracing the area with the pointer while the base remains stationary. How? I literally cannot explain it. Math and witchcraft, I suppose.

◀ Unlike the mechanical version to the right, digital planimeters make perfect sense. The pointer is moved around the perimeter of an area on a map or blueprint, multiple sensors measure the movement, and a computer does the math to calculate the area.

▶ This coordinatograph is by far the largest, rarest, most beautiful, and most useless precision instrument I own.

▼ A creep gauge doesn't tell you how much of a creep you are; instead it tells you if a crack in your foundation wall is getting worse. The half with a printed grid is screwed to the wall on one side of the crack, and the half with crosshairs is screwed to the other side. If the position of the crosshairs changes over time, you need to worry.

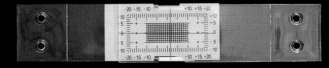

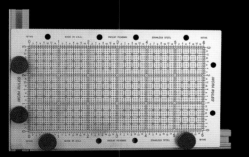

▲ Common T squares and uncommon grid rulers measure two directions at once.

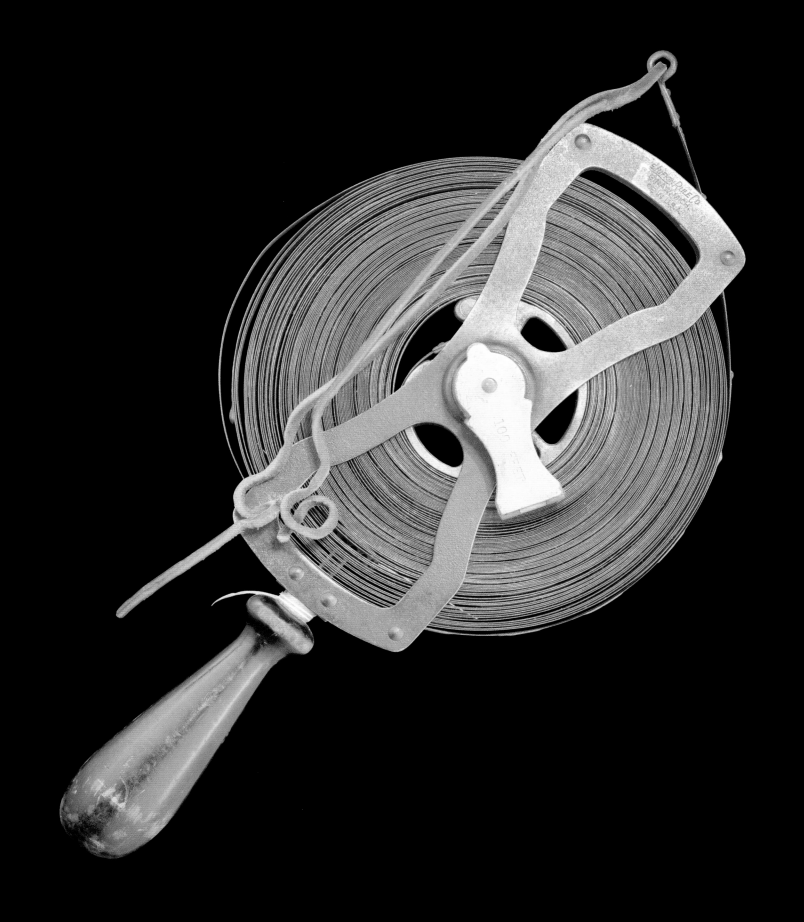

TAPE MEASURES

PRIOR TO THE INVENTION of steel measuring tapes, the most accurate way of measuring medium distances was with tremendously inconvenient iron measuring chains. Flat steel tapes were revolutionary, but the real revolution came in 1922 with the invention of the automatic retracting, convex-concave pocket tape measure, surely one of the most useful inventions of all time. A pocket tape that literally fits in an average pocket can measure distances up to 30 feet (10 m) quickly and easily within $\frac{1}{32}$ inch (less than 1 mm). Slightly larger versions go up to 300 feet (100 m), far longer than any practical chain.

Among the multiple clever features in a modern tape measure is the clip on the end. It always feels like it's loose, but this is not a flaw, it's a feature! The amount by which the clip can slide is equal to the thickness of the bent-over tab of the clip. That way you can push the end up against a wall, or pull it against the end of a board, and either way the measurement will start in the right place.

Steel is the superior material for tape measures because it's nearly impossible to stretch, but fiberglass is lighter, softer, and more durable. I have a 300-foot (91 m) fiberglass tape that I can stretch several inches over its whole length by pulling moderately hard, but that's fine, I don't expect it to be accurate beyond an inch or two. For nonlinear or curved measurements, like measuring on the body for tailoring, fiberglass or even cloth tapes are much preferred for their softness.

◀▶ The distance marks on this beautiful old 100-foot (30 m) steel tape are individual bits of engraved metal soldered onto the sturdy tape! It must have taken forever to make.

▶ This is a modern reproduction of a Gunter's chain similar to those used in the 1700s. The only measurement it can make is the full length between two marks at opposite ends of the chain. I have no idea why someone is making modern Gunter's chains, but I appreciate the effort.

◀ The mark in the window shows the measurement starting from the back of the case.

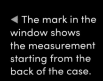

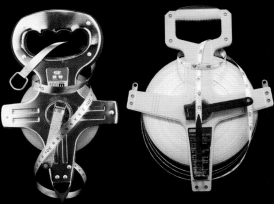
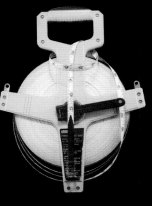

▲ Both these tapes are about the same length (300 feet / 100 m respectively). The stainless steel one at left is smaller and stiffer, but the tape is easy to kink and kind of sharp along the edges.

▶ These specialized tape measures are used progressively farther out along a human arm, starting with the upper arm (for fitness), wrist (for sizing bracelets), and finger (for fitting rings).

▲ Possibly the most useful measuring tool ever invented, the common pocket tape measure.

▲ A laser rangefinder is a good tool for medium distances: up to 130 feet (40 m) for this one but much farther for fancy models.

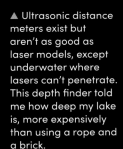

▲ Ultrasonic distance meters exist but aren't as good as laser models, except underwater where lasers can't penetrate. This depth finder told me how deep my lake is, more expensively than using a rope and a brick.

PROTRACTORS

CIRCLES ARE DIVIDED into 360 degrees, thanks to the Babylonians, who thought there were 360 days in a year (they were wrong, there are 365.26). Each degree is split into 60 "minutes" and each minute into 60 "seconds," just as hours are divided into minutes and seconds.

Angles are usually measured with a protractor, which is just a half circle with marks typically every one degree. How big is a degree? Pretty small. I like to visualize it by how far a long rod moves when it's rotated by a degree. For example, if you have a rod a mile (1.6 km) long, and you rotate it by one degree, the far end will move by 46 feet (14 m), which really isn't very much when you consider how long the rod is.

A good machinist's protractor like the one on the left can measure angles to within one or two minutes of arc: one minute is just about 9 inches (230 mm) at the end of the 1-mile rod. High-grade indexing heads can be accurate to one second of arc, or about ⅛ inch (4 mm) at the end of the rod. There are even some remarkable indexing heads that are accurate to ¹⁄₁₀ of an arc-second, or ¹⁄₆₄ inch (0.4 mm) a mile out. (Fun fact: the optical resolution of the Hubble Space Telescope is only a bit higher at one-twentieth of an arc-second.)

Protractors are not the only way of measuring very small angles: you can also do it with the bubbles on the next page.

▲ This upscale school-style protractor is made of brass, with marks every one degree.

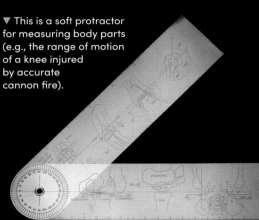

▼ This is a soft protractor for measuring body parts (e.g., the range of motion of a knee injured by accurate cannon fire).

School protractors have one mark on their scale for each degree. This one has a vernier scale that lets you read the angle to within one-thirtieth of a degree (2 minutes of arc). Straight and right-angle extensions move into a range of positions for measuring or marking inside and outside angles.

◄ This reproduction cannon inclinometer is meant to be fastened to the side of a cannon barrel to help aim it at the correct angle. The pointer hangs down, so you can measure angles relative to vertical.

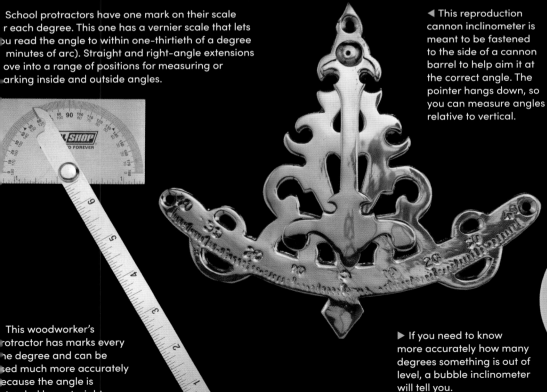

This woodworker's protractor has marks every one degree and can be used much more accurately because the angle is extended by a straight edge for easy marking.

▲ Some angles are more equal than others. This jig lets you set a miter saw accurately to common angles needed for boxes with three-, four-, five-, six-, eight-, and twelve-sided frames.

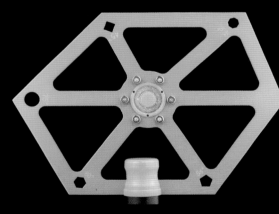

▶ If you need to know more accurately how many degrees something is out of level, a bubble inclinometer will tell you.

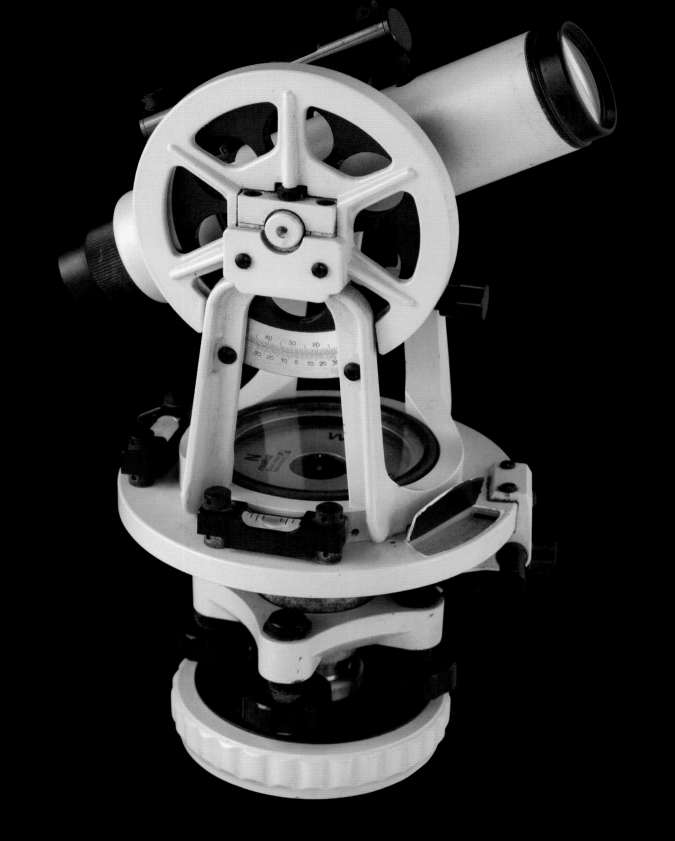

LEVELS

IT'S NOT HARD to check whether a level is accurate, and you don't need a known level surface to do it. Put the level down on any *reasonably* level surface and look at the bubble. It may be exactly centered or slightly off—just remember where it is. Rotate the level end to end and look at the bubble again. If it was slightly to the left before, it should be slightly to the left again. Alternately, use a wedge on one side of the level to get it to read perfectly flat, then rotate it and see if it still reads perfectly flat. In my experience, it rarely will.

Cheap levels usually don't include any way to calibrate them (which you could trivially do by slightly rotating the vial within its housing). Better levels specify how accurate they are and have adjustment

screws so you can calibrate them.

A machinist's level like the one below is pretty useless for common tasks like leveling picture frames or floors; it's simply *too* sensitive. But it's great for aligning large machine frames. For example, our quilting machine has two rails each 12 feet (3.6 m) long and 12 feet apart. They need to be very accurately parallel to each other, or the beam riding between them will twist as it moves. Measuring diagonals tells you they are square to each other, but not whether they are twisted out of parallel. This is extremely difficult to measure, but I could use the level below to get both rails almost perfectly level, which necessarily means they are also parallel to each other.

▲ The fanciest form of sight level is called a theodolite. This chunky Italian model has etched glass scales readable to less than one minute of arc, illuminated by a mirror that reflects sunlight into the body of the instrument. My modern digital theodolite, too ugly to picture here, is readable to one second of arc, but isn't actually that accurate.

◀ A transit combines an accurate bubble level with a telescope and two protractor scales, allowing you to measure both vertical and horizonal angles at the same time. The theodolite shown to the right does exactly the same thing but with a more accurate design that doesn't look as cool from the outside.

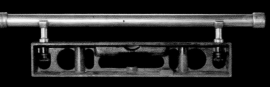

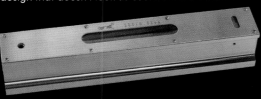

▲ A simple sight level has a telescope with crosshairs exactly in line with an accurate level, for finding level as far as the eye can see.

◀ A fancy form of sight level called an automatic level has a pendulum mechanism inside which ensures that the crosshairs in the telescope are always showing you exact level.

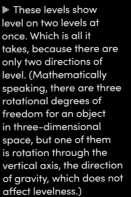

▶ These levels show level on two levels at once. Which is all it takes, because there are only two directions of level. (Mathematically speaking, there are three rotational degrees of freedom for an object in three-dimensional space, but one of them is rotation through the vertical axis, the direction of gravity, which does not affect levelness.)

▲ This machinist's level promises an accuracy of 0.02 mm/m, or 0.00002 inches/inch. That's about eight seconds of arc or about 1 ¼ inches (32 mm) at the end of a 1-mile (1.6 km) rod. It's hard to get the bubble centered in a level this sensitive!

▲ Carpenter's levels are typically about 4 feet (1.2 m) long.

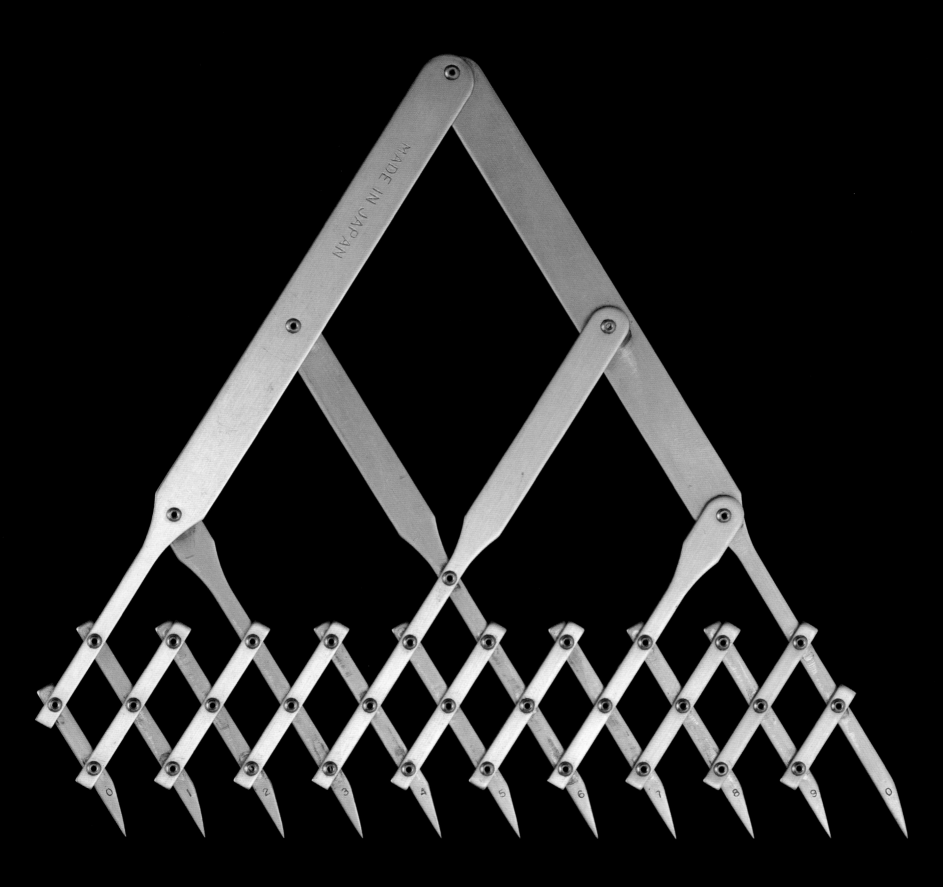

CALIPERS

THE CALIPERS HERE are used to measure dimensions without actually assigning a number to the measurement. Instead of using a ruler to determine that a board is, say, 37 mm wide, you set a caliper around it and determine that it is, well, as wide as the calipers are set to, whatever that is. How is this useful? Well, perhaps you just want to mark the width on another board so you can cut a matching slot. It doesn't matter what the dimensions are, just that they are the same.

Alternately, you could set the caliper around the board, remove it, and then hold a ruler against the jaws of the caliper to measure the dimension indirectly. This can be useful if the edge of the board is irregular so you can't get an accurate reading with the ruler directly against it. It's also useful for measuring the diameter of rods, which can't be done directly with a ruler.

Equal-spacing calipers extend the no-numbers-needed feature to splitting up a dimension evenly into a given number of divisions. For example, six buttons down the front of a shirt: the exact spacing will be different depending on the size of the shirt, but it's always six evenly spaced positions.

The clever clockmaking calipers on this page let you adjust the spacing between two gears until it's perfect, allowing them to spin smoothly without backlash. Then you can transfer the spacing to a brass plate using the two built-in center punches, without ever knowing the numerical measurement.

If you *do* need to assign a number to your caliper measurement, the tools on the next page will handle that for you.

▶ These large old calipers can be used to measure around something, or inverted to measure an inside dimension, maybe the diameter inside a pipe or the width of a slot.

◀ This magnificent equal spacing divider ensures perfectly even spacing of its eleven points by supporting most of them all the way back to a common origin. It is smooth and very satisfying to open and close.

▶ Calipers come with straight points for measurements on a surface, points angled in for outside measurements, and points angled out for inside measurements.

▲ This is an iris mechanism, like the ones found inside camera lenses, but sold as a variable circle drawing or measuring template. The leaf vanes open and close when you rotate the outer rim.

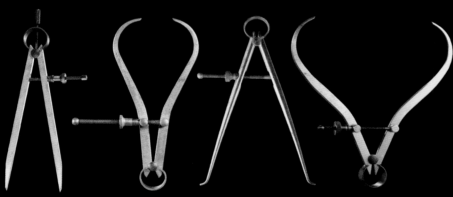

◀ The ancient Greeks decided that the "Golden Ratio," about 1.618 to 1, was the most beautiful mathematical relationship. For example, the Parthenon's width and height have this ratio to each other. Elegant Golden Ratio calipers automatically create the Golden Ratio between their pairs of jaws. They are advertised mainly to help you achieve the perfection of ancient Greek architecture on your face with makeup and eyebrow trimming.

◀ This specialized caliper measures clock gears and automatically marks their ideal separation on a plate, without ever determining the numerical value of that separation.

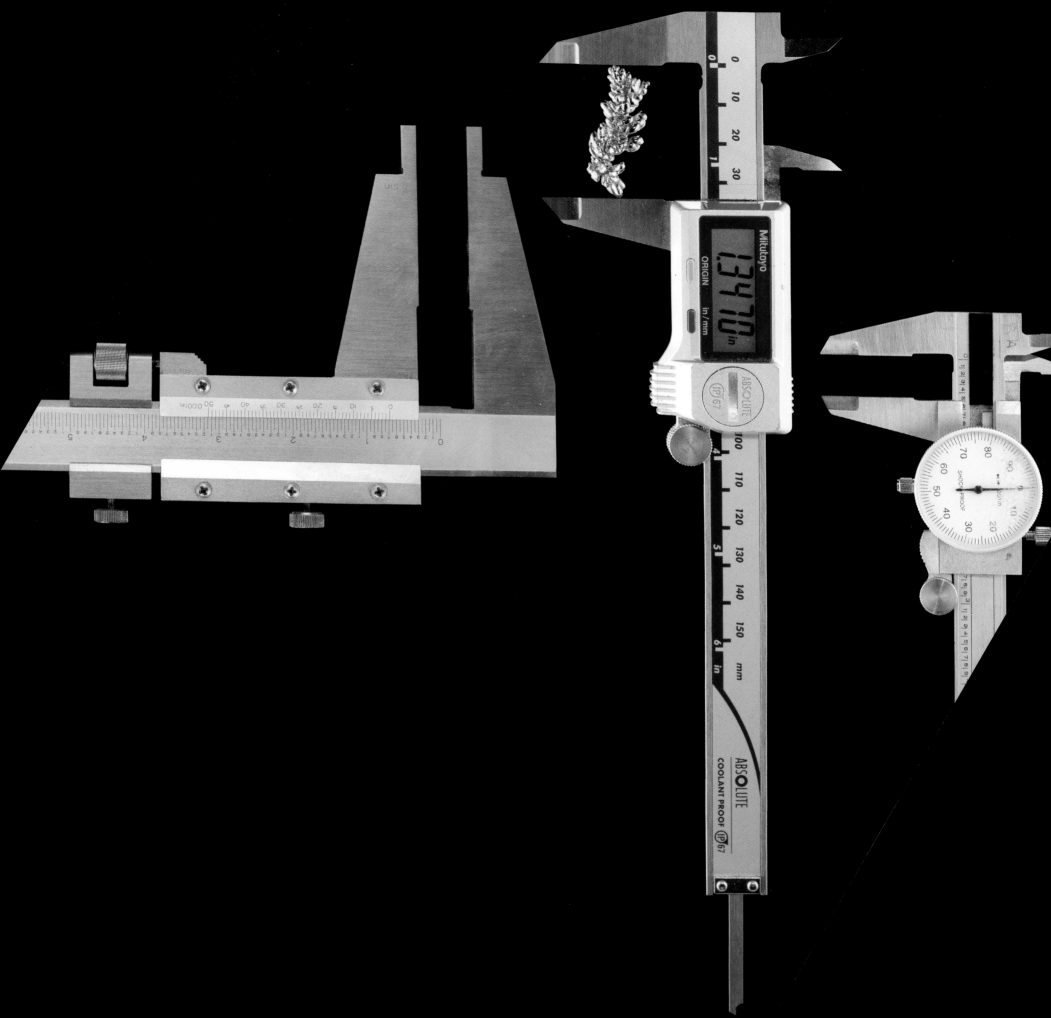

MEASURING CALIPERS

PRECISION BEYOND the level of rulers is the domain of calipers and micrometers. As we will see, these tools can achieve astonishing levels of precision. The first step is a measuring caliper. In large machine shops you can find them up to several feet (over a meter) long, though usually they are 6 inches (150 mm), with one jaw fixed to the end of a scale and another that slides along the scale. They typically measure to within $\frac{1}{1,000}$ inch (0.025 mm).

General-purpose calipers are designed so the same instrument can measure four common situations: outside dimensions (length or thickness of a piece of material), inside dimensions (width of a slot or diameter of a hole), depth of a hole, and step (offset from one level to the next). This multifunction design must naturally make compromises all over the place. There are plenty of other tools that do one thing at a time, but do it better.

Beyond these, there are a tremendous number of special-purpose calipers, a few of which you'll see here before we move on to a particularly useful variation on the next page.

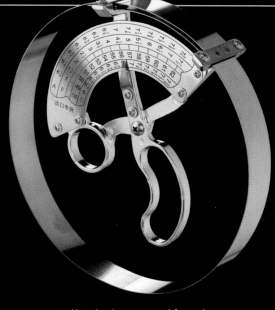

▲ Hat size is measured from the inside with these scissor calipers.

◀ Vernier calipers use a vernier scale, located on the sliding jaw, to reliably read their position to ⅟₅₀ of one division on the main scale. Dial calipers are much easier to read, but more delicate and more expensive. Digital calipers are dirt cheap, can read in metric or imperial measurements, can be zeroed at any position to do relative measurements, and don't work when the battery, which you don't have a spare of, is dead.

▼ Hinged calipers are generally less accurate than sliding ones, but they can come close. This one is accurate to ⅟₁₀₀₀ inch (0.025 mm).

◀ Deep jaw calipers are great for reaching into tight spots, but introduce potentially large errors if the slide is not set perfectly, allowing the jaws to flex out of parallel.

▼ These calipers magnify the dimension for easy reading. They are designed for measuring wood being worked down to a target thickness.

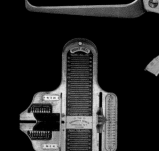

▲ Gauges for fitting shoes are a kind of everyday caliper.

▶ The "pelvimeter" is a sort of quack medical device for measuring pregnant stomachs.

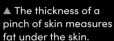

▲ The thickness of a pinch of skin measures fat under the skin.

▶ Dental calipers measure old teeth to fit replacements.

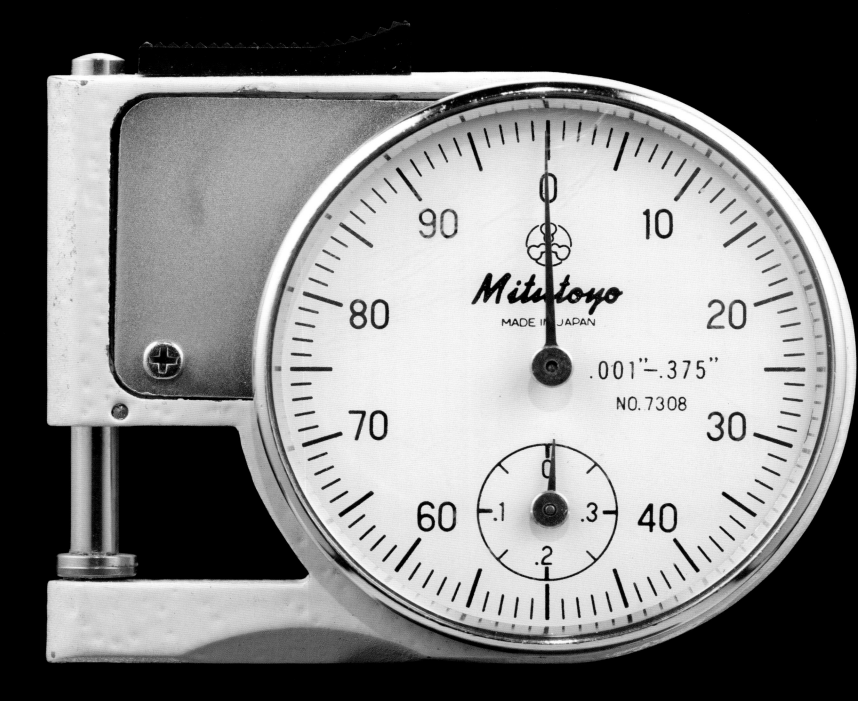

THICKNESS GAUGES

THICKNESS GAUGES are sort of a midway measuring tool between calipers and micrometers, which we'll cover a little bit later on. Their intended purpose is measuring the thickness of sheet material. Their accuracy comes from the fact that, unlike measuring calipers, the measuring mechanism is directly in line with the jaws. There is no hinged pivot point or long lever arm to flex, just a straight rod, which is an inherently more accurate design.

Some thickness gauges have a spring that keeps the jaws open when not in use. The jaws are pressed together against the resistance of the spring to achieve the measurement. Others are the opposite: a spring keeps the jaws closed and you use a lever to open them and take the measurement. The latter design is more accurate, because it ensures that every measurement, including when the device is being calibrated with known reference blocks, is made with the same amount of measuring pressure.

There are some special-purpose thickness gauges that work without moving parts. Eddy current gauges have a coil of fine wire in the nose, which is fed a high-frequency alternating current. If the gauge is very close to a piece of sheet metal, for example separated only by the thickness of a layer of paint, the alternating current creates a matching eddy current in the metal underneath, which can be measured by the instrument and translated into a measurement of the thickness of the paint.

▶ This thickness gauge is sturdy and well made, despite being quite inexpensive.

◀ I got this fine old thickness gauge at an antiques store. It claims to be accurate to ⅟₁₀₀₀ inch (0.025 mm), and I've confirmed that it is, despite most likely not having been calibrated for decades. It has a spring that closes, rather than opens, the jaws, contributing to its accuracy.

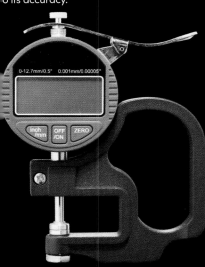

▲ This digital model can be read to ⅟₁₀₀₀ mm, or 0.00005 inches.

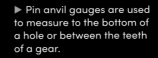

▶ Pin anvil gauges are used to measure to the bottom of a hole or between the teeth of a gear.

◀ This eddy current thickness gauge works only after it's been calibrated for a given type of paint and sheet metal backing. But once calibrated, it's fast and works without moving parts.

▼ This automotive paint thickness gauge is simply a magnet mounted on a spring: you stick it to the car, then see how far you can pull the rod out before the magnet lets loose. Not very accurate, but certainly able to tell if an area has been patched over with putty or fiberglass.

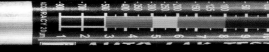

DIAL INDICATORS

DIAL INDICATORS, and their digital relatives (which are also called dial indicators even though they don't have a dial), are like thickness gauges without the other jaw to establish the zero point of the scale. As such, dial indicators don't give absolute measurements, only *relative* ones: Is this block thicker or thinner than this other block, and by how much? How much material was machined off on the last pass? How much is the surface of this bar moving when it turns in the lathe?

A dial indicator can be mounted above a flat base to turn it into something like a thickness gauge, but often it's more useful mounted at a strange angle pointing at some part of a machine or workpiece, measuring relative movements of the thing it's in contact with. For that use, magnetic mounts clamp themselves to some nearby part of the machine while an adjustable arm brings the indicator where it needs to be.

The hardest part of making a good mechanical dial indicator is eliminating backlash. In theory the dial should always read exactly the same value when the rod is at the same position, but in practice it always depends at least a tiny bit on the direction from which the rod arrived at that position: Was it being pushed in or moved out when it got to the position? Backlash is caused by friction and play (looseness) in the gears, which can be minimized but never completely eliminated. Digital dial indicators don't have gears and thus have much lower backlash.

▲ Mounting a dial indicator above a cast-iron or granite base turns it into an uncalibrated thickness gauge.

◀ This reasonably good dial indicator has divisions of ¹⁄₁,₀₀₀ mm (about ¹⁄₂₀,₀₀₀ inch). The big pointer makes one full revolution per 0.1 mm, while the small pointer goes around once per 5 mm. Over its 5-mm (about ¼-inch) range, the main pointer turns fifty times! Which means that when you push the rod in, the pointer spins *fast!*

▶ Magnetic mounts are a flexible way to mount an indicator.

◀ Digital indicators make it easy to read a specific number from their display, when the reading is stable. But dial indicators are often used in situations where the reading is continuously changing, for example when the probe tip is up against a rotating workpiece in a lathe. Then a mechanical pointer is better because reading fast-changing digits is nearly impossible.

▶ Not all dial indicators measure in-line. This one measures the sideways deflection of a pointer.

▶ This indicator measures deflection in two directions, left-right and front-back, which makes its name, 3D indicator, a lie. (Recognizing this, it's also commonly called a coaxial indicator.)

▲ This special-purpose indicator measures the position of a cutting tool descending from above in the spindle of a milling machine.

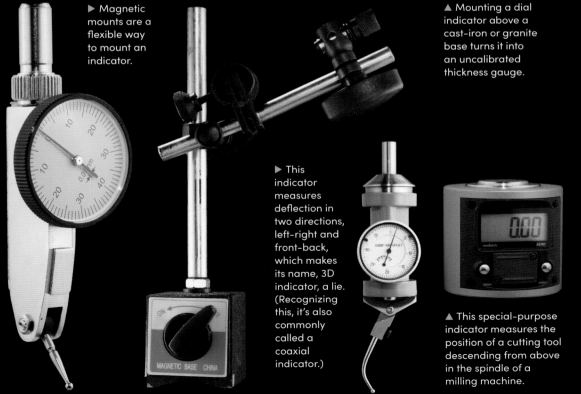

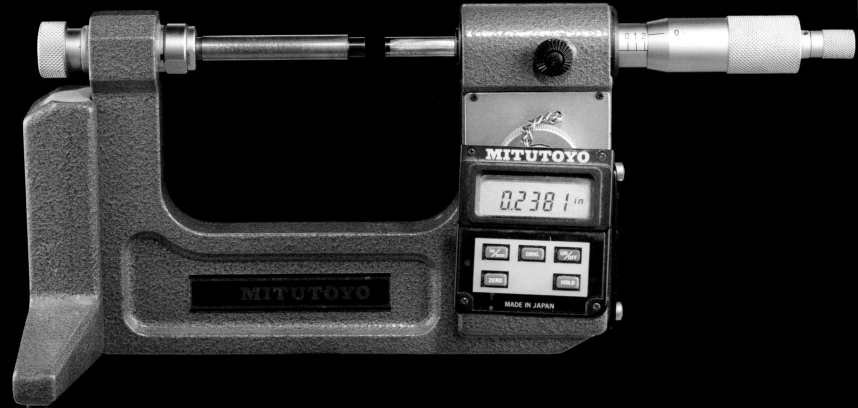

MICROMETERS

AT LAST, WE HAVE arrived at micrometers, the most accurate measuring tools commonly found outside of national standards laboratories. Unlike calipers and thickness gauges, which have freely sliding jaws, micrometers have a fine-pitch screw that turns to open and close them. This takes much longer than just sliding the jaws of a caliper—a typical micrometer has to be turned forty times to move 1 inch, or twenty turns to move 1 centimeter—but in exchange for this added labor, it offers an accuracy of at least $\frac{1}{10,000}$ inch or $\frac{1}{1,000}$ mm, about ten times more accurate than typical calipers.

An accurate measuring mechanism is useless if it isn't mounted in a frame that can hold a fixed separation with at least the same degree of accuracy.

Micrometers typically have a wide, thick C-frame, not because they need it for strength, but because they need it for stiffness. Even though only very slight pressure is exerted between the two ends, a thinner frame could flex enough to throw off the measurement.

Digital micrometers have the same precision screw as regular micrometers, and the same capacitive position-measuring mechanism as digital calipers. But the electronics are used to measure the rotational position of the screw, not the actual opening width as they do in a caliper. Since the opening moves by only $\frac{1}{40}$ inch, or ½ mm, per full turn of the screw, the electronics can read out the opening to much higher resolution.

This page features "normal" micrometers. It gets weirder from here.

▲ Digital micrometers are fine too.

▶ Micrometers never have screws over 1 inch (25 mm) long, but unmounted micrometer *heads* are available in longer sizes.

◀ Bench-mounted micrometers can have much thicker, stiffer frames than hand-held models, because weight is not a problem. The anvil on this one can be adjusted to give it a wider-than-normal measuring range, but the screw still only moves by 1 inch (25 mm).

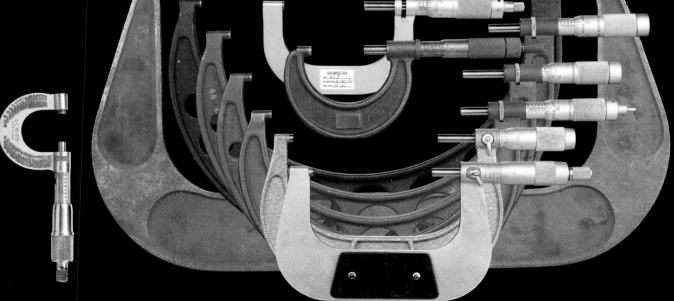

◀ It's nearly unheard-of for a micrometer screw to have an adjustment range longer than 1 inch (25 mm), so you need to have a separate micrometer for each 1-inch measuring range. Usually they come in a matched set stored in a nice box, but I'm taking the opportunity to also show you many different styles. And I don't have a matched set.

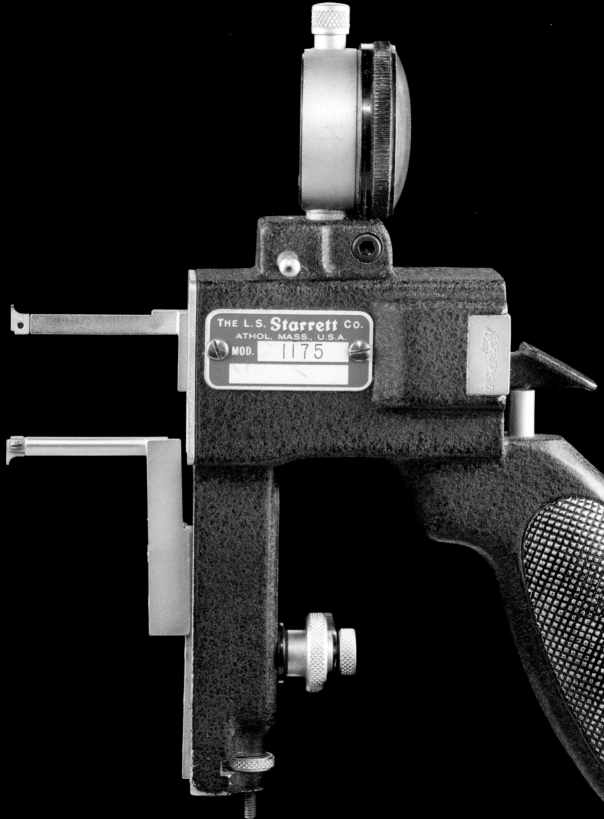

SPECIAL MICROMETERS

NUMEROUS SPECIAL micrometers have evolved to measure in a wide variety of situations, including oddly shaped holes and difficult-to-reach spaces.

Measuring small inside dimensions is particularly difficult, because for maximum accuracy the instrument needs to fit entirely between the surfaces being measured (e.g., inside the hole if you're measuring a hole). That avoids the error introduced by jaws reaching out sideways, as in a caliper, which can always flex or twist out of line. But of course there's a limit to how small a micrometer can be, which leads to all sorts of attempted solutions, none of them ideal but each of which is the best that can reasonably be expected for a particular circumstance.

▶ This bore gauge has an internal lever that translates the width of a slot or the diameter of a hole into movement of a rod in its handle, which is measured by the dial indicator at the top. It must be carefully calibrated before it can achieve any degree of accuracy.

◀ This is by far the most expensive micrometer I have (it's actually more of a caliper than a micrometer, but it's so accurate, and so expensive, that I give it honorary micrometer status). It's used to reach down into a hole to measure the depth of a groove cut inside the hole. A lever moves the jaws close together so they can be squeezed into the hole. Releasing the lever then expands the jaws inside the groove, and a spring provides a consistent measuring pressure. The dial has graduations spaced at ½₀₀₀ inch (0.01 mm).

▶ These are passive bore gauges. They expand with a spring to fill the space between two surfaces, then lock in place with a twist of the handle. After removing them from the hole or slot, you measure the faces of the gauge with a normal micrometer.

▼ Inside micrometers with their measuring faces in line with their screw do exist, but are limited to fairly large inside dimensions because the whole instrument has to fit between the surfaces being measured. This model lets you measure inside diameters down to 1½ inches (38 mm), or up to 8 inches (200 mm) with extension rods.

SPECIAL MICROMETERS

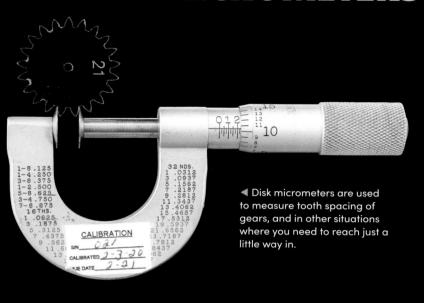

◄ Disk micrometers are used to measure tooth spacing of gears, and in other situations where you need to reach just a little way in.

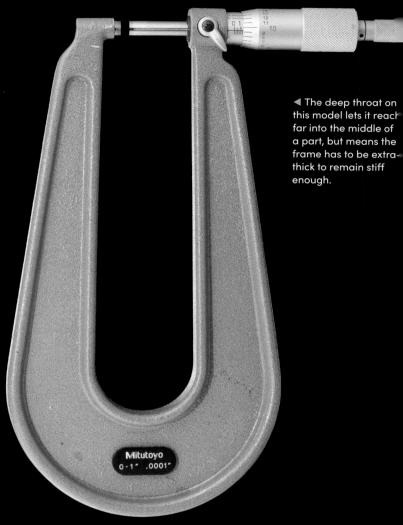

◄ The deep throat on this model lets it reach far into the middle of a part, but means the frame has to be extra-thick to remain stiff enough.

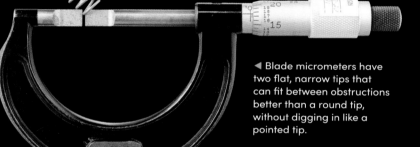

◄ Blade micrometers have two flat, narrow tips that can fit between obstructions better than a round tip, without digging in like a pointed tip.

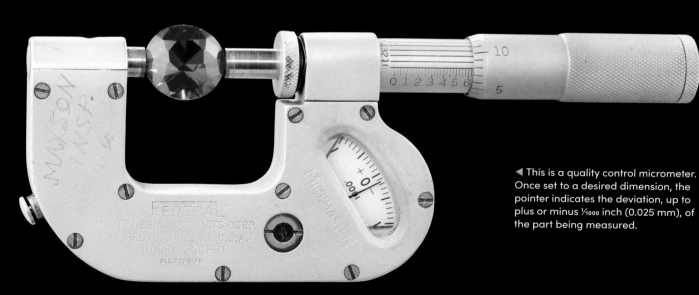

◄ This is a quality control micrometer. Once set to a desired dimension, the pointer indicates the deviation, up to plus or minus $\frac{1}{1000}$ inch (0.025 mm), of the part being measured.

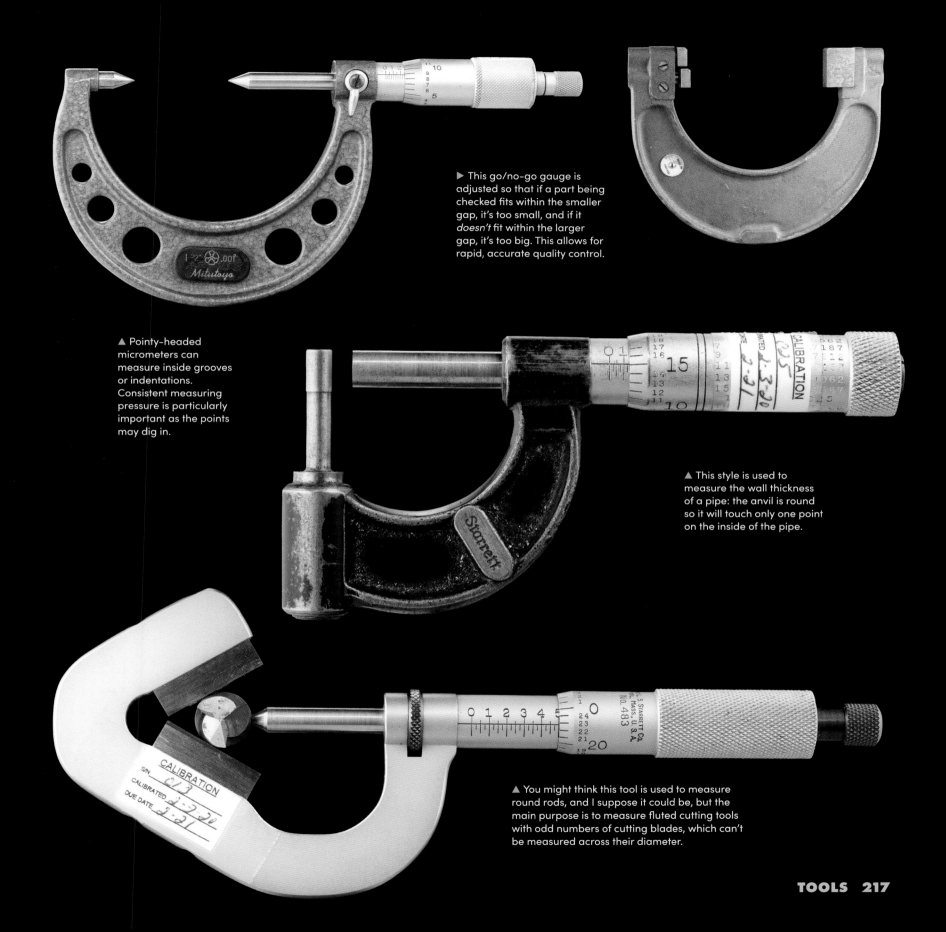

▶ This go/no-go gauge is adjusted so that if a part being checked fits within the smaller gap, it's too small, and if it *doesn't* fit within the larger gap, it's too big. This allows for rapid, accurate quality control.

▲ Pointy-headed micrometers can measure inside grooves or indentations. Consistent measuring pressure is particularly important as the points may dig in.

▲ This style is used to measure the wall thickness of a pipe: the anvil is round so it will touch only one point on the inside of the pipe.

▲ You might think this tool is used to measure round rods, and I suppose it could be, but the main purpose is to measure fluted cutting tools with odd numbers of cutting blades, which can't be measured across their diameter.

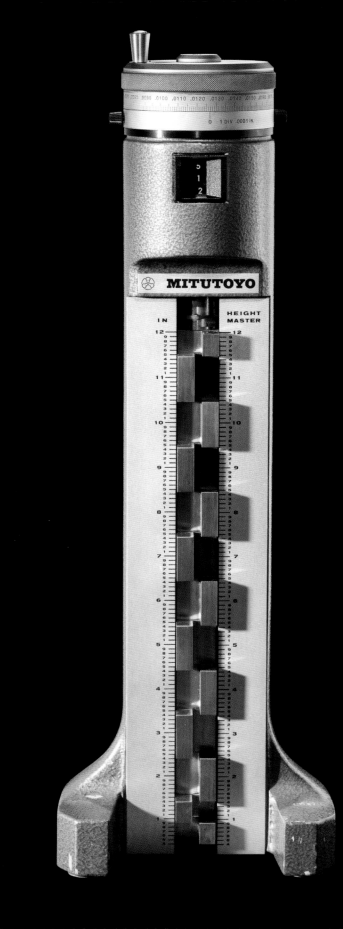

HEIGHT GAUGES

HEIGHT GAUGES are basically a variation on calipers where the fixed jaw is replaced with a foot meant to stand on a flat surface, such as a milling machine table or precision granite flat (see next page).

Depth gauges also sit on a flat surface, but they have a rod that protrudes *through* their foot, reaching down into a hole or slot below the surface. Depth gauges differ from height gauges, micrometers, and dial indicators in one interesting way: inexpensive, inaccurate versions are widely available. That's because there is a unique market segment that needs cheap depth gauges, and lots of them.

As anyone trying to sell you tires will tell you, it's not safe to drive a car whose tires have worn down to the point that there is little or no depth left to the grooves in the tread. You can tell if your tire tread is dangerously low just by looking at the tires, but to *sell* you new tires, it's helpful to have an instrument that puts a number on just how tenuous your hold on life would be, should you continue driving on your current death traps. Thus is born the market for cheap tire tread depth gauges, which can't really be accurate no matter what, since rubber is soft and the surface of a tire is irregular.

▶ You can only adjust the micrometer in this precision depth gauge over a range of 1 inch (25 mm), but extension rods let you measure a hole of any depth up to 6 inches (152 mm).

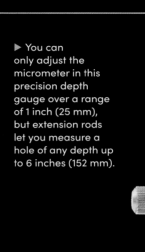

MADE IN CHINA

◀ This fine old Mitutoyo Height Master gauge, often informally known as a Cadillac gauge, has a stack of twelve precision gauge blocks, each exactly 1 inch (25 mm) high, with alternating upper and lower surfaces. A dial at the top lets you move the whole stack up and down over a range of 1 inch, with gradations on the dial marked in ten-thousandths of an inch. In other words, you can position either the top or the bottom of a block anywhere between 0 and 12 inches (305 mm) in increments of $1/10,000$ inch.

◀ This vernier height gauge is built just like a caliper, but with a foot on one end, allowing it to stand upright on a granite flat.

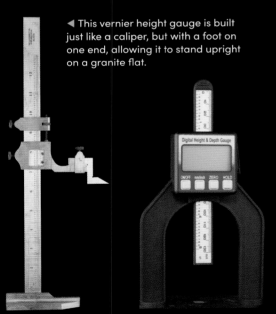

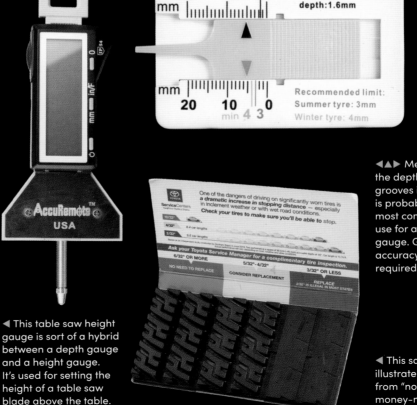

Standard minimum depth: 1.6mm

Recommended limit:
Summer tyre: 3mm
Winter tyre: 4mm

◀▲▶ Measuring the depth of the grooves in a tire is probably the most common use for a depth gauge. Great accuracy is not required.

One of the dangers of driving on significantly worn tires is *a dramatic increase in stopping distance* — especially in inclement weather or with wet road conditions. Check your tires to make sure you'll be able to stop.

Ask your Toyota Service Manager for a complimentary tire inspection.

8/32" OR MORE	5/32"-4/32"	3/32" OR LESS
NO NEED TO REPLACE	CONSIDER REPLACEMENT	REPLACE 2/32" IS ILLEGAL IN MOST STATES

◀ This table saw height gauge is sort of a hybrid between a depth gauge and a height gauge. It's used for setting the height of a table saw blade above the table.

◀ This sales display is meant to illustrate the stages of tire wear, from "no-problem" to "give-us-your-money-now-for-your-own-safety."

GRANITE FLATS

ON THE PREVIOUS pages we learned about height gauges, which are only as good as the surface they are sitting on. If it's not very flat, you can't get a meaningful measurement from the gauge. So specially made precision flat surfaces are an integral part of the process of using height gauges.

There are two common sorts of very flat surfaces: machined cast-iron tables (for example in a milling machine) and precision granite flats. Stone might seem like a surprising material to use as a precision measuring surface, but stone flats are flatter than anything that can be made of metal. All metal blocks have internal stresses and variations that result in slow creep over months and years. Granite is already millions of years old, and any stress has long since settled down.

Granite blocks are also, surprisingly, more forgiving if you drop something heavy on them. Yes, they will chip, resulting in an unusable spot on the stone, but it won't ruin the whole stone, because you can just avoid that spot. If the same thing happens to a metal table, there will not only be a visible dent, but also a bulging-up around the dent as the metal is deformed. This bulge is not visible and is thus much harder to avoid.

Granite is used not only for flat surfaces, but also for the most accurate right-angle blocks, straight edges, and step blocks. These tools can be fantastically expensive compared to their metal versions, but only the granite versions are accurate and stable

enough to serve as reference standards against which metal parts can be measured.

The biggest precision granite flats, used in locomotive and ship's engine plants, can be dozens of feet (12 m or more) long, and 3 feet (1 m) or more thick. Needless to say, they cost a fortune, unlike the biggest ones I have, which I use as lawn furniture and paid $80 each for.

Decades ago there was a company in my town that made aluminum hard disk platters using ultra-precise polishing machines mounted on the stones you see here. As technology progressed, the requirements for these platters became tighter and tighter until the machines were no longer good enough, and they, along with their mounts, became obsolete. Dozens of the mounts were sold at auction to a local stone dealer, and I happened to pull up in their lot just after they had unloaded them. Blocks were piled up everywhere, blocking the driveway and generally making a nuisance of themselves, so the owner offered to sell me a bunch cheap just to get them out of their hair.

The sad part of this story is that I also had a couple thousand pounds (about 1000 kg) of the scrapped aluminum platters made on these stones, but the whole crate was stolen out of my shed, and now I just have a small box of them. Oh well. On the next page you'll meet one of the few instruments that could measure the thickness of the platters accurately enough to determine that they didn't meet the new standards.

▶ This small granite flat is used as the base for holding a dial indicator.

▲ When these blocks were new and being used for their intended purpose, their two mounting surfaces were flat and parallel to within millionths of an inch, and they were worth a fortune. Now they are scrap and worth next to nothing. I rented a rough-terrain forklift to arrange them as lawn furniture in my front yard.

◀ My granite surface plate is only 18 by 24 inches (450 x 600 mm), but already it has to be 4 inches (100 mm) thick to be stiff enough to maintain its accuracy of about 2/10000 inch (0.005 mm) maximum deviation across the whole plate.

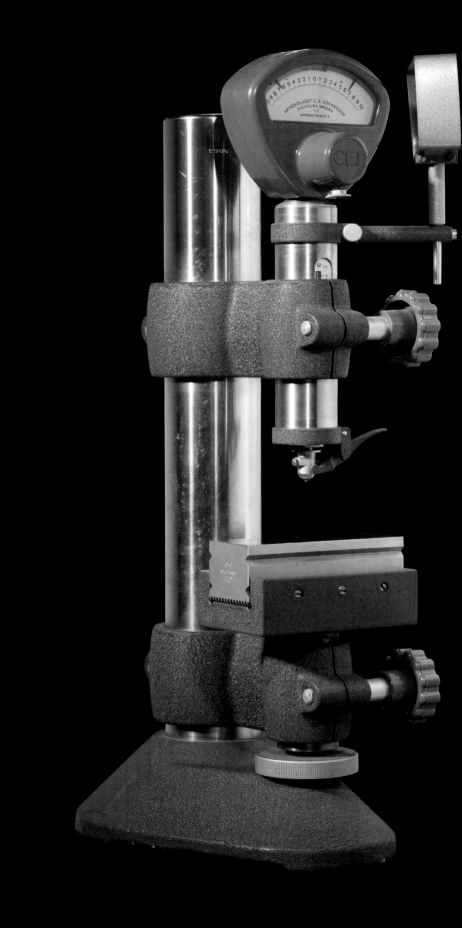

MIKROKATOR

THIS IS THE INSTRUMENT that made me reconsider the size of light. Wait, light has a size?

Light is a wave and every wave has a wavelength, defined as the distance from one peak of the wave to the next. Visible light occupies a sliver of wavelengths between about 400 and 750 billionths of a meter (nanometers, or nm for short). The practical effect is that you cannot *see* something smaller than about 500 nm (the wavelength of green light) because it's literally smaller than the light you're trying to see it with.

So how big is 500 nm? Half of a millionth of a meter? My gut feeling, my intuition about light, had always been that it is *extremely* small. So small that you could never directly perceive its size in, say, the movement of some mechanical device. This instrument, which I ran into at random and paid $100 for at auction, blew that intuition right out of the water.

It is a precision height comparator, brand name Mikrokator, made in Sweden probably in the 1960s. You put something, typically a very carefully made block of metal called a gauge block, under the probe

and adjust the indicator to the zero position in the middle. Then you replace the gauge block with something you want to measure, and the pointer shows you the difference in height between the two—as long as that difference is very, very small. The whole scale from one end to the other is plus or minus $1/10,000$ of an inch (0.0025 mm). In other words, what is the limit of accuracy of a typical micrometer is the *whole range* on this thing.

The fine divisions are $2/1,000,000$ of an inch. One millionth of an inch is about 25 nm. That means the divisions on this scale mark off increments of 50 nm. That means a typical 500 nm wavelength of green light is *ten divisions* on this scale. The whole range of the scale from one end to the other is just ten wavelengths!

Wow. This purely mechanical device is directly, mechanically, reading out differences in height down to less than $1/10$ of the wavelength of visible light. What's more, the magnifying glass implies that you're meant to be able to reliably read the position of the indicator to a fraction of one division, so maybe you can read this to about 10 nm, or $1/50$ of a wavelength.

That quite frankly blew my little mind—but only because I was being dumb about it. In retrospect, I really shouldn't have been so surprised. I knew that gauges able to read to $1/10,000$ inch (0.0025 mm) are commonplace, and not really considered super-accurate. I have had gauges like that for years, and all that time a trivial calculation would have shown me that $1/10,000$ inch is only about 5 wavelengths of green light. So even these common shop tools are able to come close to measuring individual wavelengths.

This thing is fifty times more sensitive, which is a lot, but not a *lot* lot, not like on a different planet. And yet, to this machine, light is big—literally off-the-scale big if you're talking about even just a dozen wavelengths. This has forever changed my view of the size of light: I will never go back to thinking of it as impossibly tiny.

With this stunning instrument we have arrived at the end of our journey through the world of measuring tools, and will now return to our regularly scheduled cutting, burning, pounding, and squeezing.

◄ Everything about this tool is designed for stiffness and stability. The column is *solid* steel. There are no bearings in the measuring path, only flexible spring mounts with zero backlash. The probe tip is a polished ruby sphere. Measuring pressure is supplied by a calibrated spring. To use it, both the instrument and the things being measured must be kept at a constant temperature for many hours to settle down, and the room temperature cannot vary by more than a fraction of a degree.

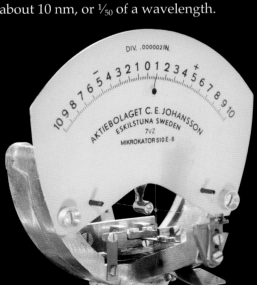

DIV. .000002 IN.

10 9 8 7 6 5 4 3 2 1 0 1 2 3 4 5 6 7 8 9 10

AKTIEBOLAGET C. E. JOHANSSON
ESKILSTUNA SWEDEN
7VZ
MIKROKATOR 510 E-8

◄ This mechanism has to be simple because there's not enough movement going on to drive anything complicated. The heart of it is nothing more than a thin ribbon twisted in opposite directions on either side of a little ball of glue that holds a pointer. When the ribbon is stretched even a tiny bit, it untwists by an amount that is proportional to the amount of stretch. The metal of the ribbon is not getting longer, just adjusting to occupy a longer space by allowing the twists to unwind. The pointer is a fine glass fiber so thin it's nearly invisible, making the painted arrow on the end appear to fly through the air.

GRABBERS

THERE ARE MANY variations on a theme when it comes to grabbers and squeezers. The variety comes from the huge range in size, shape, temperature, and fragility of the things being grabbed. Tweezers are at one end of the spectrum, followed by salad tongs. Massive steel jaws that can pull heavy pallets or rip small trees out of the ground reside at the other end of the spectrum.

Not included in this category are any tools that use screws or hydraulics to squeeze: those come later. All the tools here work either by direct human squeezing or by a clever application of leverage, whereby the force of pulling on them increases the clamping force.

The classic example of such a self-tightening squeezer is the Chinese finger trap, a toy woven out of reeds. You can put your finger in easily, because when the tube is pushed together, making it shorter, its diameter increases. But if you try to pull your finger out, the tube is stretched longer, which causes it to tighten around your finger. The harder you pull, the tighter it holds on, causing great distress in small children caught in its merciless grip.

Ice tongs are another example of what amounts to a one-way latching mechanism. Movement into the jaws tends to push the jaws open, but because of the way the pivot point is arranged, trying to pull outward on the jaws instead causes them to close tighter.

If you increase the length of the handles and/or decrease the length of the jaws on a grabber, you start being able to exert significantly more pressure, and soon land in the territory of pliers.

▲ One of these is for grabbing hot canning jars out of a boiling water bath, the other is for grabbing babies who are being difficult before they are even born.

▼ This grapple is meant to clamp to an overhead rafter or beam and support a rope or chain for lifting hay. Just don't stand underneath it!

◄ This grabber is for dragging pallets from the front of a truck to the door at the back, where they can be picked up by a forklift.

▼ Chinese finger trap.

◄ Wire puller that works just like a Chinese finger trap, used to pull electrical cables through walls and conduit.

◄ Lab tongs insulated with asbestos. Not for kitchen use, please.

► Cervical biopsy forceps, or horror movie eyeball pluckers, you decide.

▲ These exotic tweezers are for pulling off watch hands. A rotating turret at the front lets you choose four different pegs to push into the axle holding the hands, like the world's smallest gear puller.

▲ Carbon fiber–tipped tweezers are for delicate, static-sensitive electronic components.

▲ Fence wire pullers grip the wire automatically: the harder you pull, the harder they hold on.

► Apparently if you grab a horse by the upper lip, it will calmly follow you around. Google "equine lip twitch" if you don't believe me.

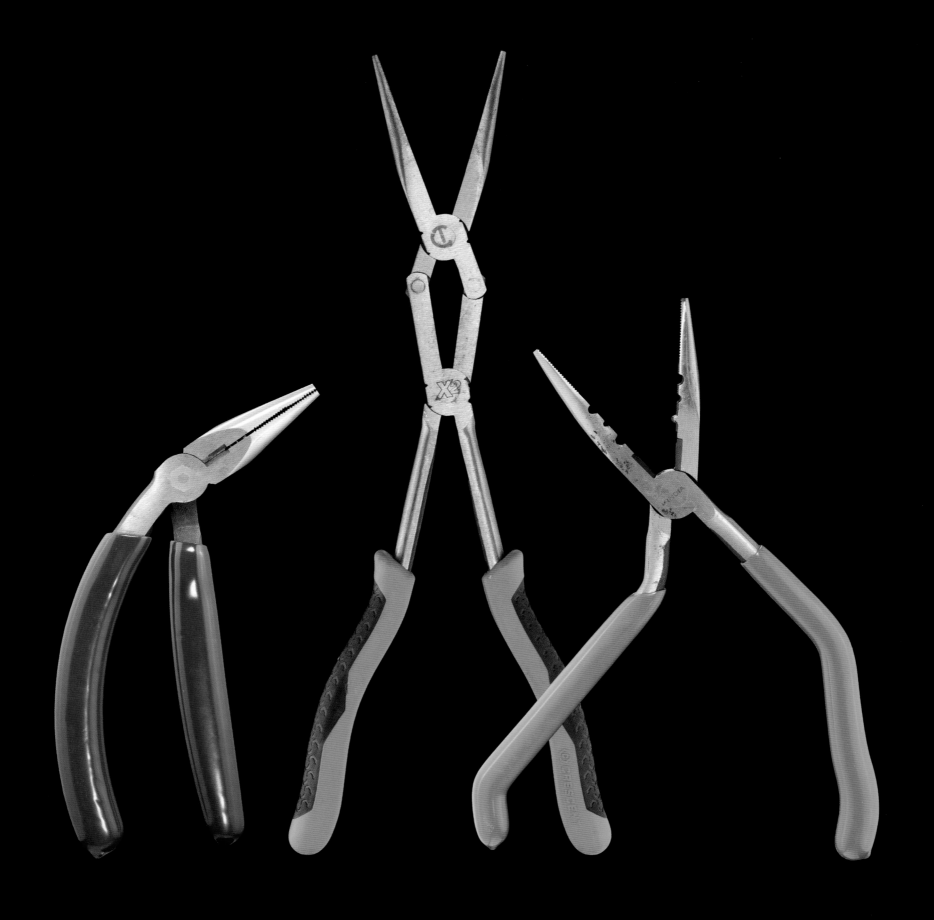

PLIERS

PLIERS, LIKE BIRD BEAKS, come in many styles, depending on whether you need to crack a thick-shelled wire nut with short, stout jaws or reach deep into a flower to bend a retaining tab. They bend and stretch to reach hard places, and they open like a snake's jaws to fit around the largest prey.

The most basic type of pliers, found everywhere on the planet, are two-position slip-joint pliers. They are inexpensive to make, with a loose-fitting pivot that does not need to be machined after forging. The looseness of the joint makes them a bit sloppy to work with, but also means that a badly rusted pair will usually work just as well as a new one. Fancier pliers have a fully machined joint that keeps the jaws perfectly aligned, but will seize up quickly if left out in the rain.

Needle-nose pliers are almost as common as blunt pliers. They come in a wide variety of lengths, with smooth jaws for jewelry making and serrated jaws for rougher work. Beyond these common pliers is an awesome array of specialized kinds.

◀ People are always trying to come up with a new angle on pliers.

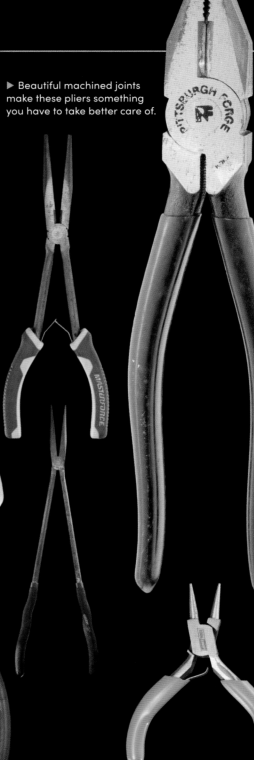

▶ Beautiful machined joints make these pliers something you have to take better care of.

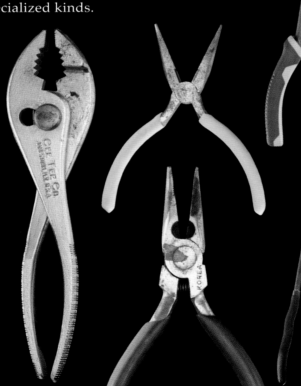

▲ These ubiquitous slip-joint pliers have a joint that can be moved to two positions, one where the jaws close completely and one where they can fit around larger objects.

◀▲ Some of these pliers look . . . jowly? Maybe it's just me, but I think they are very funny.

▲ Pinocchio would have made a good pair of needle-nose pliers.

▲ Jewelry-making pliers are tiny!

SPECIALIZED PLIERS

PLIERS JAWS GET pretty crazy. The ones on this page are just scratching the surface: I could not possibly include all the specialized variations found in the wild, and that's not including the whole next page of pliers that think they are wrenches.

◀ These Jar Jar Binks–looking pliers are used for closing folded metal seams on the back side of car wheel wells. The turkey wattle is a brace for pulling nails. The laughing alligator? There are no good theories about why these were made or what they were used for.

▼ These jeweler's pliers are for bending precious metal wire or bar into rings of different diameters.

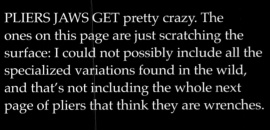

◀ SwitchGrip! It's two pliers in one! The handles flip completely around to bring either regular or needle-nose plier jaws into play.

◀ These multi-pliers make waves in the end of a sheet metal duct so it will fit inside another one.

◀ These are for screwing a water hose onto the back of a washing machine while awkwardly balancing over the top and trying to reach down to where you can't see properly.

▶ Pliers for pressing out tight spots in shoes.

▲ This beak would be great for cracking nuts, but is instead for crimping hog rings (which can go in a hog's nose but are more commonly used to fasten together wire fence panels).

▲ These are also not for cracking nuts. They are for cracking teeth prior to extraction.

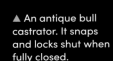

▲ An antique bull castrator. It snaps and locks shut when fully closed.

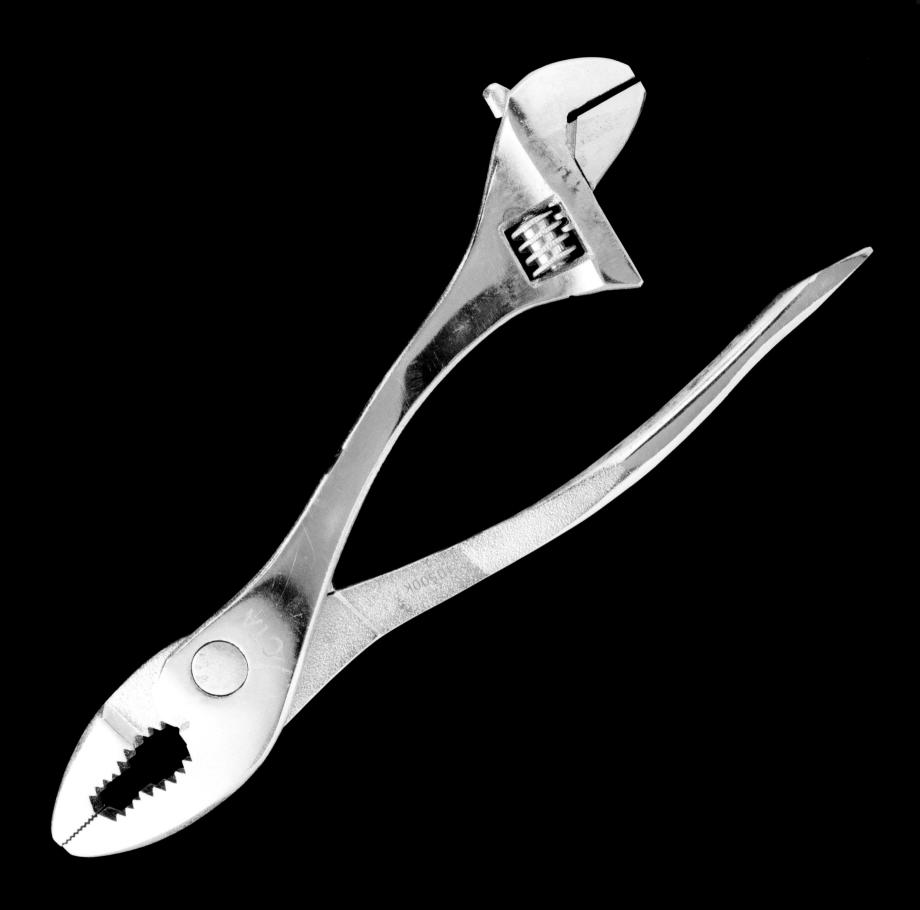

PLIER-WRENCHES

USING A PAIR OF PLIERS to turn a bolt is perhaps the most embarrassing activity any self-respecting craftsperson can be caught in the act of performing. It's simply not done! Except it is, by everyone. Like picking your nose, everyone at one time or another uses a pair of pliers as a wrench, they just learn to wait until no one is looking. Unlike with nose-picking, tool manufacturers have designed a zoo of tools meant to remove the social stigma of using pliers as wrenches. One brand goes so far as to explicitly call their tool a "pliers wrench" as if that's just perfectly fine.

There are two approaches to socially acceptable plier-wrenches. One is to have flat jaws and some way of keeping them parallel, so they firmly grip two sides of a nut, just as a crescent wrench would. The other approach is to have 60-degree notches in each jaw, which together grip four of the six sides of a hexagonal nut. These have the advantage of looking like they were designed for this specific job.

Is it OK? Yes, go ahead, be free. Use pliers on nuts. For all I care, you can use perfectly ordinary pliers too. Just don't use any of these tools on nuts that are extremely tight, because all of them rely on your grip strength to stay closed, and all of them will eventually slip. Probably when someone is looking.

◀ This is an old (patented 1916) take on sliding, parallel-jaw pliers, named the Plierench by its inventor. It's a pretty cool design, and even has a modern fan base of collectors.

◀ Who could doubt the usefulness of a combination pliers and crescent wrench? Anyone who's tried to use one of these, that's who. The pliers-side handle is located in exactly the wrong place when you try to use the wrench side. So much so that you'd be tempted to use the pliers instead.

▲ Unlike all other slip joint pliers, these have a cam mechanism that keeps the jaws exactly parallel at all times, justifying their name: pliers wrench.

▲ The marketing materials even show how the notches in the jaws can grip four sides of a nut, to reassure you that this is OK.

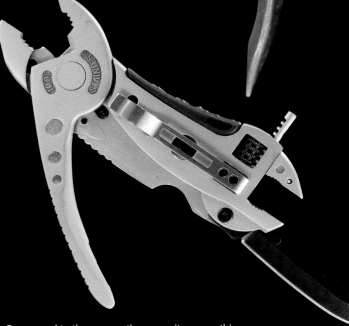

▲ Compared to the one on the opposite page, this modern contraption is a better-made and more useful version of a combination pliers and crescent wrench. For one thing, the pliers lock shut, so they stay out of the way when using the wrench.

▶ These automotive battery nut pliers are for older people who just don't care anymore what anyone thinks.

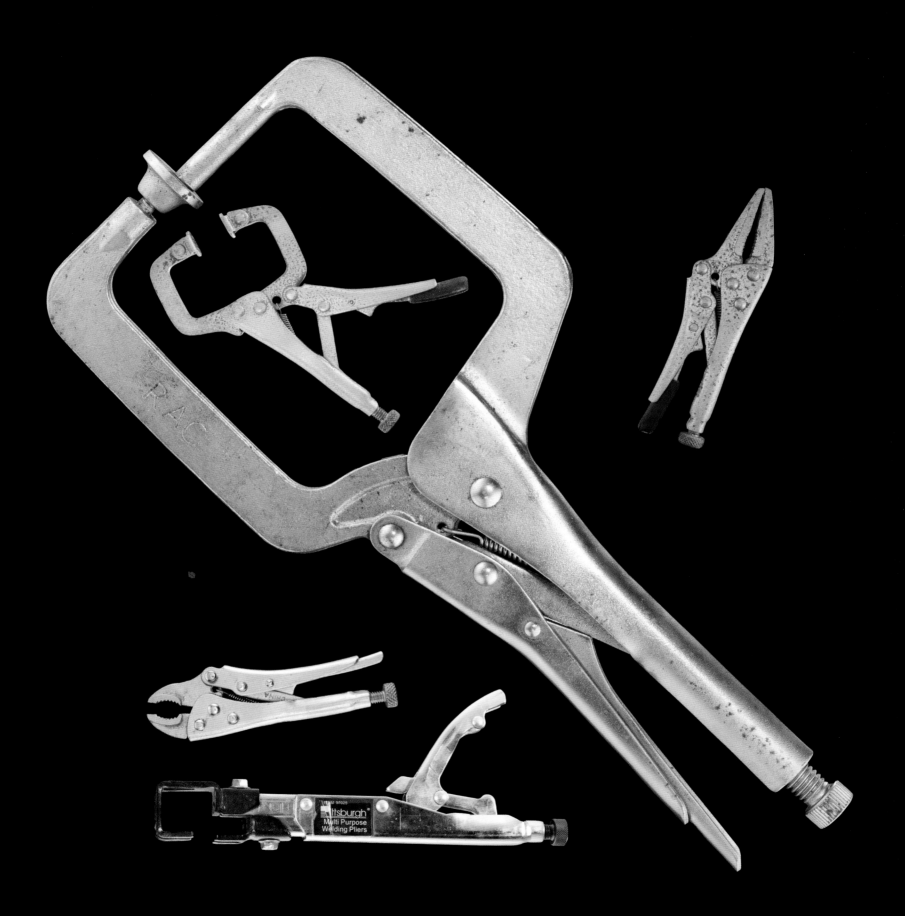

VISE-GRIPS

"VISE-GRIP" IS A trademark of the Black+Decker company, but that's like saying Photoshop is a trademark of Adobe or that Kleenex is a trademark of Kimberly-Clark. Nobody cares. The key to all vise-grip pliers, regardless of brand, is the point in their range where the leverage becomes effectively infinite. As you close the handles, the jaws close quickly at first, then more and more slowly, with more and more leverage, until finally the jaws snap to the other side and lock in place, maintaining the grip with no further effort. It's like the way you can "lock" your knees or elbows by letting them bend slightly in the wrong direction.

Importantly, you can use a thumbscrew at the back to choose exactly where in the range this point of infinite leverage occurs,

so you can apply a tremendous amount of squeezing force to items of any diameter.

Vise-grips are almost indescribably useful. If I could have only one tool in the universe of pliers and wrenches, it would be a vise-grip. You can use them like ordinary pliers. You can grip things with more force than with any other hand-held tool. You can clamp them onto nuts and bolts and use them like a wrench. You can grab the heads of stripped-out screws or pull nails with them. They make a perfectly decent pipe wrench. And as the name implies, you can use them like a mini vise to hold workpieces. Some of them can even be used to clamp wood, though that task is usually best left to the more traditional clamps on the next page.

◀ The Vise-Grip brand is now made in China, while the original Vise-Grip factory in America was bought by Malco, which now sells vise-grips under the Eagle Grip name. So which is the real one?

▼ Instead of an adjusting screw, these have a spring-loaded slide that locks in place at just the wrong moment to start squeezing.

▶ The crazy deep jaws on this vise-grip let it clamp far into the middle of a sheet of material.

▲ This crazy long one is definitely pushing the limit of how far the jaws can be separated from the handles.

▲ This antique hand clamp is a sort of predecessor to the vise-grip.

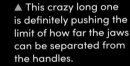

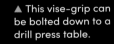

▲ This vise-grip can be bolted down to a drill press table.

▶ The Zoidberg of vise-grips?

◀ This early oddity has the locking property of a vise-grip, but not its infinite leverage.

DELICATE CLAMPS

THERE ARE A VARIETY of reasons to use clamps, and a variety of clamps to serve those needs. The clamps featured here could be described loosely as delicate clamps, those meant to avoid marring the surface of the piece you're clamping by spreading the load out.

Wooden handscrew clamps, as shown on the left, are used exclusively by woodworkers, who are often precious about them, as they are about block planes. Don't be fooled. A $10 handscrew clamp from a discount store works just as well as a $100 version from a boutique

woodworkers' supplier. These clamps are versatile because you can independently adjust the opening at the front and back, so you can set the angle between the jaws to any position you like. Pro tip: the fastest way to move the jaws in and out is to grab both handles and crank them around each other, as if you were cranking the pedals on a bicycle. This moves both ends of the jaws in the same direction at the same time.

On the next page we'll look at some clamps that are more about force than diplomacy.

▶ The oldest handscrew clamps are made entirely of wood, even the screws. Modern ones have steel screws that work much better.

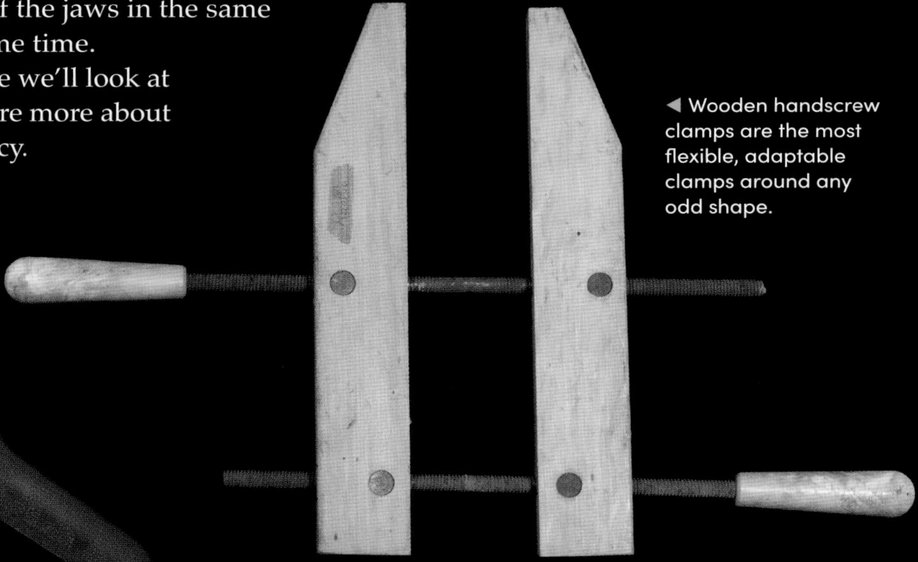

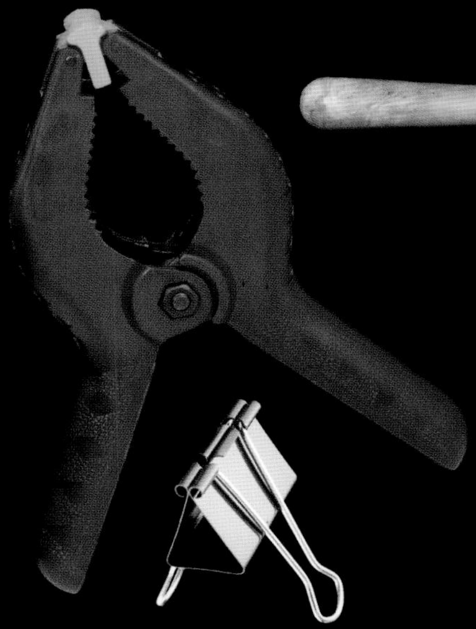

◀ This looks like a spring clamp, but it isn't meant to hold anything. It's a welding ground clamp (hence the massive volume of brass and the terminal for attaching a thick wire).

▶ Spring clamps, even clothespins and binder clips, are strong enough for many gluing jobs: just be sure to use a lot of them at a time, which spreads the load.

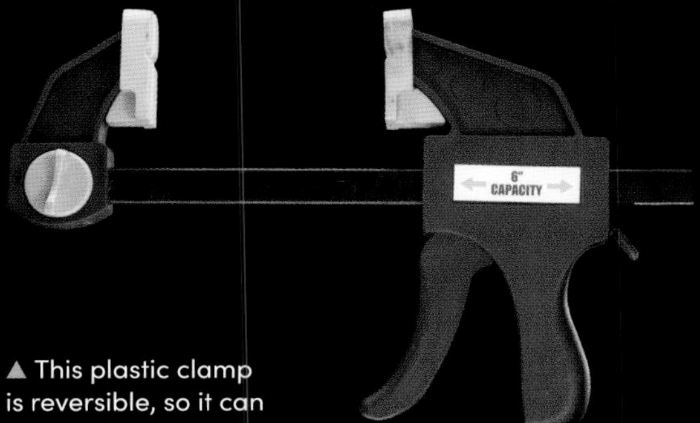

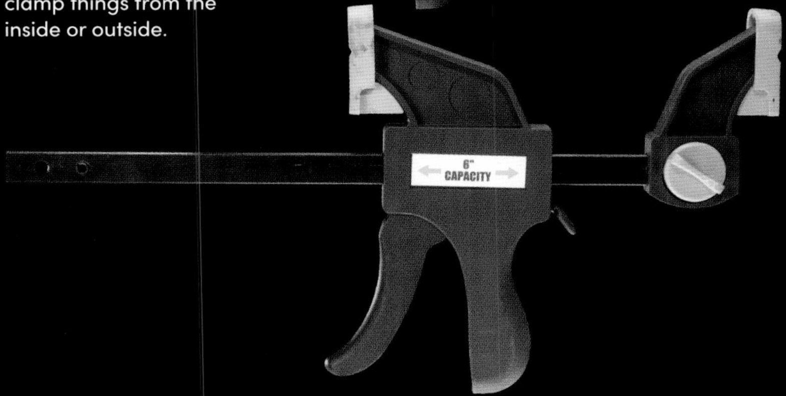

◀ Wooden handscrew clamps are the most flexible, adaptable clamps around any odd shape.

▲ This plastic clamp is reversible, so it can clamp things from the inside or outside.

◀ Small handscrew clamps can also be made entirely of metal.

6" CAPACITY

6" CAPACITY

GENERAL U.S.A. No 118 A

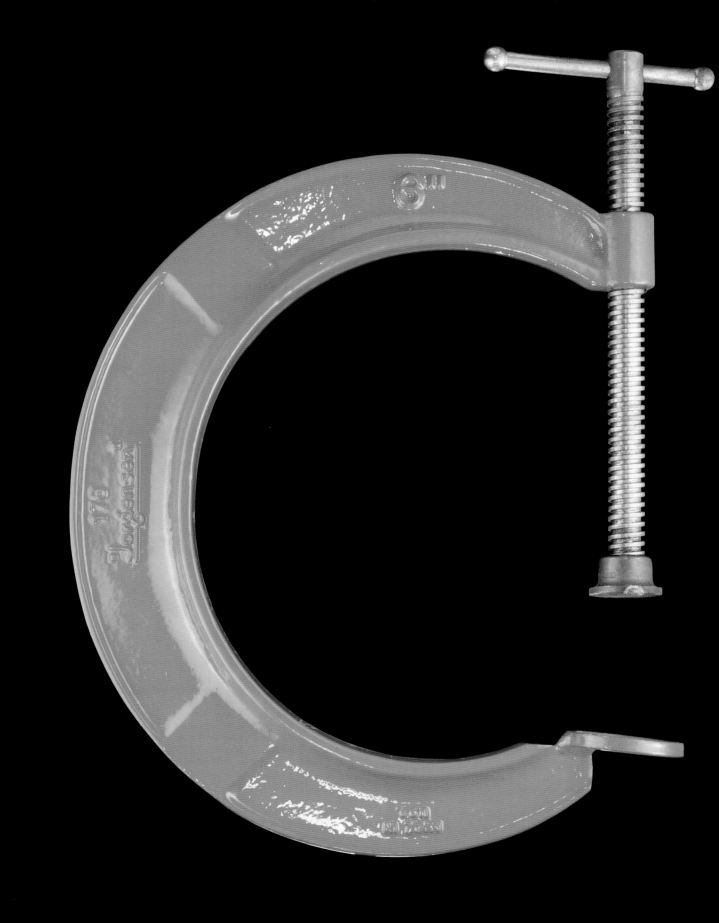

ROUGH CLAMPS

THE MAIN THING to know about clamps is that you need more of them. Doesn't matter how many you have, you should get more. While the clamps on this page can squeeze pretty hard, it's almost always better to use more of them with less force on each. This is especially important when clamping wood, but even with metal construction you don't want to warp or dent things needlessly.

C-clamps and pipe clamps are at the upper end of performance in terms of the amount of squeezing force you can get from a clamp. If you're in need of more force, you'll want to move on to the next page.

▶ Pipe clamps are a variation on bar clamps where you buy the two jaws and supply your own standard iron water pipe. The advantage is that you can get as long or short a pipe as you need.

◀ This is hands down the most gorgeous C-clamp I've ever seen. The shape is elegant, the color is cherry, and it's completely blemish-free. Just lovely. I could not possibly ever use it, lest its pristine condition be assaulted.

◀ This is a C-clamp in an old Wild West font. It was made by the Peck, Stow & Wilcox company, founded in 1870, bankrupt in 2003, land bought by developers, currently an empty field. The story of America.

▶ Bar clamps are like C-clamps with a wider, faster adjustment range because you can slide one jaw along the bar.

▶ This clamp grabs and holds a bone during orthopedic surgery, a fairly athletic activity not unlike woodworking.

▶ Comically thicc C-clamp.

▲ There are several approaches, not commonly seen, to making bar clamps more convenient.

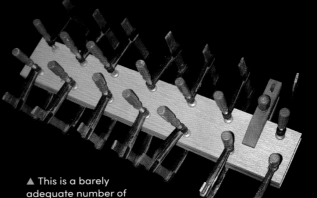

▲ This is a barely adequate number of clamps.

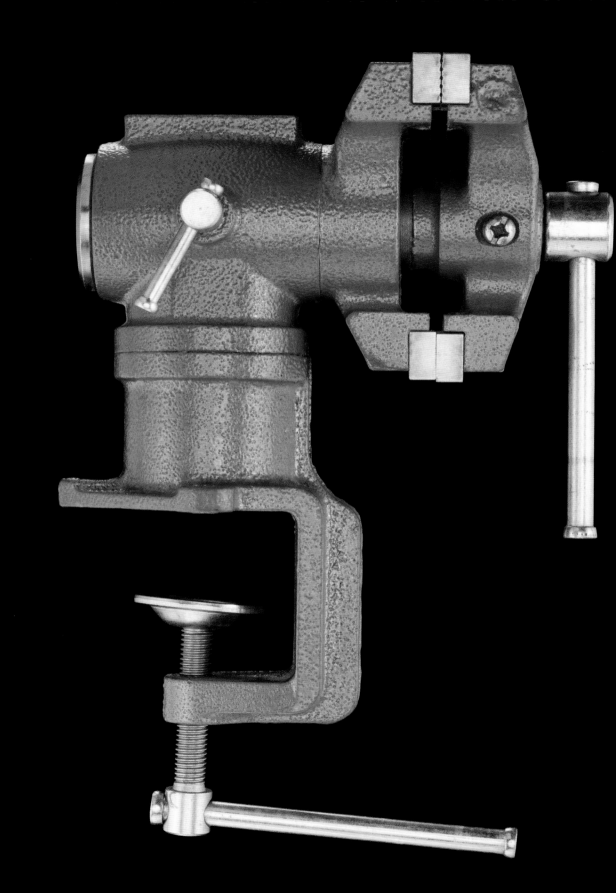

SMALL VISES

VISES ARE LIKE CLAMPS but more so. They are generally meant to be used mounted to or at least resting on a workbench. The ones on this page are small and specialized. Some are really quite dainty. On the next page we'll see that vises can also be some of the heaviest and most brutish tools in the shop.

By the way, I would like to mention that vise and vice are two entirely different words. A vise is the tool we're talking about here. The word derives from the Latin vītis, meaning the tendrils of a vine (used to twist and bind). A vice is a thing you're not supposed to do, and it derives from the Latin vitium, meaning a defect or imperfection. It's possible that I wrote an entire draft of this book using vice everywhere I should have used vise.

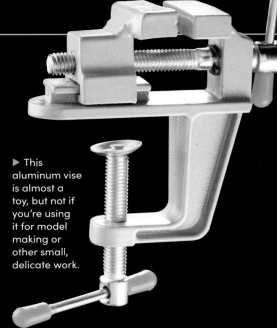

▶ This aluminum vise is almost a toy, but not if you're using it for model making or other small, delicate work.

◀ This vise isn't very big, but it's chunky and satisfying. I have at least five of these that I can think of.

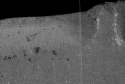

◀ I may have many vises, but this isn't one of them, because it's a nutcracker.

◀ Small cast-iron vises are clearly meant for serious use, despite their miniature size.

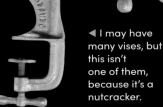

▼ My grandfather had a nutcracker exactly like this. I assumed he made it himself, given that he was an inventor, but now I'm not so sure: I got this one from a shop in China decades after he died.

▲ This *beautifully* made, precision-machined vise holds three generations of Apple AirPod wireless headphones without scratching them.

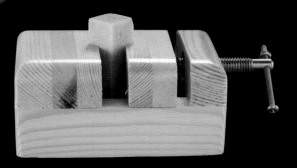

▲ This cute little wooden vise is used to hold square bars of soft stone while a street vendor carves your (usually Chinese) name into the face.

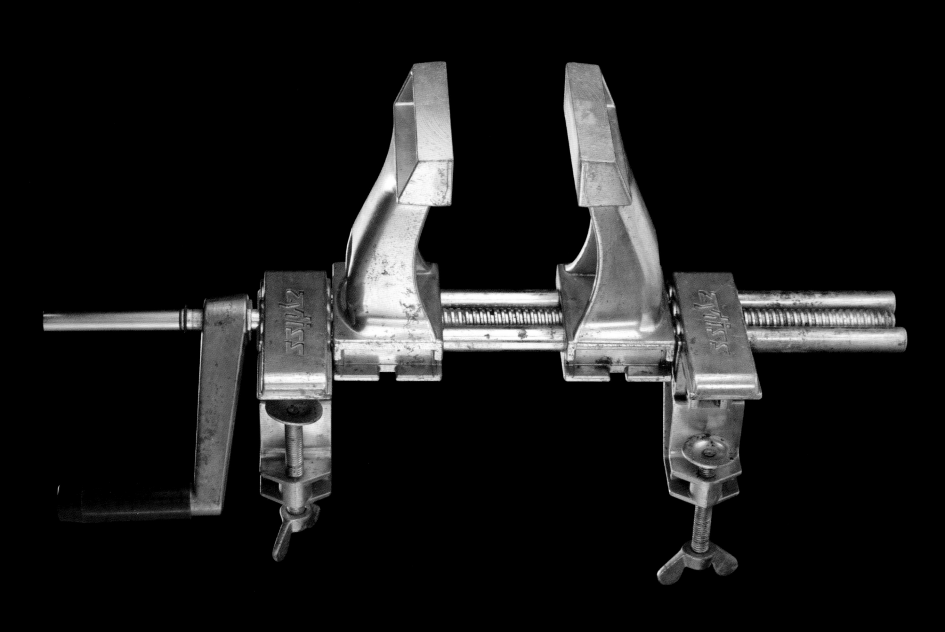

BIG VISES

A GOOD METALWORKING bench vise, like a proper anvil, should be heavy. Brutishly heavy. Some tools last a lifetime if treated well. A bench vise will last a lifetime when beaten on, yanked around, and generally abused like few other shop tools. If your bench vise doesn't have a few dings on it, you're not doing it right.

Vises for woodworking, often made of wood themselves, are just as big, but less brutish. Cutting or drilling into them is frowned upon, especially the kind that are an integral part of a wooden workbench.

These vises are all meant to hold anything you can throw at them. They are general-purpose vises, and every workshop needs to have at least one good bench vise. On the next page we'll see some fascinating examples of specialty vises.

▲ This vise has no handle: instead, compressed air pushes the jaws closed. It would be used for repeated clamping and unclamping in a production situation.

◀ I'm fond of this Swiss-made aluminum vise, mainly intended for woodworking, because I had one as a kid. (This one.) It's lightweight, but sturdy enough, and it can be configured in many different clever ways.

▶ This was my first serious vise, bought with money I made in high school working in a chemistry lab every Friday night. You could say it was my main (and only) squeeze for years. The whole jaw assembly can be rotated or flipped over for clamping pipes, and the area behind the jaws can be used for hammering, like an anvil.

▼ This is a terrible vise, sloppy and weak because it's made of welded plate steel instead of cast-iron. But wow does it open w—i—d—e!

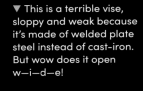

▲ This small bench vise has a mini-anvil complete with horn on the back, making clear that hammering is expected and acceptable. The second set of jaws nested inside the main ones don't shoot out like in the movies, but instead are used to hold pipes.

▲ This vise takes the anvil thing so far you could say it's more of an anvil with vise attached.

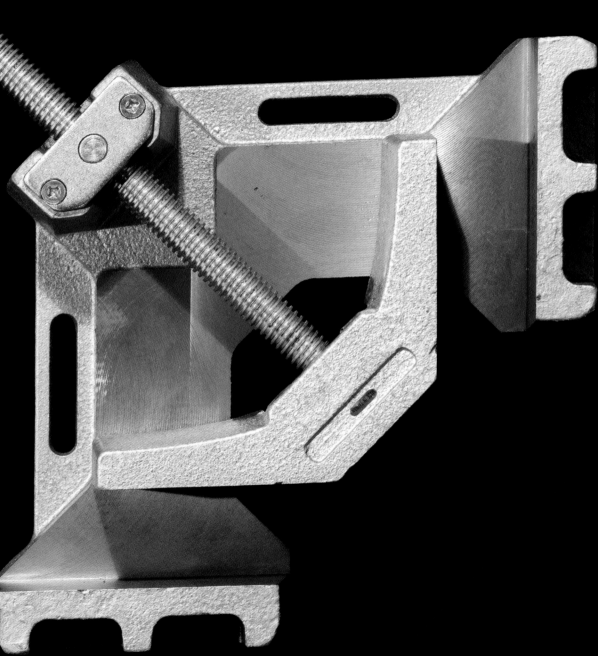

SPECIAL VISES

THE HEAVIEST, STRONGEST vises are those used to hold blocks of metal on milling machines. I've got a couple that I should not lift for the sake of my back, even though they are relatively small examples of the species. They need to be monstrously thick because not only do they have to keep a grip on their work while it's being pushed on with great force by a milling bit, they also have to prevent flex or movement. Even a thousandth of an inch of deflection would be unacceptable during a precision machining operation.

Large-diameter steel or cast-iron pipes are another application that nurtures large vises. Pipes need to be held up, kept from rotating, and secured for cutting, all of which require heavy-duty clamping forces.

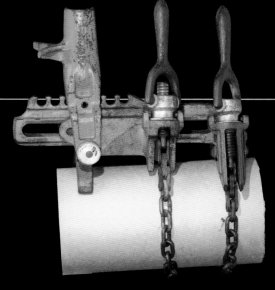

▲ This is no ordinary pipe vise. It's two pipe vises, with a ratchet mechanism that lets you forcefully pull them closer together. It's used to join up sewer pipe by ramming the straight end of one length of pipe into the bell end of another.

◀ This unreasonably heavy corner clamp is used for welding steel frames. The shape of the jaws keeps them away from the corner where the joint will be welded.

▼ The handles on machinists' vises come off, so they don't get in the way during machining operations. These things are basically solid steel all the way through.

▼ This "sine vise" has a set of precision pivot points that, with a stack of gauge blocks and some math, can be set to a very precise tilt angle.

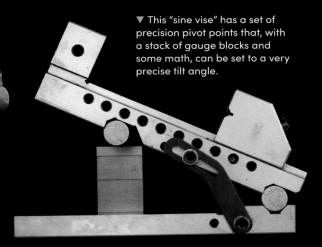

◀ If you want to cut threads on the end of a pipe, you need a pipe vise to prevent the pipe from turning (threading takes a *lot* of force, all of it in the turning direction).

▼ This pipe dog or pump puller vise is used to lift well pipe out of a well. The hinged part on the right grips tighter if the pipe tries to slide back down. To release it, you step on the pedal on the far right.

▲ Vises have main screws with threads whose sides are vertical, rather than slanted like normal threads. This allows the screw to apply force along its length without the threads being pushed inward by their slope.

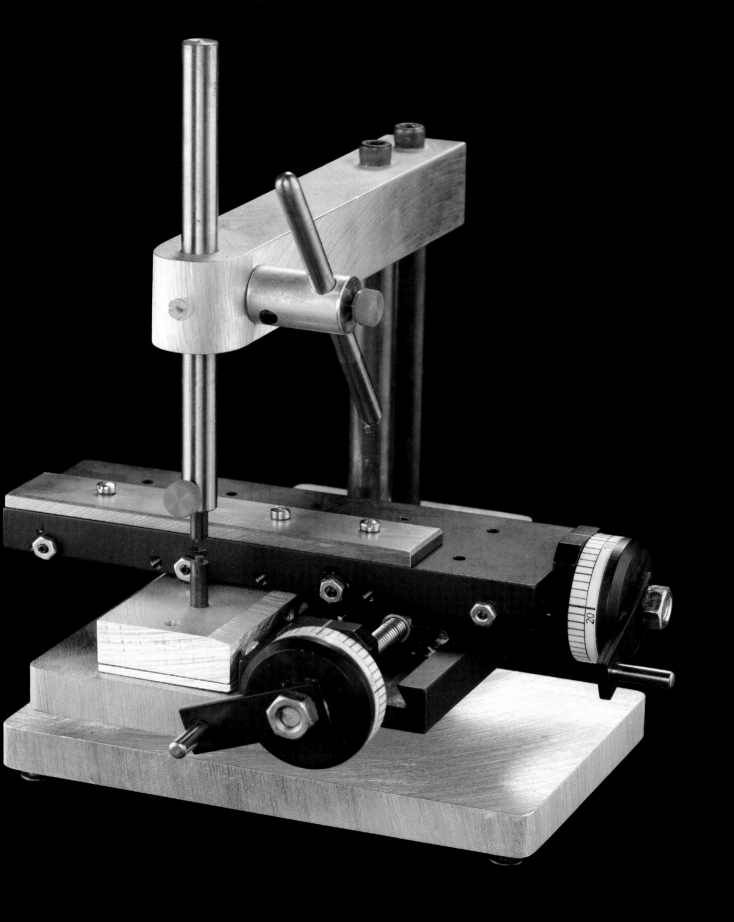

PRESSES

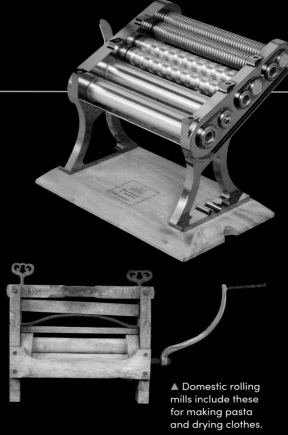

SOME OF THE LARGEST machines in the world, the size of multistory buildings and costing tens of millions of dollars, are hydraulic stamping, molding, and forging presses. These are so important to manufacturing that after World War II, American and Russian forces scrambled to capture and study the superior German presses vital to their fighter plane production. I don't have any of those.

On a more domestic scale, arbor presses and shop-sized hydraulic presses are great for pressing bearings into pulleys and just generally squeezing things harder than is possible in a vise. A common shop press can exert force up to 20 tons (18,144 kg). In contrast, my favorite press at the University of Illinois shows off its 1,500-ton

(3,000,000-pound or 1,360,000 kg) capacity every year by crushing concrete cylinders for the amusement of local schoolchildren. It has two large lead screws that move the head up and down rapidly, but when it comes time to squeeze, the screws don't turn, instead huge hydraulic cylinders under the floor pull the whole screw assembly down, pulling the head with it.

Rolling mills create miles of sheet steel, but can also delicately roll out a few grams of gold into a bar for making a finger ring. Other types of presses apply heat to transfer images to T-shirts, or flatten curly hair. Press brakes bend sheet metal by squeezing it into a V-shaped die. (I have a small one shown on page 169, and a *tiny* one on this page.)

▲ Domestic rolling mills include these for making pasta and drying clothes.

◄ This delightfully precise pin press has an x-y micrometer table and a lever that pushes a pin down to mark spots very accurately.

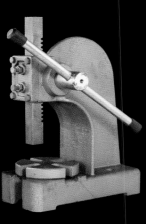

▲ Arbor presses use a small pinion gear to drive a rack gear down with up to a ton or so of force.

◄ Who doesn't love a good concrete crushing demonstration? The floor shakes and the children shriek when the column finally gives way.

▼ Rolling mills have two polished steel rollers that can be adjusted to a precise separation and then turned in opposite directions to squeeze out soft metals.

◄ This itsy bitsy teeny tiny press break can fold little bits of brass into little corners, up to 90 degrees.

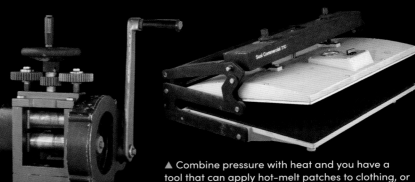

▲ Combine pressure with heat and you have a tool that can apply hot-melt patches to clothing, or transfer images to T-shirts.

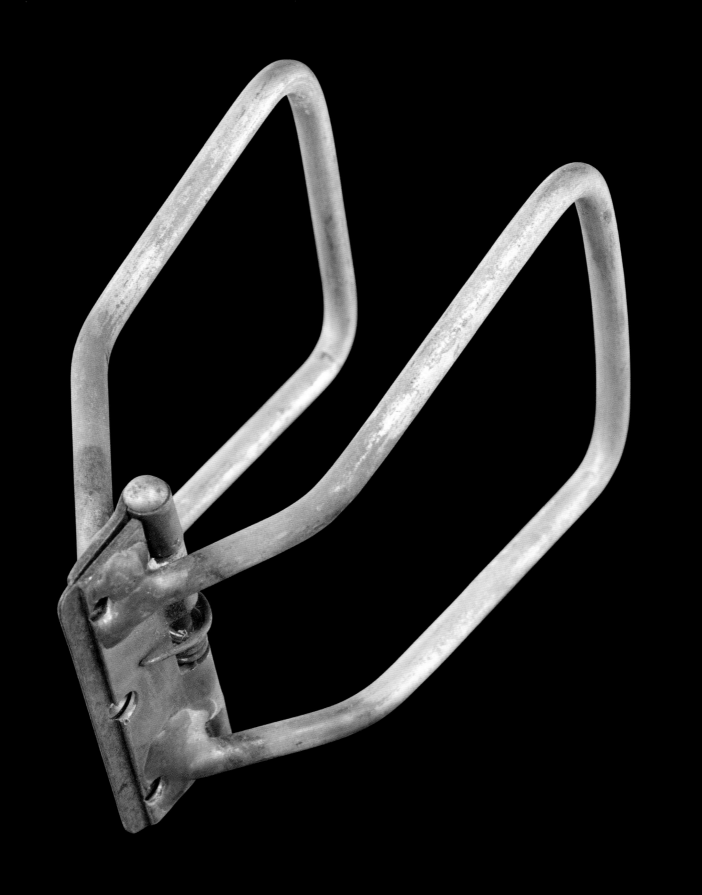

SPREADERS

WE'VE JUST SPENT many pages squeezing things together with progressively more force. Now we're going to undo all that by looking at tools that spread and open.

One of my favorite spreading tools is a pair of separating pliers I made myself out of a hinge and some bent steel rods. When the first-generation Macintosh computers came out, opening the case required a special tool to gently but firmly pry apart the two halves. Apple, ahead of its time as usual, tried to discourage people from being able to open the case themselves, and did not provide a tool for this job. So I had to make my own, as did many other people.

This tradition continues to the present day, when you need specialized tools—more complex with every generation—to get into an iPhone. One of the most useful is a pair of suction cup anti-pliers, which grip and firmly pull apart your kid's phone when it needs yet another new screen.

Snap ring pliers are another common example of a spreader tool. Snap rings can be either internal (fitting into a groove cut inside a hole) or external (fitting into a groove cut in a rod or axle). Removing an internal snap ring can be accomplished by squeezing its ends together. To remove an external one, the ends need to be stretched apart, increasing the diameter of the ring until it comes out of the groove. (At which point it will immediately fly across the room, never to be seen again, which explains the popularity of replacement snap ring assortments.)

▶ Surgical retractors and speculums are biological spreaders.

▶ One of many tools required to open a modern cellphone.

◀ It's a battery clamp spreader, for when you can't get the battery clamp back over the terminal on your car battery, and you're too proud to use a screwdriver to wedge it open.

◀ I made this tool to open first-generation Macintosh computers in 1984.

▼ When you squeeze the handles of this snap ring tool together, the jaws either move together or apart, depending on the position of a clever selector lever.

▲▶▼ Hats, shoes, and the fingers of gloves all sometimes require stretching.

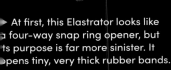

▶ At first, this Elastrator looks like a four-way snap ring opener, but its purpose is far more sinister. It opens tiny, very thick rubber bands.

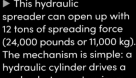

▶ This hydraulic spreader can open up with 12 tons of spreading force (24,000 pounds or 11,000 kg). The mechanism is simple: a hydraulic cylinder drives a wedge between two jaws.

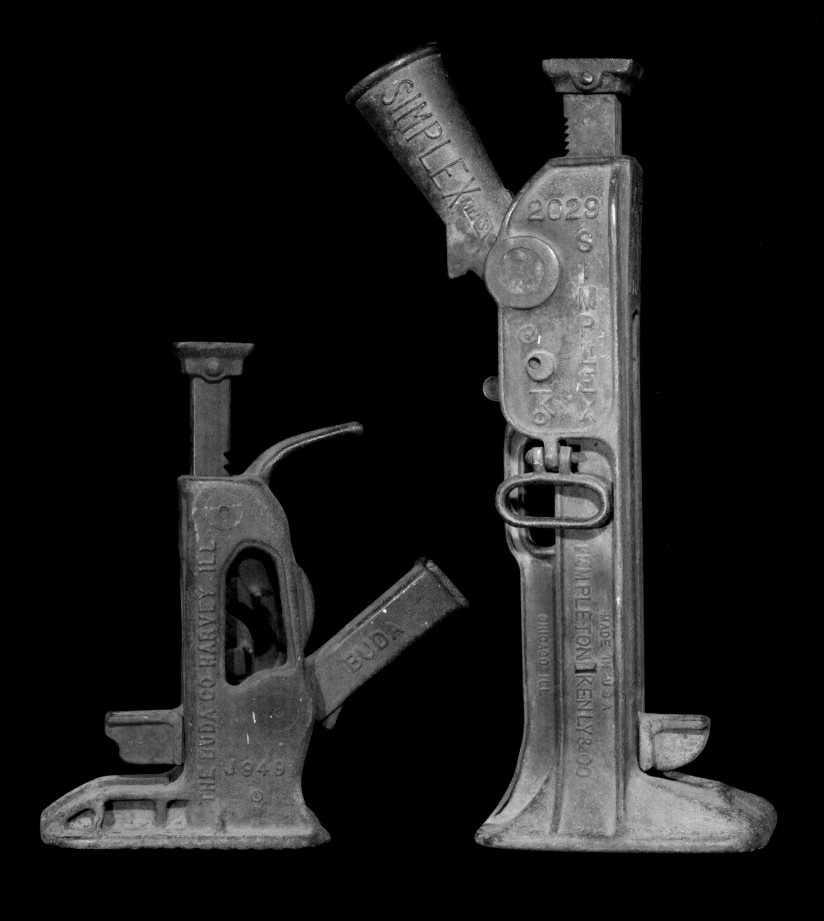

JACKS

JACKS ARE SPREADERS used to separate a thing from the thing it's sitting on: they fight gravity rather than some mechanical obstruction. It's important to remember that jacks have only one job: lifting. They are not for keeping things up in the air while you work under them. Any mechanism that can move up can also move down. After lifting with a jack, you always need to put a jack stand or two under the car before working under it. (Jack stands also have one job:

keeping things up in the air once they have been lifted by a jack. Anytime one fails to do that, there is a lawsuit and a recall of the defective stands.)

Some jacks are even more specialized: they are spreaders designed to separate you from the ground. The safety implications of that are obvious, so you should probably not, for example, buy one at auction and immediately start using it to run yourself and your kids up and down for fun.

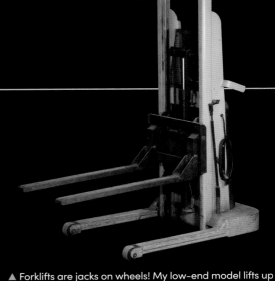

▲ Forklifts are jacks on wheels! My low-end model lifts up to 1 ton (907 kg) with an electric motor driving a hydraulic pump, but you have to push it around manually.

◀ These things are commonly referred to as railroad jacks, though they can just as well be used on large trucks. They are strong enough to lift ten ordinary cars.

▶ The scissor jack you get in the trunk of most cars is *just* strong enough to lift the car it came with, hopefully.

▶ This is an older style of jack, now largely replaced by more convenient hydraulic jacks. The ratchet flips to one side or the other, depending on whether you want to raise or lower the jack.

◀ A hydraulic floor jack is a much better way of lifting a car, but heavy and awkward to keep in the trunk.

▶ Hydraulic bottle jacks come in many sizes, for home use to lift typically between 2 and 20 tons (1,814 and 18,144 kg), and for industrial or construction use up to hundreds of tons.

▶ This jack may look like an antique, but this type is still widely used. Sometimes known as a hi-lift jack because it goes up much higher than other designs.

▲ This "Handy Herman" lift will take you about 30 feet (9 m) up in the air with surprisingly little wobble. I paid $220 for it at auction. I do not, yet, regret the purchase, and I've had it for over twenty years.

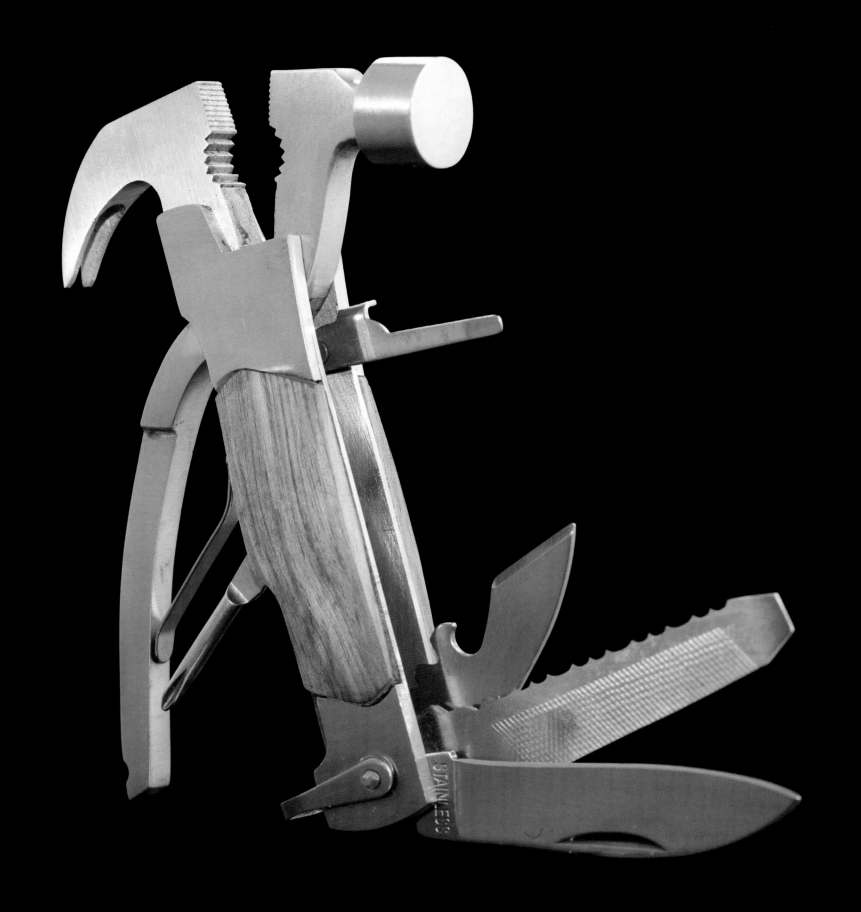

MULTI-TOOLS

Multi-tools are so much more fun and interesting than they are useful. With the possible exception of the Swiss Army knife and its close relatives, there are just too many compromises involved for them to be serious everyday tools. Which has not stopped them from being wildly popular as gifts, for others and oneself. It certainly hasn't stopped me from buying nearly every variety I encounter.

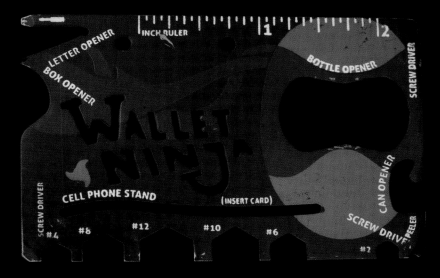

▶ Swiss Army knives are the original multi-tool. They come in sensible and not-sensible sizes.

◀ This is my favorite mini-multi-tool, just because of how well it's made.

▼ Lovely, just lovely.

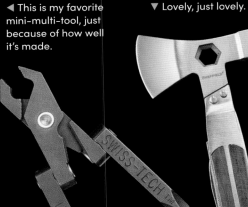

SWISS-TECH ™

LETTER OPENER
BOX OPENER
INCH RULER
1
2
BOTTLE OPENER
SCREW DRIVER
WALLET NINJA
SCREW DRIVER
CELL PHONE STAND
(INSERT CARD)
CAN OPENER
SCREW DRIVER
PEELER
#4   #8   #12   #10   #6   #2

◀ I almost got this thing taken away by airport security when they found it in my wallet, but it ended up being OK because there's no knife edge.

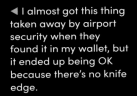

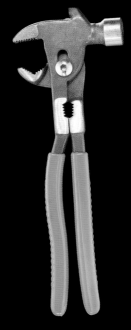

▶ The ultimate camper's and mechanic's multi-tool.

▶ Can there be any more versatile multi-tool than one that lets you both light a campfire and trim your toenails?

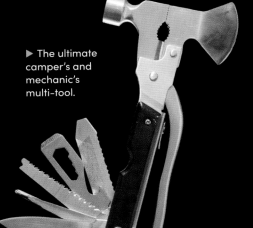

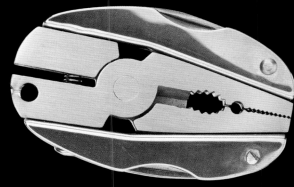

▲ This one has more features, but its rough edges ruin the feel.

▲ There are two things you're not supposed to do with pliers: use them on nuts and hammer with them. These pliers are designed to do both.

ACKNOWLEDGMENTS

SO MANY PEOPLE have influenced and contributed to my life with tools that it's scary to even try to list them. Of course my dad, who showed me how to saw and drill, and my mom who showed me how to knit and sew. My uncle made a big impression on young me with the drill I talk about in the introduction to this book. My shop teacher in high school, whose name I unfortunately don't remember, let me have free use of the lathes and milling machines after class hours: that was a great thing for him to do and I wish I could properly thank him for it.

My friend Donald's father Harry Barnhart introduced me to the world of farm shed tools: sledgehammers, hacksaws, acetylene torches, and Carhartt overalls with the rich smell of motor oil infused in them. Donald's friend Dean Rose taught me about forging and smithing, while wearing the skin of Donald's former pet goat.

In more recent years my friend and resident of my farm Bobby Crowe introduced me to the world of concrete tools. My girlfriend's son Toby took an interest in welding during the writing of this book, and together we put together a pretty good collection of various generations of welders, plasma cutters, grinders, surface prep tools, and a remarkable metal-cutting circular saw that unfortunately didn't make it into my life in time to be included in this book.

I owe a special thanks to the auctioneers of the Midwest and their usually deceased clients whose estate auctions were the source of many of the most interesting tools in this book. There's nothing like a tool auction to introduce you to a random assortment of tools at least a few of which you've never seen before and can't live without.

Of course, no acknowledgments section of a book of mine would be complete without mentioning my longtime photographer colleague Nick Mann, who contributed about half the pictures in this book before having twins and dropping of the face of the earth in terms of time available for not dealing with babies.

My sustaining and frequently cooking girlfriend Maribel, and my children (who are now fully functional adults!) were a great help through the various panics that occurred while I was working on the book.

Finally I would like to do the opposite of thanking the county government of Champaign County, Illinois, for buying the building my studio was located in and forcing me to move *all my tools* at the worst possible time during the completion of this book.

PHOTO CREDITS

All photos in this book were taken by either Nick Mann or Theodore Gray, except for the following:

page 69: map of aggregate hardness from MK Diamond Products

page 119: laser cutters from GU Eagle Advanced Automation

page 139: power meat saw from Jarvis Wellsaw

page 171: the author seated by Mike Walker

page 195: Egyptian ruler from Alain Guilleux

INDEX

ALSO AVAILABLE BY THEODORE GRAY

FOR ADULTS

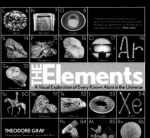

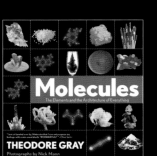

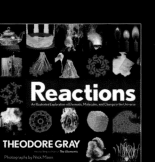

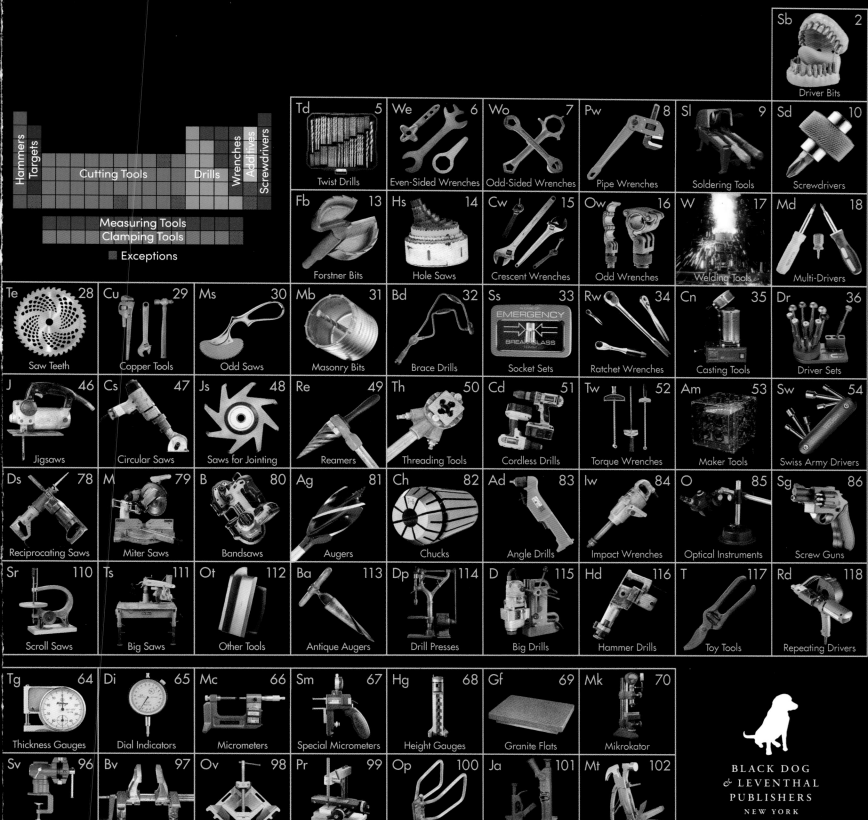

Hammers
Targets
Cutting Tools
Drills
Wrenches
Additives
Screwdrivers
Measuring Tools
Clamping Tools
■ Exceptions

Sb 2 — Driver Bits

Td 5 — Twist Drills
We 6 — Even-Sided Wrenches
Wo 7 — Odd-Sided Wrenches
Pw 8 — Pipe Wrenches
Sl 9 — Soldering Tools
Sd 10 — Screwdrivers

Fb 13 — Forstner Bits
Hs 14 — Hole Saws
Cw 15 — Crescent Wrenches
Ow 16 — Odd Wrenches
W 17 — Welding Tools
Md 18 — Multi-Drivers

Te 28 — Saw Teeth
Cu 29 — Copper Tools
Ms 30 — Odd Saws
Mb 31 — Masonry Bits
Bd 32 — Brace Drills
Ss 33 — Socket Sets
Rw 34 — Ratchet Wrenches
Cn 35 — Casting Tools
Dr 36 — Driver Sets

J 46 — Jigsaws
Cs 47 — Circular Saws
Js 48 — Saws for Jointing
Re 49 — Reamers
Th 50 — Threading Tools
Cd 51 — Cordless Drills
Tw 52 — Torque Wrenches
Am 53 — Maker Tools
Sw 54 — Swiss Army Drivers

Ds 78 — Reciprocating Saws
M 79 — Miter Saws
B 80 — Bandsaws
Ag 81 — Augers
Ch 82 — Chucks
Ad 83 — Angle Drills
Iw 84 — Impact Wrenches
O 85 — Optical Instruments
Sg 86 — Screw Guns

Sr 110 — Scroll Saws
Ts 111 — Big Saws
Ot 112 — Other Tools
Ba 113 — Antique Augers
Dp 114 — Drill Presses
D 115 — Big Drills
Hd 116 — Hammer Drills
T 117 — Toy Tools
Rd 118 — Repeating Drivers

Tg 64 — Thickness Gauges
Di 65 — Dial Indicators
Mc 66 — Micrometers
Sm 67 — Special Micrometers
Hg 68 — Height Gauges
Gf 69 — Granite Flats
Mk 70 — Mikrokator

Sv 96 — Small Vises
Bv 97 — Big Vises
Ov 98 — Special Vises
Pr 99 — Presses
Op 100 — Spreaders
Ja 101 — Jacks
Mt 102 — Multi-Tools

BLACK DOG
& LEVENTHAL
PUBLISHERS
NEW YORK

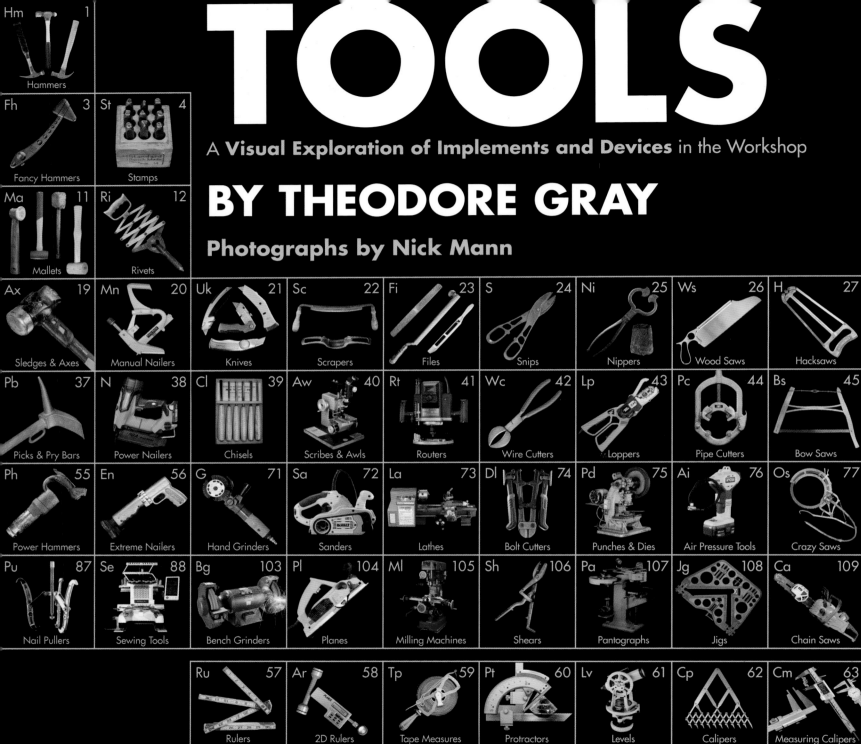

TOOLS

A **Visual Exploration of Implements and Devices** in the Workshop

BY THEODORE GRAY

Photographs by Nick Mann

Hm 1 — Hammers			
Fh 3 — Fancy Hammers	St 4 — Stamps		
Ma 11 — Mallets	Ri 12 — Rivets		

Ax 19 — Sledges & Axes	Mn 20 — Manual Nailers	Uk 21 — Knives	Sc 22 — Scrapers	Fi 23 — Files	S 24 — Snips	Ni 25 — Nippers	Ws 26 — Wood Saws	H 27 — Hacksaws
Pb 37 — Picks & Pry Bars	N 38 — Power Nailers	Cl 39 — Chisels	Aw 40 — Scribes & Awls	Rt 41 — Routers	Wc 42 — Wire Cutters	Lp 43 — Loppers	Pc 44 — Pipe Cutters	Bs 45 — Bow Saws
Ph 55 — Power Hammers	En 56 — Extreme Nailers	G 71 — Hand Grinders	Sa 72 — Sanders	La 73 — Lathes	Dl 74 — Bolt Cutters	Pd 75 — Punches & Dies	Ai 76 — Air Pressure Tools	Os 77 — Crazy Saws
Pu 87 — Nail Pullers	Se 88 — Sewing Tools	Bg 103 — Bench Grinders	Pl 104 — Planes	Ml 105 — Milling Machines	Sh 106 — Shears	Pa 107 — Pantographs	Jg 108 — Jigs	Ca 109 — Chain Saws

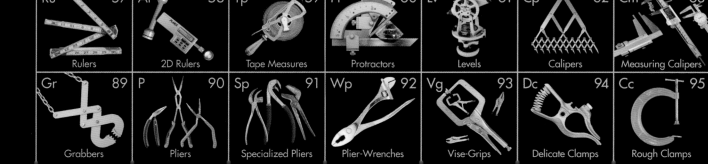

Ru 57 — Rulers	Ar 58 — 2D Rulers	Tp 59 — Tape Measures	Pt 60 — Protractors	Lv 61 — Levels	Cp 62 — Calipers	Cm 63 — Measuring Calipers
Gr 89 — Grabbers	P 90 — Pliers	Sp 91 — Specialized Pliers	Wp 92 — Plier-Wrenches	Vg 93 — Vise-Grips	Dc 94 — Delicate Clamps	Cc 95 — Rough Clamps